Thinking with Feeling

Are emotions good or bad for thinking and learning?
Have you ever wondered why a good lesson of one year falls flat in another?
Why do students behave the way they do?

Teachers are expected to foster productive thought, yet the neglect of emotion in the classroom in favour of intellect, means teaching and learning is often not as effective as it might be. *Thinking with Feeling* explores what we mean by productive thought, its interrelationship with mood and emotions, how teachers can manage that interaction to improve teaching and learning and what teacher trainers could do about it.

Synthesizing the most important international research in the field, it offers a framework for productive, purposeful thought – deduction, understanding, creative thinking, wise thinking and critical thinking – and explains how mood and emotion can support and also impede learning. It considers the effect of the interplay of emotion and intellect on classroom behaviour, on students' public performance and performance in tests, and how emotional labour can affect the teacher.

Illustrated with examples from practice, this challenging, thoughtful study offers education professionals a basis for understanding the interaction of emotions and cognition and making it a successful partnership in order to improve teaching and learning.

Douglas P. Newton PhD, DSc teaches and researches in the School of Education at the University of Durham, UK. He has written and co-authored many books on education and teaching – including *Teaching for Understanding*, which is now in its second edition – and researches extensively on various aspects of thinking and ways of fostering learning.

'In today's world, there is often so much emphasis placed on the intellect that the interaction between feeling and thinking is rarely identified, let alone addressed. Nonetheless, emotions can and do have a powerful effect on cognition and learning. Doug Newton has done a masterful job in connecting 'sense and sensibility' in both theoretical and practical ways. After reading this book, thoughtful, sensitive educators will realize that they have been touched by something very special.'
– *Dr Ken McCluskey, Dean and Professor of Education, University of Winnipeg, Canada*

'This book addresses a frequently ignored area in schools by challenging our understanding about the interaction of moods, emotions and cognition in the classroom. It reflects on how deductive thinking takes place within an emotional climate, explores the complexity of creative thinking and problem solving and discusses the role and effects of moods and emotions in the development of wisdom. Crucially, it offers teachers invaluable practical advice on developing and sustaining productive thought in the classroom, and offers an important contribution towards understanding how emotion–cognition concepts inform quality teaching and learning.' – *Professor Mike Younger, Cambridge University, UK*

'Too often we ignore the crucial role of emotion in learning. Here is a book that will help schools understand the relationship between emotion and cognition, something that will help teachers understand their students' learning in subtle, powerful ways. Professor Newton manages to bring an impressive level of academic study to the classroom in a book that is fascinating and useful for parents, teachers and administrators interested in the role of emotion in thinking. This analysis of the driving force behind motivation and learning is a must for schools interested in taking the learning to a new level.' – *Dr Conrad Hughes, Director of Education, International School of Geneva, Switzerland*

'Teacher education and learning in schools is mostly based on cognition. But human beings are led by emotions. Newton's book is a Copernican change in thinking about teaching; he gives a deep and differentiated emphasis on all the emotional dimensions that affect learning. I recommended this book to all my graduate students to change their thinking about teaching in a way that is really helpful for the students.' – *Professor Dr Astrid Kaiser, Institut für Pädagogik, Carl von Ossietzky University of Oldenburg, Germany*

'This book quite rightly shines a long overdue light on how emotions affect teaching and learning.' – *Sir Paul Grant, Headteacher, Robert Clack Academy, London, UK*

'This book makes a welcome contribution to our understanding of the interplay between emotion and cognition in learning. It explores the role of feelings in influencing the kinds of thinking that tend to be valued in education. Professor Newton sets out to argue that thinking is more likely to be productive if emotions and reason work in harmony and that managing the partnership between the two can lead to more efficient and productive thinking. The chapters address important implications for teaching and learning and teacher education, providing valuable recommendations for practice.' – *Professor Sue Robson, School of Education, Newcastle University, UK*

Thinking with Feeling

Fostering productive thought in the classroom

Douglas P. Newton

Routledge
Taylor & Francis Group

LONDON AND NEW YORK

First published 2014
by Routledge
2 Park Square, Milton Park, Abingdon, Oxon OX14 4RN

and by Routledge
711 Third Avenue, New York, NY 10017

Routledge is an imprint of the Taylor & Francis Group, an informa business

British Library Cataloguing in Publication Data
A catalogue record for this book is available from the British Library

Library of Congress Cataloging in Publication Data
Newton, Douglas P.
Thinking with feeling : fostering productive thought in the classroom / Douglas P. Newton.
pages cm
1. Thought and thinking—Study and teaching. 2. Reasoning—Study and teaching. I. Title.
LB1590.3.N54 2014
370.15'2—dc23
2013033790

ISBN: 978-0-415-81982-4 (hbk)
ISBN: 978-0-415-81983-1 (pbk)
ISBN: 978-1-315-81656-2 (ebk)

Typeset in Bembo
by Cenveo Publisher Services

Printed and bound in the United States of America by Publishers Graphics, LLC on sustainably sourced paper.

To Lynn

Contents

Figures

Tables

Preface

Norman (2002), thinking about technological design, relates that when he makes tea he chooses a teapot to match his mood, and then the tea tastes superb. It's the same with relationships – the intellect alone does not make for a happy marriage or satisfying employment. From the trivial to the significant, moods and emotions matter. They matter in education, too, often more than the intellect, and can make the difference between success and failure. Yet they are largely ignored; only the intellect receives attention, cultivation and exercise. In the classroom there sits an emotional elephant that many try to ignore. On and off, over the last ten years or so, while I've concerned myself with fostering productive thought, I've thought about that elephant and how it can thwart the best of intentions. At the same time, interest in research on moods and emotions and how they interact with cognition has grown so that it is now possible to say something about the subject which, hopefully, is useful.

Education and psychology are disciplines which should inform one another but they are, nevertheless, different and have their own concerns, vocabulary and goals. Bringing them (and other disciplines) together to inform educational thinking and practice in a practically meaningful way is not always easy. Thinking processes and products as they are conceived in education tend to be large complexes of mental activity which are not always mutually exclusive and do not always map readily onto more distinct notions in psychology. Nevertheless, an attempt to bridge the divide is potentially useful provided that it remains practically meaningful to a wide range of educators who must function effectively in a variety of contexts. The approach I have taken is to illustrate some kinds of purposeful thought which tend to be highly valued in education and to describe how they interact with moods and emotions in their respective chapters, thereby building up a picture in steps. It turns out that those interactions are sometimes good for thought, sometimes bad for thought, but always essential. The trick is to know when these interactions are likely and what to do about them.

I have been greatly encouraged by the response of several colleagues who readily recognize that teaching and learning is emotional labour. I should add that engaging with the interaction of emotions and the intellect is also to engage with the Ancient Greek exhortation: know yourself.

D.P.N.

Chapter 1

Second thoughts
Sense and sensibility

Human thought frequently, perhaps always, bears the stamp of emotion. Academic activity is no exception; it is a matter of thinking and feeling and the feeling can determine whether the thinking is successful or even takes place at all. Given that, it is surprising that teachers may plan for the intellect but not for the emotions. This neglect has a long history and may be transmitted from one generation of teachers to another, as novice teachers simply imitate what they see. This chapter outlines the interaction of thinking and feeling and indicates its potential to shape productive thought. Subsequent chapters will explore this interaction in more detail and consider its implications for fostering particular kinds of productive thought.

Productive thought

Productive thought is potentially powerful and enabling. Being able to make sense of the world, think things through to a conclusion, create a solution to a problem, act wisely and judge the quality of thought allows us to meet and deal with the challenges and vicissitudes of life. For instance, if you understand how force relates to momentum, rocket science could be the job for you; knowing how your boss is likely to respond can help you plan your bid for promotion; and teasing out what underlies a politician's rhetoric might lead you to vote for someone else. Productive thought – teasing more from and making more of the known – has the potential to help someone meet the demands of a challenging world.

Sense

Surely, learning rocket science, justifying a promotion and considering a politician's proposals are just matters for the intellect? The emotionless android Data, of the Starship Enterprise, had only his intellect to depend on. He turned the handle and out came the mental products, all of which were absolutely rational, unsullied by emotion. Human thought can be like this, but when it is, it still has a tendency to take short cuts, it does not always explore every alternative, and it fails to mention its departure from the logical straight and narrow (e.g. Kahneman & Tversky, 1979). As Spellman and Schnall (2009: 118) put it, 'the rational human is neither rational nor human'.

Sensibility

Sensibility is our receptiveness to emotional effects and it is greater than we might like to think. All the big decisions in life, like who to marry, where to live, whether or not to accept a job in another city and what to do with that lottery win, are partly shaped by emotion. Even the relatively small things, like what to do on your day off or which shoes to buy can depend on your mood. There is a way of taking decisions on the toss of a coin which recognizes the importance of emotions. If the coin comes down heads, do it; but, if that doesn't *feel* right, don't do it. A decision can be logical but not the right one for you (Spicer, 2004; Sylvester, 1994). And, sometimes, emotions simply outweigh logic. Norman (2002), the designer, describes how his intellect told him his black and white computer screen did everything he wanted but his emotions told him to replace it with a colour monitor. We also relate to others through our feelings, sometimes to the exclusion of sense. Stephen Fry (1998) describes how he judged people he visited as a child according to the make of their lavatory cleaner. Even 'dispassionate', academic research is driven by emotion. Neumann (2012: 8) describes how 'the systematic exploration and analysis of selected aspects of our world relies on feeling [as much as] thinking, knowing, and learning'. In effect, people do it because it offers interest, excitement and pleasure, which outweigh the periods of tedium and frustration. The point is that, like it or not, our thoughts involve emotions. But this does not mean those thoughts are irrational, or the decisions are wrong, or that emotions are always bad for thought.

A fluid partnership

Immordino-Yang and Damasio (2007) have described the interaction of thinking and feeling (more properly, cognition and emotion). On the one hand, there is High Reason, where the intellect reigns, as in the thoughts of Data. On the other hand, there is the purely emotional response, uninformed by reason – if a snake was suddenly to appear, you would leap back with a surge of fear. But between these extremes, and where most of our thinking lies, cognition and emotion interact. What we store and recall is shaped by this interaction and we remember highly emotive events more than the unemotional, we fill our minds with worries which deflect attention and occupy mental space, we note that our creativity is enhanced by some states of mind more than others, we do what we feel is in our best interests rather than what we reason to be so (and we justify it afterwards), and we look for personal relevance in events to motivate us. Such effects enter into the various kinds of productive thought. This means that mental products can change with mood and emotion. For instance, the essays of depressed college students can include more gloomy, sad references and make more self-reference than those who are not depressed (Rude et al., 2004). If moods change, so do the essays. Emotion shapes the landscape we think in. What is foremost in our minds, what we attend to and how we process the information can depend on the prevailing state of mind (Spicer, 2004).

For over two millennia, there has been a tendency to see this as bad for thought (Phelps, 2006). Plato talked of the rational mind struggling to master the emotions, like a charioteer (reason) with unruly horses (the spirit and the appetites) (Kristjánsson, 2007; Laidlaw, 2012; Sokolon, 2006). Two thousand years later, Descartes reaffirmed the division between reason and passion (Damasio, 1994). This helped to shape the attitudes of later generations. Thomas Jefferson, for instance, saw American independence as confirming that what matters is reason alone (Lehrer, 2009). Kant (1785/2002) took this to its limit, but a somewhat solitary voice, that of Hume (1739/1978), argued that 'passions' have the prime role in directing affairs, although they may be modified by reason. Deutscher (2011) has demonstrated that, while neither view is entirely tenable in its extreme form, reason and emotion are inseparable. Lehrer (2009: 20) goes further: 'If it weren't for our emotions, reason wouldn't exist at all.' Nevertheless, emotions are commonly seen as primitive responses which impede good thinking, a nuisance, unreliable guides to action, obstacles to clarity of thought and 'the sand in the system' (Koole, 2009; Oatley & Jenkins, 1996; Ragozinno et al., 2003; Spicer, 2004).

This stark division into desirable reason and unwelcome emotions has been challenged by direct observation. Damasio (1994) described it as Descartes' error: we are not computing machines with an unfortunate tendency to be emotional; far from being an encumbrance, 'emotions are vital … to intelligent action' (Evans & Cruse, 2004: xii; Mayring, 2003; Pekrun, 1992, 2011; Wundt, 1907 in Zajonc, 1980). Damasio (1994) described one of his patients whose emotional system was severely impaired. The unfortunate man was unable to make decisions which were clearly in his best interest. Had it been the intellectual system that was compromised, the emotional system may have looked out for him much as it does for your pet dog. In the human brain, however, the two systems co-exist, there are numerous connections between them and they communicate with one another, sometimes harmoniously and sometimes discordantly (Sylvester, 1994). Cambria et al. (2009: 32) explain that, 'Although we often tend to separate sense and sensibility, there is no such hard line in our brain between rationality and emotions … emotions are often the product of our thoughts while our reflections are often the product of our affective states.' Plato's charioteer may fight to subdue the horses but can go nowhere without them (Laidlaw, 2012). Thought is more likely to be productive if emotions and reason work in harmony.

This is not to say that there is no such thing as rational thought or that irrationality is acceptable (Fried, 2011; Sylvester, 1994). We have two systems doing their best to keep us out of trouble and help us thrive (Evans, 2004; Hänze, 2003; Oatley & Jenkins, 1996; Pekrun, 2006). In evolutionary terms, the emotional system is the older of the two and is probably shared to some extent with some other animals. It can be fast, automatic and unconscious and it can be informed by rational thought (George, 2009). In the distant past, it became tuned to the dangers of the ancestral environment and has written in it what Gross (2002) has called the 'Wisdom of the Ages'. The other system, that of the intellect, can be a bit of a plodder in comparison and is more limited in capacity, but is more open to reflection and management. It can be very rational, but is, nevertheless, imperfect. But without emotion it can lack direction. Knowing and managing the partnership between these systems could make thought more efficient and productive.

Nevertheless, the partnership between the emotions and the intellect is not always an easy one. Sometimes emotions impede thought, as when anxiety in an examination blocks recall and fills space needed for conscious thought. Sometimes, it behaves like Tweedledum and Tweedledee, pointing firmly in opposite directions, as when reason indicates one course of action but emotion urges us to take another. But emotion also makes many decisions feasible by narrowing the options to what matters to us. Ideas and events automatically pass through our personal what–matters–to–us filter where those of little relevance are put aside. The result is quickly signalled by an emotional response that may also prompt us to take action (Evans, 2004). This filter behaves as though it has a built-in bias favouring a state of pleasure or contentment so that we are likely to prefer and choose what make us feel good (Phillips, 2003). Without something to look after our general well-being in this way, we could soon find ourselves in difficulty (Charland, 1998).

The interplay between thinking and feeling does not pass unnoticed in everyday life, and we experience it in literature. Indeed, emotions are the bread and butter of fiction writers (Oatley, 2002; 2009). Joseph Conrad (1904/1994), for instance, described the impact of emotion on the thinking of Sotillo, one of his characters in *Nostromo*: 'Sotillo had spent the morning in battling with his thoughts; a contest to which he was unequal, from the vacuity of his mind and the violence of his passions.' Here, emotion was supreme but this is not always so. In *Le Grand Meaulnes*, Alain-Fournier (1913/1966) described reason's mastery of emotion in a young woman's decision not to marry: 'She had made herself think that such happiness was not for her, that the boy was far too young, that he had made up all the wonderful things he described to her.' But feelings can also motivate thought and action. Moisevitch, in Chekhov's *The Steppe* (1888/1991), 'was embarrassed at the sight of the money. He got up, and, as a man of delicate feeling unwilling to pry into other people's secrets, he went out of the room on tiptoe.' And emotions can reward us with pleasant feelings, encouraging us to prolong the agreeable situation. De Carvalho, writing of life in Roman Spain in *A God Strolling in the Cool of the Evening* (1997), described a senator's response to a book: 'He was smiling, delighted, still savouring in his thoughts the dialogues he had just heard.' Equally, emotions are everywhere in teaching and learning and they 'profoundly affect students' engagement and performance' (Pekrun & Linnenbrink-Garcia, 2012: 259). How emotions do this can also be quite subtle and pass unnoticed. In teaching, there can be a tendency to plan for the intellect alone, but not for moods and emotions, and how they might interact to make a productive partnership.

Thinking with feeling in the classroom

This interaction has largely been ignored in education, except by a few, such as the American teacher, philosopher and educational theorist John Dewey (1859–1952) (Adler & Obstfeld, 2007; Hargreaves, 2000; Immordino-Yang & Damasio, 2007). Dewey recognized that the schism between the intellect and emotions was unfortunate. He valued, in particular, the motivating role of interest and curiosity (Dewey, 1916; 1938/1998). More recently, some have seen emotional development and regulation as potential goals. Bloom's 1956 taxonomy of educational objectives, for instance, began with the cognitive domain; the affective domain was added later, but they were not related. Anderson and Krathwohl's revision of the taxonomy acknowledged the involvement of affect but is confined to the cognitive domain (Moseley et al., 2005). Immordino-Yang and Damasio (2007: 3) contend that this lack of attention to the relationship is a serious omission as, 'we feel, therefore we learn'. Even subjects which expunge emotions from their discourse, such as physics, can arouse the breadth of emotions from 'interest, intrigue, fascination and enthusiasm [to] boredom, disillusionment, frustration and fear' (Alsop & Watts, 2000: 21). Alsop and Watts have come to believe that learning science involves the emotions as much as it does the intellect. In other subjects, like history, Wulf (2011: 92) believes it needs to be 'emotionally anchored in the imagination of the students to give it a presence and relevance for the future'.

Educational institutions, like most places where people gather and interact, are awash with emotions which inevitably bear upon cognition. Teaching and learning involve both cognitive and emotional labour and could benefit from planning with both in mind (Fried, 2011; Schutz & Lanehart, 2002). Amongst other things, the learning environment can make a difference. Strictly speaking, this could include its colour, layout and smell. For instance, Moss et al. (2003) found that the smell of lavender reduced intellectual performance while rosemary increased it. The mood or other changes produced by these odours affected reaction times, attention to task, and memory. The effects of seemingly minor environmental properties like these have been found elsewhere, although they can be complex (e.g. Cupchik & Krista, 2005). The physical environment, however, is generally a given, so there may be little a teacher can do with it other than remove distractions, make it visually attractive and organize it to suit the task in hand. Some environments, however, can add considerably to the emotional labour of learning. O'Regan (2003) interviewed some older

Australian students about their online learning and found frustration, fear, anxiety, apprehension and embarrassment, brought about by the vagaries of the digital systems, lack of control or mastery of the processes and the public exposure of thoughts and work. Emotions like these are likely to be counterproductive in any environment. There were, however, occasions of enthusiasm, excitement and pride when things went well. Generally, students can benefit from environments which minimize the former and maximize the latter feelings.

Then there is the subject or topic to be learned. First, learners can bring moods and emotions to their learning which affect their engagement and, at times, their recall (Forgas, 1995). For instance, students feeling sad who are asked to pass judgment on events or the actions of people may unconsciously take a more negative view than they would had they felt happy. There can be a tendency for people in different moods to process information in different ways (Gaspar, 2004a). Of course, the task itself can generate emotions which may help or hinder learning. Even very young children learning to read can feel ego-protective about their performance (Poskiparta et al., 2003). This can become very significant amongst older students, so that emotions become affective filters which determine the nature of their interaction with the subject. In foreign language learning, the student's emotional state can obstruct or enable reception and performance. Fear of the loss of self- and peer-esteem when publicly exposing inadequacies in a language can be a powerful block to learning, while those of a different temperament, less concerned with the regard of others, succeed (Richards & Rodgers, 1986). In cultures where the public exposure of inadequacy or loss of face is felt to be humiliating, the emotions generated by the risk can be very strong. Older students learning a foreign language in Australia, for instance, found performance in front of peers and the teacher to be embarrassing, unnerving and frightening and made them blush and tremble. Even having a sensitive teacher only partly eased the emotions (Cohen & Norst, 1989). This effect is not, of course, confined to learning a foreign language (O'Regan, 2003).

Even young children can show some knowledge of the interaction of thinking and feeling. Using story-like scenarios in the USA with children from about 5 years old, there is evidence of a belief that thinking positively in bad situations will improve feelings. In the other direction, they also tend to recognize that feeling sad can adversely affect thinking in school (Bamford & Lagattuta, 2012). Of course, this is not to say that their understanding is fully conscious or adult-like or that they can manage the interaction themselves. Many of our responses to the world are automatic, unconscious and operate on an 'act now, think later' basis. The action of affective filters is an instance. Risk takers tend to approach a challenge or project positively, while risk avoiders are often more negative and have more cautious goals. Student discussion can also be strongly affect-laden and may rarely be dispassionate (Meyer & Turner, 2002). But students are not the only ones involved in emotional labour. Perhaps no one can be more involved than the teacher, who is subject to his or her own moods and emotions and at the same time is enveloped in those of the students, while also being subject to demands from outside the classroom. This can make teaching a stressful occupation, even for the teacher with some ability to manage those emotions (Sylvester, 1994; Wilson, 2004).

There's more to productive thought than intellectual ability

Intellectual ability is not the only player in the thinking game. Moods and emotions are players, too, and, instead of simply being the sand in the system, they can be the oil (Spicer, 2004). Feeling positive about science and mathematics, for instance, is associated with achievement in those subjects (Ng et al., 2012).

But thinking only in terms of sand and oil, hinderer and facilitator of rational thought, is too narrow. Emotions can and do act in this way, but they can also provide quick and prudent responses to appraisals of the immediate world, which can prompt us forcefully to action (Nussbaum, 2001). It has been argued that the emotional system itself is essentially rational and also contributes usefully to other rational processes (Frank, 1988; Sripada & Stich, 2004). And there may be times when the prevailing emotion is neither sand nor oil and indicates only an indifference to events.

In education, emotions can make a difference to thinking and learning. For instance, feelings of well-being and optimism and tendencies to self-motivate and control impulsivity can be associated with attainment. Rodeiro et al. (2009) believe that emotional abilities can have more influence on students' success than their intelligence. Whatever a student's cognitive ability, emotional responses can help or hinder performance or, on occasions, leave it untouched (Dogan, 2012; Frederickson & Furnham, 2004; Gumora & Arsenio, 2002). The central concern here, however, is not with the development of what has been called students' emotional intelligence, although that is a matter to consider. Instead, it is about not ignoring the emotional elephant in the classroom and taking what it does into account in order to make teaching more effective, and learning better and more enduring. Of course, there are other creatures in the classroom, too, and it is important not to give emotions the exclusive role enjoyed by the intellect for some two millennia – that would simply replace one omission with another – but it serves to emphasize that, when it comes to thinking, the intellect isn't everything.

Looking ahead

This thumbnail sketch needs elaboration. Kinds of productive thought commonly seen as worthwhile in education, and some general matters to do with emotions, will be described next. After that, the interaction of thinking and feeling in different kinds of productive thought will be outlined, each chapter concluding with implications for teaching and learning and some recommendations for practice. Various broader matters also involve the thinking–feeling partnership and bear upon productive thought. These can, for instance, affect assessed performance, students' responses to the learning context more widely and teachers and their role. These are addressed in succeeding chapters. The final chapter brings the various strands together and considers implications for teacher education and training.

Chapter 2

Purposeful, productive thought
A framework

Asked how he passed his time, an old man said he sometimes sits in the sun and thinks, and sometimes he just sits in the sun. Of course, thinking – the mental management and processing of information (Colman, 2003) – is not optional, there is no just sitting in the sun. But the purpose of that thought is very varied. It ranges from, for instance, idle daydreaming to the effortful construction of meaning, and this may be the distinction the old man was making. This chapter outlines common kinds of purposeful, productive thought as they are conceived in education.

Fertile thoughts

Productive thought

Productive thought is the successful, purposeful, mental processing of information which goes beyond what is given (e.g. Glatthorn and Barron, 1991). It may take the bare bones of information and tease out a conclusion hidden in the marrow. Or it may go further and make mental connections which give the information a personal meaning, or which enable the solving of a problem, or the planning of an acceptable course of action. It is a complex kind of mental activity that typically requires the thinker to represent, analyze, relate, synthesize or otherwise manipulate that information consciously and unconsciously. 'Cognition' is the term commonly used to describe these mental activities. Productive thought, then, draws strongly on cognitive processes to go beyond what is given (e.g. Gregory, 1998). It is a powerful kind of thought, highly valued for its potential to meet new needs and situations, support independent action and avoid exploitation. Reproductive thought, on the other hand, is the recycling of information, as when recalling a telephone number or following step-by-step instructions like those of an algorithm in mathematics. Reproductive thought is useful and, in a world where nothing changes, memorization and habits may serve a lifetime but that world has gone for most of us. Productive thought, however, helps us cope in a changing world. This is not to say that reproductive thought, facts and figures are not important. But being able to think productively is a very valuable asset, which owes a lot to the intellect (Newton, 2012a).

Frameworks for productive thought

Moseley at al. (2005: 49 et seq.) review eleven frameworks describing kinds of productive thought as educational goals. By productive thought, they mean, 'analysis, synthesis and evaluation and various combinations of these and other processes, when they lead to deeper understanding, a defensible judgment or a valued product'. It includes planning, imagining, reasoning, problem solving, generating ideas, considering opinions, taking decisions and making judgments. Generally, the frameworks focus on the goals of creative thinking, problem solving and critical thinking [for example, de Bono's lateral and parallel thinking tools (de Bono, 1985); Paul's model of critical thinking (Paul, 1993); Petty's six-phase model of the creative process (Petty, 1997)] but they also include other productive thinking goals, such as reasoning and understanding (for example, Jewell's reasoning taxonomy for gifted children [Jewell, 1996) and Petty's framework)]. Moseley et al. (2005) offer a broader view of productive thinking which includes reasoning, understanding, creative thinking and problem solving and they point out that having the ability, skill or capacity for productive thought is necessary but not sufficient, there must also be dispositions which make the capable person inclined to use them. Perkins et al. (1993) described these dispositions as being able to sense the appropriateness of a particular kind of thought, as feeling an impetus to use it and as having the ability or capacity to use it. Wisdom as a prospective candidate for inclusion or, at least, the dispositions and personal attributes which contribute to it, largely post-dates these frameworks.

Purposeful, productive thought in education

Peirce, the philosopher, has pointed out that we think for a purpose (see Poggiani, 2012). Academic thought, as it is encouraged in the classroom, has particular purposes and is labelled accordingly. Reference in programmes of study, for instance, is made to purposeful thought, such as making a deduction, constructing an understanding and engaging in creative and critical thinking. In the classroom, it is practically useful to describe thought in such terms rather than fragment them into their underlying mental processes. Moseley and his colleagues' review is useful in this respect. It indicates what these broader kinds of thought might be and suggests how they might relate. For instance, it is suggested that reasoning, understanding and creative thinking are kinds of productive thought which should be exercised in the classroom (Moseley et al., 2005), while Knauff and Wolf (2010) add that these also help us meet life's problems beyond the classroom.

Deductive reasoning

Broadly speaking, reasoning includes the making of a variety of inferences: deductive, inductive, statistical and strategic inferences are just a few. These enter into a variety of kinds of productive thought, commonly distinguished in other ways. A common expectation in education is that students should 'think it through', generally meaning that they should deduce consequences from conditions in an 'if … then' sequence to 'come to a conclusion'. For example, in mathematics, they might have to follow a proof of Pythagoras' theorem. This kind of reasoning is expected to be logical and certain. In some other subjects, deduction is often less certain. Deductive reasoning may also contribute to the other kinds of productive thought and can be supported by allowing students to use pencil and paper to extend their memory capacity. Human deductive reasoning is not infallible and is subject to information–handling limitations, lapses in attention and wishful thinking (Garnham & Oakhill, 1994).

Causal understanding

Understanding is the construction of meaningful, coherent wholes of initially disparate items of information by inferring patterns and relationships between them and connecting them to prior knowledge. Of particular importance are inferences, which enable the construction of hypotheses, theories, explanations and causal understandings. For instance, students could be expected to develop a causal understanding of the topography of the landscape in accordance with the laws of nature. In such circumstances, such an understanding may enable prediction. In history, however, 'causal' understandings and explanations of historical events have plausibility but are less certain and there are no completely reliable predictions (Newton, 2012a). The construction of a causal understanding may be supported by, questioning, for instance, which directs attention to relevant information at the appropriate time (Newton, L.D., 2013a). On the other hand, understanding can be hindered by explanations which assume prior knowledge the student does not have.

Creative thinking

Creative thinking and its cognate twin, problem solving, is about constructing possible worlds which are more or less novel, definitely appropriate and prefer-ably mentally elegant, parsimonious or economical (Newton, 2010a). In a real sense, creative thinking can be an extension of the process of understanding into the construction of coherent, meaningful structures that are at least novel to the student in some way. The onus for productive thought, however, is often more on the student in creative thinking than it is in understanding. What counts as understanding in different domains is different and, similarly, what counts as creativity depends on the domain. The terms 'novelty', 'appropriateness' and 'parsimony' and the relative emphasis on each may change to suit the domain. For instance, in art, appropriateness can be described as rightness-of-fit (Newton & Donkin, 2011). In science, a young student might be shown a phenomenon and be invited to explain it and then construct a practical test of that potential explanation. In art, a child might be asked to make a self-portrait which would let a visitor know something about the child's nature. Creative thinking may be supported by having students consider 'What if?' scenarios. It can be hindered by shortage of time and pressure to perform.

Wise thinking

Wise thinking aims to bring relevant understandings together in a coherent way, embedding them in a wide context, often involving living things, in order to construct possible courses of action and their consequences and to choose the most appropriate action (Baltes & Smith, 2008). Wise thinking can call for deduction, understanding and creative thinking to achieve this end. In real world scenarios, it typically needs an ability to construct comprehensive relationships and involves values, ethics, morality and a balancing of self-interests with the interests of others. For example, when exploring the impact of people on the environment, students would learn of the demise of various species of flora and fauna. They could be asked to consider the wisdom of re-introducing species like the wolf, given the changes that have occurred since its demise. This would involve embedding ecological, geographical and agricultural understandings in wider, human contexts and drawing on values to determine what action, if any, would be appropriate. Helping students remove the partitions between subjects may facilitate such thinking. With younger students, having them see the world through the eyes of the wolf introduces the need to take multiple perspectives. Wise thinking may be hindered by tasks that call for experience which is beyond the students' comprehension.

Critical thinking

Views of critical thinking vary, but in essence its role is to evaluate the quality of thought in order to improve it or judge its credibility (Moseley et al., 2005). On this basis, it is purposeful and potentially productive. This quality control may be applied to existing thought structures but can also guide thought in action, aiming to make the production sound and worthwhile. When applied to the thoughts of other people, it must reconstruct what it appraises and it may be supported by, for instance, knowledge of common reasoning errors and the provision of a scaffold to guide the criticism which, for instance, directs attention to the need to examine underlying assumptions. It can be hindered by unconscious biases and prejudices. In other words, as with all kinds of human thought, it is not infallible (Thayer-Bacon, 1998).

More general supportive strategies

In addition to the strategies which foster specific kinds of productive thought, some are more broadly useful and include, for example, concept maps where learners note and relate their thoughts on paper (e.g. Novak, 2010). Questions that direct attention to what matters and prompt particular kinds of processing to suit the immediate needs of the task can, of course, can be used in a variety of contexts (Janssen & Hullu, 2008; Newton, L.D., 2013a). Self-talk, silently or quietly talking something through can support productive thinking, as it can help the learner to focus and engage in appropriate processing (Hardy et al., 2001). There are many tested strategies available to the teacher for supporting productive thought, and some, like isolation in a quiet place, may already have been acquired by students through experience in their learning. Wider-ranging are approaches which can reflect a conception of the broad purpose of education. For example, if that purpose is seen as chiefly aimed at developing certain thinking skills, prime examples of approaches to fostering such skills are *Thinking in Education/Philosophy in the Classroom* (Lipman, 2003; Lipman et al., 1980) and *Really Raising Standards* (Adey & Shayer, 1994). Some success may lie in the encouragement of conscious reflection on thinking (metacognition), particularly in connection with planning, monitoring and evaluating thinking and its products. Some may also be due to enhancing self-regulated thought, as when students manage their motivation and reasoning (Higgins, 2012). Students' conceptions of education, or what they want from it, are not necessarily the same as those of the teacher. Students may favour reproductive learning, because that is what they think is expected of them, because the subject is nothing more than a means to an end or because that is what they see as counting in tests and examinations. Pointing out what is expected and illustrating what that means in specific terms can shape students' thinking (Entwistle & Entwistle, 2002; Enwistle, 2009). Productive thought, however, can be discouraged by the kind of test and the nature of the questions teachers ask. Multiple choice questions, for instance, particularly those which reward the recall of information, tend to reduce higher level thinking. More open questions which require more effortful productive thought may be disliked by students but they are more likely to encourage higher level thought (Barnett & Francis, 2012; Peterson & Taylor, 2012; Stanger-Hall, 2012). The nature of the assessment is likely to have a significant effect on the kinds of thinking older students engage in.

Bags of beans

Thinking here is seen from a teleological perspective, that is, the kinds of thinking are distinguished by their purpose. This reflects how such terms are used in education, in the classroom and in programmes of study at all levels of teaching and learning. Nevertheless, these kinds of thought comprise more fundamental processes. Some of these processes, like recall from memory and interpretation, may be common to all. At the same time, purposeful thinking in the classroom may rarely be 'pure'. Creative thinking, for instance, may call on, amongst other things, deduction, causal understanding and a dash of critical thinking to achieve its ends. What distinguishes it is its overall purpose and, to achieve that purpose, there are differences in the kind of and emphasis on the underlying processes. For example, Peirce (1923/1998) saw differences in the certainty of the product, with deduction being the most certain, while causal understanding is, essentially, tentative (Glassman & Kang, 2011). Deduction can be seen as a self-contained process, extracting from the given what is hidden in it rather than going beyond it. Causal understanding is less contained in that it goes beyond the given to construct a coherent explanation of it, often led by the causal understanding the teacher has in mind. Creative thinking is more open and wise thinking can draw on other purposeful thought to build comprehensive understandings of the world and possible actions in it. In that sense, it is potentially very wide-ranging. Each of these kinds of thinking is like a bag of beans; each bean represents a specific, psychological process. While each bag may contain beans like the others, the bags also contain some which are different: larger, smaller and of a different colour. Those that are like the others are what the thinking has in common; those that are different (in kind or emphasis) reflect its particular purpose. Other analogies which represent purposeful, productive thinking are, of course, possible (see Newton, L.D., 2013b).

Critical thinking is, however, different. When aimed at maintaining and enhancing the quality of thought, it should show itself in all kinds of purposeful thinking. When evaluating someone's mental product, however, it looks in from the outside and makes a judgment of its worth. Figure 2.1 illustrates this by showing the examples of purposeful thought, allowing for other kinds of such thought, and showing critical thinking's pervasive role in supporting thinking quality while at the same time being capable of application from outside. It is important, however, not to see the sequence from deduction to wise thinking as indicating levels of difficulty or as a teaching progression. Difficulty and progression depend on context and task.

Where the conscious action is

Information can be maintained and processed in working memory, a term introduced by Baddeley (e.g. 1976). From a constructivist perspective, inferential knowledge cannot be transmitted to others, they have to make the connections themselves (Good, 1993); we simply provide the information and try to supply conditions which help them make the mental connections to knit the parts together into a coherent and meaningful whole (Newton, 2012a). Working memory is the term given to the mental processes which do this. They temporarily hold the information and manipulate and build it into mental structures (Dosher, 2003; Lane & Nadel, 2000). Working memory's capacity, however, is

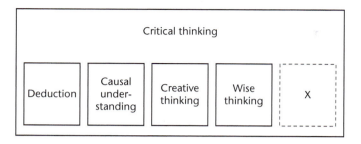

Figure 2.1 The examples of purposeful thought (X allows for others) are permeated appropriately by critical thinking while allowing that critical evaluation may, in addition, be applied after the event.

limited so that we may not be able to manipulate more than a few (three to five) 'chunks' of information at once (Cowan et al., 2005). (A chunk of information comprises lesser elements which are integrated into a coherent whole, like the way a forest is a 'chunk' representing a collection of individual trees, or when the four numbers 1, 9, 8, 4 are remembered as '1984', the title of George Orwell's book.) A mind map constructed on a notepad can support thinking similarly because, in effect, it serves as an organized extension to memory. Working memory is managed by a control or executive system which initiates, prioritizes, sequences and monitors conscious, purposeful thought, having the power to allow it to continue if it is seems to be productive and to stop it if it is not (Martin & Kerns, 2011). Thought, however, is not only conscious. What happens in working memory also depends on semi-conscious and unconscious processes, such as the recall of prior knowledge. Various accounts of this control and working memory system differ in detail, but they agree that it has its limits, it is open to distraction and it can influence and be influenced by emotions (Barkley, 1996; Just & Carpenter, 1996). Productive thought, whatever its purpose, is likely to involve this system. Usefully, students can often tell us something about what they are thinking or, at least, their conscious thoughts in working memory. What they say may be only a part of the story, but it is a window on the students' thoughts and mental skills. In the classroom, the term 'thinking' generally refers to what is conscious and happening in working memory. Cognition is wider than this, but of course much is unconscious and inaccessible.

The capacity for productive thought

Piaget's stage theory of cognitive development (Piaget, 1952) is well known and is a practically useful framework for exercising thinking abilities if not applied too rigidly. It describes some tendencies in thinking according to age, which indicate that thinking for particular purposes, although often limited, begins to emerge in young children and continues to develop into and beyond adolescence. Children 5 or 6 years old can usually solve simple practical problems and show imagination. An early tendency to be strongly egocentric begins to decline by about 6 or 7 years old. While children less than about 6 years old can be confused by causal relationships, this confusion fades and some systematic thinking develops as strategies evolve, particularly when thinking with the help of tangible objects. By 10 years old, the time taken to recall information from memory becomes less and working memory capacity behaves more like it does in adulthood, although such children, probably like some adults, may find it difficult to manipulate more than two chunks of information at once (Cole & Cole, 2001). While the ages at which these changes are complete can vary, allowing for age, experience and meaningful contexts, some form of purposeful, productive thought is possible from an early age and can be expected throughout formal education. This is not to say it will emerge fully armed; there may need to be preparation and progression towards more demanding contexts and forms of thinking. Nevertheless, there is evidence that helping children reflect on their thinking using, for instance, discussion, drawings and concept maps can improve their grasp of what is expected of them (Novak, 2010). Although children show some empathy from an early age and develop a rudimentary grasp of moral and ethical behaviour in adolescence, wise thinking may continue to develop over a lifetime. Nevertheless, the foundations for such thought may be at least strengthened over the period of formal education.

Same lesson, different outcomes

Being able to think purposefully and productively is a worthwhile asset, both in learning and in life in general. It is satisfying, engenders confidence, enables flexible responses and, at its best, supports well-being (Newton, 2012a). Ways of fostering productive thought are known and their application in the classroom can be more or less successful. But why does the same lesson have different outcomes with different students? Why does it sometimes fall flat? Obviously, more is involved in the success of a lesson than a concern for the right thinking strategy. For instance, students vary in prior knowledge, how it is organized and how they think about it. Similarly, their personalities, comfort and health vary, and their experiences, even only minutes ago, differ. Some of the differences are beyond the teacher's control. But what does affect what happens in the classroom is the interaction between emotions and intellectual mental processes and this is something the teacher can plan for and manage, albeit cautiously at first, but with increasing confidence. The next chapter outlines some important features of moods and emotions, then subsequent chapters explore in more detail the common examples of productive thought described above and how moods and emotions can interact with them.

Chapter 3

Ever watchful

Moods, emotions and appraisals

Most of us know a chair when we see one, even though it comes in a variety of shapes and sizes. Moods and emotions are similar and form a somewhat fuzzy family of mental phenomena (Parkinson, 1995). Although difficult to pin down precisely, most people can provide lots of examples (Fehr & Russell, 1984). This makes it possible to talk usefully of emotions, even though what they have in common is more like a family resemblance than a specific set of characteristics. Emotions are 'fundamental to children's academic and cognitive competence', although, today, they are generated by events far removed from those where they evolved (Garner, 2010: 298).

Matters of personal consequence

In the beginning

Like many other animals, we benefit from a rapid, automatic response system which keeps us out of trouble. Imagine walking in a forest when a snarling wolf leaps out. Information about the situation is promptly forwarded to certain parts of the brain, which swiftly screen it, initiate a response, and you leap back (LeDoux, 1998). Whatever you were thinking before is suppressed and you give your full attention to the perceived threat (Rader & Hughes, 2005; Schnall & Laird, 2003; Schupp et al., 2004). At the same time, substances are released in your body which, amongst other things, make your heart beat faster in readiness for further action. In these circumstances, you would probably call the sensation fear. Others might be alerted to the danger by your posture, involuntary cry and facial expression. This emotional system probably evolved because of its survival value (Tooby & Cosmides, 1990). But, in humans, the information is also sent to other parts of the brain, where it is reflected upon at a more leisurely pace. If you deduce that you are safe because the wolf's path is blocked, the emotional system is informed, you relax a little and experience a spreading feeling of relief. Tooby and Cosmides (1990) have argued that some of the other emotions which support our welfare may have evolved similarly. For instance, our ancestors also had a vested interest in supportive, personal relationships because the welfare of hunter-gatherers depended on them. Threats to these relationships may have produced feelings of anxiety, embarrassment, shame or guilt. On the other hand, support for them may have led to feelings of gratitude.

Emotions today

We may be biologically bound to feel fear if we see a wolf, or anxious if made an outcast, but experience adds other producers of emotions to the list so, today, we feel fear and anxiety in situations most unlike those of our ancestors (Frijda, 2004; Lahikainen et al., 2003; LeDoux, 1989, 2000; Plutchik, 1980; Prinz, 2004). For instance, a teacher mentions an activity which his young students will do soon. They perceive it to be an opportunity to satisfy their curiosity, to work independently and to demonstrate their competence, so they look forward to it with eager anticipation and some impatience. Elsewhere, some students are to sit an examination. They know their careers depend on it; consequently, they feel anxious, even agitated.

For me or against me

Life is full of situations which affect us, but we generally do not reason each one through. Instead, the emotional system appraises the situation, looking for matters of personal consequence and, if it finds some, makes a quick judgment of what it sees as the implications and lets us know the outcome, often accompanied by a feeling (Clore & Huntsinger, 2007; Reddy, 2001). The nature of the emotion reflects the perceived significance of the situation for the person concerned; that is, whether it is for or against what are, broadly speaking, the person's vested interests (Crano, 1995; Nussbaum, 2001; Prinz, 2004). This is not to say that the appraisal is always sound but it can, at least, bypass prolonged deliberation and prompt you to give attention to personal concerns, sustaining what you believe is advantageous and ending what you believe is not (Oatley & Jenkins, 1996). Matters of personal consequence are not always immediately evident. They may reveal themselves only after intellectual deliberation and, as that realization spreads to the emotional system, they are appraised and emotions like joy, anticipation, fear and anxiety are generated. Of course, at times the appraisal may reveal neither threat nor benefit, so there may be no emotional response.

The intensity of emotional responses and how well someone copes with them depends on the person: some respond excessively and have long-term academic problems, while others do not (Richards & Hadwin, 2011). Human nature and what is of personal consequence vary, so what is perceived to be a threat by one student may not be much of a threat to another. Emotional expression also depends on cultural norms of behaviour (Prinz, 2004) and there may be emotional complexes in one culture which have no name in others.

For example, the Portuguese have a word for a bittersweet blend of anxiety and happiness, *saudade*, which, it is claimed, has few parallels in other languages (Silva, 2012).

Over time, we learn that some kinds of event either threaten or promote our well-being. This can lead to a more or less sustained state of readiness to respond in a particular way (Frijda, 1986). Many students know that examinations can have lifelong consequences, so feel anxious as the dreaded day approaches. In practice, the anxiety may be more general and attach itself to a wide variety of events where performance is seen as important, including social events. At times, this can be maladaptive. In effect, the state of anxiety, triggered only in specific situations, becomes a reaction to a wide variety of life's events, not always with good cause or to good effect (Frijda, 1988; Schwartz & Clore, 2003).

Moods and emotions: redundant or useful?

Clearly of survival value in the distant past, is the emotional system now nothing more than an unwanted obstruction to sound thinking? Mulligan and Scherer (2012) have defined emotions as relatively short-lived, affective responses, directed at something specific, and triggered by an appraisal of information. Fear, anger and joy are examples. We may become aware of physical feelings associated with such emotions and, in common usage, the terms "feeling" and "emotion" can be almost synonymous. Moods are relatives of emotions and may be one of their longer-term aftermaths or can be responses to more sweeping appraisals of personal well-being. Moods such as sadness tend to last longer, are more diffuse and are of lower intensity than emotions like anger. Unlike emotions, moods can be difficult to relate to a specific event; their function seems to be to provide us with a running commentary on our current state of well-being extended over time (Hullett, 2005; Isen, 1990; Spicer, 2004). For instance, an unconscious appraisal of one's personal life may produce sadness, even depression, if life is judged to be unremittingly unpleasant. States which prove to be very long-lasting, like lifelong 'sadness', may be better described as dispositions (e.g. George & Zhou, 2002; Madjar and Oldham, 2002; Oatley & Jenkins, 1996). Do moods and emotions have the potential to make a contribution to productive thought?

Memory

The emotional system judges some situations to be matters of concern; that is, they are perceived to have consequences for our personal well-being. Potentially important, they may be situations to avoid or look for in the future. The emotional content of these situations makes them more memorable than many emotionless, routine events we meet in daily life (Armony, 2007; Cahill et al., 1996; Phelps, 2006). Traumatic events, for instance, are rarely forgotten and readily brought to mind. Recalling them easily can help us avoid them in the future. This enhancement of memory extends to socially traumatic events which cause, for example, embarrassment, regret and shame, and for which recall is not always welcome (Schunk, 2012). The emotional pains of childhood – 'pains of loneliness, boredom, abandonment, humiliation, rejection and fear … inflicted on me by other children and myself' (Fry, 1998) – are rarely forgotten, as with the longing for things denied us (Truong et al., 2013). The emotional system labels emotive experiences as more noteworthy than others and the memory gives them preferential treatment.

Motivation, attention and direction

In seventeenth-century England, Edward de Vere bowed to Queen Elizabeth I and broke wind; de Vere's embarrassment was so great that he exiled himself for seven years (Dick, 1972). Sensing a situation's threats and benefits can motivate mental and physical action. When our interests are perceived to be at stake, we give the situation our attention and strive to avoid it, change it or take advantage of it. At its simplest, if you are happy, you are likely to try to prolong your current situation; if sad, you may try to change things or escape from them (e.g. Izard, 2010; Reisenzein, 2009; Robinson, 2000). More broadly, the emotional system gives preference to one course of action over another and, in effect, gives direction to our lives. It also applies to trains of thought. Perceptions of progress result in emotions that indicate the likelihood that the current train of thought will achieve your goal. In effect, there is a built-in, continuously alert, stop–go signal which tells you when things are going well and when you might be better changing the direction of your thinking (Martin et al., 1993). If thinking is foundering, you may feel a rising impatience or frustration with it, which makes you pause and take stock. If it seems to be going well, you may feel pleasure or satisfaction (Isbell et al., 2013). When time is limited, this has enormous advantages over slow, analytical thought (Clore & Huntsinger, 2007; Zeelenberg et al., 2008). Here, the emotional system motivates and monitors purposeful thought (Spellman & Schnall, 2009).

Shaping thoughts

In drawing attention to pertinent matters the emotional system can also narrow thought to what is immediately relevant and, when there are alternative courses of action, it can measure each against our best interests and recommend one. Moods and emotions can also shape the content and processing of thought. For example, the task of writing is a demanding one for children, and emotions can sap their mental resources and make the task harder (Fartoukh et al., 2013). An investigation of thinking about terrorism showed that those who feel angry about it tend to look for its causes while those who feel sad do not

(Small et al., 2006). A sad person may also find it harder to see the wood for the trees than a happy person. Happy people tend to feel secure enough to let their thoughts 'broaden and build', while depressed people tend to focus and narrow their thinking (Fredrickson, 2004). In short, the emotional system can shape thought.

Communication

Emotional responses include signals to others about how you feel. Your smile, anger or sad demeanour may communicate your state of mind and serve as a welcome, a warning or a need for comfort (e.g. Lang, 1988). In a classroom, enthusiastic actions will probably induce students' to see what might be in it for them. This may be why headteachers rate enthusiasm very highly when selecting new teachers (Newton & Newton, 2001). Here, the effects of the emotional system serve to communicate with others.

This illustrates that moods and emotions play an important part in our thinking lives. Given the validity of our personal concerns, emotions can be rational responses to situations which bear on them. Of course, matters of personal consequence may not be relevant, sound or worthy, so emotional responses may not always be in our best interests. At times, existing moods and emotions may not be appropriate for the needs of the situation, as when happy music in a car distracts attention and makes the driver more erratic (Pêcher et al., 2009). Certain moods and emotions may facilitate thinking in one context but not in another. On occasions, moods and emotions may be brought from elsewhere and mistaken for internal comments on the task in hand. So, someone may be angry after a minor traffic accident and, still feeling annoyed, she judges students' performance more harshly than she might otherwise have done. Had she won on the lottery, her judgments could have been more generous (Forgas, 1995).

Labelling moods and emotions

Moods and emotions are clustered in various ways. A long-standing division is according to their hedonic tone or valence, that is, how they make you feel, pleasant or unpleasant. Happiness and joy generally have pleasant, positive tones; sadness and depression tend to have unpleasant, negative tones. It is also possible to be in a neutral state (Diener & Lucas, 2000). In addition, moods and emotions can be clustered into those which activate, or prompt us to action, and those which deactivate. Happiness and anger, for instance, are usually activating, while serenity and sadness tend to be deactivating. A third way of classifying moods and emotions is to sort them into those which impel us to approach and those which impel us to avoid their causes (also described as promotion and prevention-focused moods and emotions). Happiness and frustration tend to result in approach while serenity and anxiety result in avoidance. This means that moods and emotions can be more or less pleasant, more or less activating and more or less directing at the same time (Baas et al., 2008). Rage, for instance, can be a negative, very activating emotion, which prompts approach. Note, however, that these ways of labelling moods and emotions really label the outcomes of appraisals, not the emotion itself. Thus, happiness is triggered by an appraisal that indicates support for matters of personal concern. Someone else may see the same event in a different light and may feel unhappy about it.

How moods and emotions interact with productive thought depends on their hedonic tone, activation and approach-avoidance characteristics (Mumford, 2003). While moods can be more enduring than emotions, Lazarus (1991) has pointed out that some moods are fleeting and readily displaced as the situation changes. This has particular relevance for purposeful thought, as it generally extends over a period of time. Emotions and moods can grow, fade and change in a stream or flow of affective experience (e.g. Vandekerckhone & Panskepp, 2009; Watson, 2000). Teaching benefits from planning but it also calls for responses in the course of teaching. Seeing moods and emotions in terms of their hedonic tone, activation or approach-avoidance characteristics is a useful way of thinking about and working with the flow of events and their manifold interactions in busy classrooms. Nevertheless, it is a simplification, albeit a practically useful one. For example, anger may be activating and prompt approach, but is it always a negative emotion? Consequently, some believe that it is better to focus on the effects of particular moods and emotions. Research directed at specific emotions can also inform practice, particularly where it is related to what have been called academic emotions, like anxiety, boredom and anticipation.

Academic moods and emotions

Strictly speaking, any mood or emotion may be involved in the processes of teaching and learning, but Pekrun and his colleagues (1992, 2011; Pekrun et al., 2006) have found that some tend to occur more than others. Amongst North American students, for instance, positive and negative emotions were reported equally often. Amongst the former, enjoyment, hope, pride, relief, gratitude and admiration were common; in the latter were anger, boredom, shame, contempt and envy. Anxiety was the emotion most often reported, both in connection with examinations and in the classroom. If a student feels unable to master a topic, he believes he has little control of his learning and enjoyment decays and anxiety grows. If he finds personal relevance in a topic, he is more likely to feel interest. In addition, moods and emotions generated elsewhere can be brought to academic study. These, too, can interact with thought and can affect it (Forgas, 1995). It is generally believed that schools should be happy places, as children learn better when they feel good. This may make learning enjoyable but it does not always make thought efficient or entirely productive. For instance, when locating particular shapes in pictures, happy 10- and 11-year-olds took longer to find the shapes than sad children (Schnall et al., 2008c). It seems that being happy hinders systematic searches and dealing with detail. Nevertheless, this is *not* to suggest that teachers should strive to make classrooms gloomy and students unhappy – there are significant benefits from feeling good, not least being better health (Fredrickson, 2003; Otto, 2001). It is possible to consider moods, emotions and intellectual needs in planning, instruction and assessment without prejudicing a positive ethos in the classroom (Popp et al., 2011).

Emotional development

This matters only if students have emotions and they are generated by appraisals of the personal relevance of situations. It is clear that infants in the first few months of life display expressions that look to us like emotional responses of happiness, fear, sadness, anger and disgust. Teasing causes frustration and odd antics produce wariness. Izard (1991) interprets this to mean that we are born with a small set of basic emotions which support our survival. It is, of course, difficult to be certain that an infant feels what we feel in response to different situations, so this does not rule out the possibility that what we see as fear in an infant's face may be something else. Some argue that, rather than being born with a few fully fledged emotions, we are equipped with more fundamental components which become linked in various ways to form what we call emotions (e.g. Fogel et al., 1992). Another possibility is that infants' emotions are simply positive or negative, so they feel their present situation as pleasant or unpleasant. Only later does this differentiate into particular emotions (Oatley & Jenkins, 1996). During the second year, however, the more complex social and self-conscious emotions of pride, shame, embarrassment and guilt may become evident. These children also recognize emotions like distress and amusement in others (Dunn, 2003).

Children between 2 years 6 months and 6 years can identify events which make them happy, afraid, angry or sad, and there is evidence that it is the children's appraisals of these events which give rise to these emotions. Younger children can feel angry when their goals are obstructed. If the obstruction seems insurmountable, they may simply feel sad. Older children, however, are more inclined to baulk at the reasons for the obstruction (Stein & Levine, 1999). Studies of 3- to 6-year-olds' explanations of emotions in the USA showed they can understand that emotions can stem from expectations of situations (Lagattuta, 2007; Sayfan & Lagattuta, 2008). In one story, a boy had his teddy bear stolen. Later, he was described as agitated by the sight of the thief and the children explained that it was because he thought the thief might steal his other toys. Another study examined children's thinking about the effects of emotions on test results (Amsterlaw et al., 2009). In one story, a child on her way to school lost her teddy bear and so was sad. At school, she had to do a hard mathematics test. Like adults, the majority of the children (5–7 years) predicted that feeling sad would impair her test performance. When the mood was a happy one, they predicted it would enhance performance. The older children were able to account for the effects in ways similar to adults, usually by reference to the effect of emotion on attention. They saw negative emotions as reducing attention and positive emotion as enhancing it. Interestingly, some argued that being happy could also reduce attention and performance,which seems a remarkably perceptive prediction for such young children to make. By 5 years of age, children have begun to understand that feeling pleased stems from seeing that events have worked out as they wanted. Similarly, they can see that surprise indicates a mismatch between expectations and reality (Hadwin & Perner, 1991). This suggests an emerging grasp of the role of appraisal in the generation of emotions. From this relatively early age, children can talk about their feelings and those of others in a rudimentary way (e.g. Lagattuta, 2007).

By the time a teacher sees these children, they have begun the path towards adult emotional behaviours. Children of school age are beginning to assess situations intuitively and relate them to their expectations, goals and perceived well-being. The age at which this comes together seems to be 7, but children still have some way to go in, for instance, the control of emotional expression, the management of emotions and the grasp of contrary, ambivalent emotions (Oatley & Jenkins, 1996). The brain continues to develop well into adolescence. Puberty increases emotional arousability and a tendency to seek sensation and take risks. A grasp of emotion-eliciting situations progressively increases. In later adolescence, reappraisals of such situations may now take place, making them acceptable by finding, for example, a silver lining in them or accepting that things could be worse (Berk, 2012; Garner, 2010; Steinberg, 2007).

On this basis, the emotional system functions from an early age, aspects of it continue to develop into adolescence, and at all ages, there is the potential for an interaction between emotions and cognition. Should teachers wish to manage this interaction, they need to recognize moods and emotions in their students.

Recognizing moods and emotions

The feelings associated with moods and emotions are personal and private but they can produce effects which could be noticed by a teacher. For example, what teachers notice are students' facial expression, posture, gaze, and the tone, volume and speed of speech. While these may not be precise indicators of mood and emotion and are open to pretence, they are the immediate sources of information we draw on when judging another's state of mind. For instance, in as little as twenty seconds, young adults can predict altruistic tendencies from their observations of emotions expressed when others make social decisions (Fetchenhauer et al., 2010).

Recognizing emotions and moods in others is a part of what some have called emotional intelligence. Goleman (1995) believes that expert teachers have it, perhaps without being aware of it. It could be that some ability to recognize emotions in others is innate, but it also develops with experience. Certainly, many can recognize emotions like anger, fear, happiness, sadness and surprise from facial expression and vocal tone (Keltner et al., 2003; Scherer et al., 2003). The ability varies from person to person and is generally better when observing those who are known well and from familiar cultures (Elfenbein & Ambady, 2003; Elfenbein et al., 2002). This suggests that teachers are likely to have some success in recognizing emotions in those they teach, particularly when they know them well. Moods, however, are generally milder and more diffuse than emotions and may be more difficult to identify.

D'Mello et al. (2008), when making their electronic 'AutoTutor' responsive to the users' emotions, tested two 'accomplished' teachers' recognition of students' moods and emotions and did not find it was reliable. However, only two teachers were involved, they were not familiar with the students and there were no vocal clues. Subsequent training with Ekman's Facial Action Coding System (Ekman & Friesen, 2003) greatly improved the teachers' mood and emotion recognition (Graesser et al., 2006). Teachers are likely to have some ability to recognize emotions and moods in their students, particularly students they know. Even when the ability is not strong, it is open to development through practice and training and, if all else fails, teachers can ask students how they feel. Students from an early age seem able and willing to talk about their academic emotions.

Managing the interaction

Recognizing emotions is one thing, but putting that knowledge to good use is what matters. Often referred to as emotion regulation, the modification of moods and emotions to foster productive thought may be initiated by the teacher or by the student. Some may feel reluctant to manage the moods and emotions of others; it has a smell of manipulation about it and, perhaps, of tinkering with something intimate and personal. Nevertheless, we frequently do it when we cheer others up, calm them down or deflect their attention from distressing events, and we rarely think twice about it. In the classroom, we try to catch interest and inspire and we sometimes disappoint students with our feedback, make them anxious with tests and sad with the results. Similarly, we may calm young children with a tranquil story and never give it a second thought.

Few would argue against helping learners feel happy about what they do, but most would hesitate at deliberately making someone sad, particularly when it is a trusting child. Feeling socially rejected can encourage artistic creativity but would we want to foster creativity by making art students, young or old, feel socially rejected? When the emotion–cognition interaction needs to be considered, the ethical suitability of what is proposed is important, as with any intervention in another person's life. For instance, a teacher should guard against inducing a habit of emotional excess or lasting negative moods. Levinson (1999) argues that if managing moods and emotions does not alter a student's fundamental emotional character, then it is reasonable to do so. On this basis, many emotion and mood management strategies are unlikely to be controversial. At the same time, teachers tend to be open with students about their motives. For example, they tell them that a particular activity was chosen because it will interest them.

Young children are unlikely to be conscious of emotion regulation until parents bring the expectation to their attention at about 6 years of age, depending on the culture (Oatley & Jenkins, 1996). 'Big boys don't cry' is an example, often accompanied with a strategy, such as 'Be a brave little soldier.' Such children are generally dependent on adults for help with managing their emotions and for coping strategies and, of course, that depends on the adults' sensitivity and knowledge of appropriate strategies. During the elementary or primary school, children's dependency on adults declines, to be replaced by peer dependence (Durkin, 1995). Later, those near adulthood who can regulate their moods have more success regulating positive moods than they do negative moods (Hovanitz et al., 2011).

Just because regulatory strategies have not been taught to students does not mean they have none. Emotions may be self-regulated from an early age to some extent by using strategies acquired unconsciously or by imitation. Young children, for instance, will simply walk away from what makes them feel emotionally uncomfortable. Distraction is a common strategy for dealing with negative emotion throughout life. Such strategies may not always be the best, but they probably have some useful effect. For those who can regulate their moods and emotions, drawing attention to the need for a mood change can work, so supportive feedback need not be confined to intellectual matters (Forgas & Vargas, 2000).

Emotional intelligence tends to mean different things to different people (Zeidner et al., 2012). According to Mayer et al. (2008a), it comprises the ability to perceive emotions, understand emotions, use emotions to facilitate thinking, and manage them to achieve goals. In the context of fostering productive thought, these could amount to an ability to perceive, understand and regulate the interaction of moods and emotions with the intellect to further that thought. This specific application of emotional intelligence does not seem to have attracted as much direct attention as improving behaviour, or promoting mental health and social competence (Elias et al., 2001; Mayer & Cobb, 2000). Each is a worthy end, but so is fostering productive thought. There is evidence that emotional intelligence can predict academic success better than some traditional indicators of academic intelligence and personality (Mayer et al., 2008b; Van der Zee et al., 2002). The development of emotional intelligence in students is not, however, the main aim here. Instead, it is to point to the value of knowing about the emotion–cognition interaction and managing it to optimize productive thought.

But managing moods and emotions is not always as easy as it sounds. For instance, simply asking someone to think positive thoughts, 'buck up' or 'just forget about it' has mixed results. Those who would manipulate moods and emotions give it a lot of thought. Charity workers, for instance, know that a positive mood tends to make us less critical and more likely to donate, so they use a small gift to make the recipient feel positive, obligated and generous (Isen, 1990). Similarly, music in shops lessens our spending restraint (e.g. Augustine & Hemenover, 2009; van Goethem & Sloboda, 2011). There are simple strategies which can make a difference to academic emotions, too. For example, imagining a happy event can counter a depressed mood (Dalgleish et al., 2009; Holmes et al., 2009; Vitters et al., 2009).)

In conclusion

Emotions may have evolved to protect our well-being, but they are not simply a vestigial inheritance from the past. As Bower expressed it, 'Emotion is evolution's way of giving meaning to our lives' (1992: 4). In the process, moods and emotions can motivate and prompt action. Levenson (1999: 481) put it well: 'Emotions serve to establish our position vis-à-vis our environment, pulling us towards certain people, objects, actions and ideas, and pushing us away from others.' Moods and emotions are also important in the workings of the intellect, particularly when the situation is personally or socially significant (Izard, 2007, 2010). The interaction of emotions and cognition starts early in life and teachers are likely to have some ability to recognize moods and emotions in their students, particularly when they know them well. Given that, there is the possibility that teachers may take this emotion–cognition interaction into account in their planning and teaching. Like old world maps, the map of emotion–cognition interactions still has patches of *terra incognita*, but enough is known to enable us to explore these interactions in the context of teaching to foster purposeful thought (Tamir, 2011). Subsequent chapters examine these interactions in the exemplars of purposeful thought and consider how that thought might be made productive.

Chapter 4

It stands to reason

Deductive thinking

This chapter describes a kind of mental activity often exercised in formal education, the act of deduction, and an obvious candidate for the High Reason of Immordino-Yang and Damasio (2007). It illustrates, largely through the interpretation and deductive inferencing processes and by the effects of the emotional climate, that, even though it is at the 'cold' end of the thinking spectrum, it is not as disconnected from emotion as some might imagine. Some of these connections will be illustrated and implications for practice considered.

Thinking it through

Reasoning is the process of making inferences (Poggiani, 2012). The inferences can be ends in themselves or may contribute to other kinds of productive thought. One kind of reasoning which is expected in education, and is frequently an end in itself at all levels, is the act of deduction, particularly of the kind '*If* that is so, *then* this follows'. In mathematics, for instance, students are expected to deduce that '*If a* is greater than *b* and *if b* is greater than *c, then a* must be greater than *c*.' In studying a language, they may be expected to learn certain verb declensions as exemplars and, subsequently, *if* a new verb has the same form as one of these, *then* students should assume its declension will be the same, at least in the first instance (Hammerly, 1975). In science, and as Archimedes deduced, students are to grasp that *if* the volume of water displaced by the king's crown is less than the gold given to make it, *then* some of the gold is missing. Strictly speaking, productive thought of this nature does not add new information to what is given, but takes what is given and squeezes a consequence or conclusion from it (Gilhooly, 1996; Harman, 2011). Teachers at all levels expect students to follow trains of thought which rely on one or a series of deductions. For this reason, deduction has been chosen to illustrate a fairly specific but important kind of thinking which is often an end in itself in the classroom and can contribute significantly to other kinds of thought. Although popularly associated with domains like mathematics and science, it is used widely. Students are set tasks involving the making of deductive inferences and may be expected to add the conclusions to their stock of knowledge (Harman, 2012).

Deductive reasoning produces a conclusion which commands belief on the assumption that its premises are true (Wagner & Penner, 1984) and so is an obvious candidate for the gold standard of reliable, logical thought, free of emotion – Damasio's High Reason, the archetype of cold, rational thought. Blanchette and Richards (2010: 562) point out that such reasoning is one of the higher kinds of thought which 'help us navigate a complex world'. Indeed, subjects like mathematics are in the curriculum partly because they provide experience of the power of deductive, logical, cold reasoning (e.g. Rosenstein et al., 1996; White, 2010). Regardless of how you feel about it, if one widget costs £2, then seven widgets cost £14. It is a powerful antidote to wishful thinking and a defence against exploitation, at least when buying widgets.

Nevertheless, human deductive reasoning is not infallible. Reasoning generally involves conscious processing in working memory, perhaps to construct a mental model of a situation and to manipulate it. It is, however, limited by working memory's capacity (DeWall et al., 2008; Johnson-Laird, 2010). Adults may be able to hold and mentally manipulate two or three premises at once but more can be quite taxing (Halford, 1993). When overloaded, people may simply give up or respond with what feels right. A computer can be obliged by its programming to explore all the options. The human mind is neither compelled to do so, nor has to be exhaustive in its efforts (Johnson-Laird, 2010). At the same time, it also has a tendency to go beyond the given and produce a world-wise interpretation of a thinking task. We know, for instance, that we can sometimes obtain a discount when we buy more than one widget, so seven widgets may cost less than £14.

To compound the problem, information is often incomplete in real life contexts. Choosing a healthy meal from a restaurant's menu is an example (Garcia-Retamero & Rieskamp, 2008). The menu rarely tells all, so people choose in a variety of ways, perhaps on how the food is prepared or on what goes into it or on the supposed simplicity of the dish. Each of these produces a different *if*, so that the *then* results in a different meal. Even when information is present, someone's conclusion can depend on how it is presented. For example, people are loss-averse, so if one choice highlights the potential loss while the other highlights the potential gain the latter will attract more attention even when the loss is the same (Byrne et al., 2000; Lehrer, 2009). At times, we may also avoid the slow and demanding path of logic and become heuristic thinkers because it can be quicker and easier (Evans, 2008). This happens when time is short, but the cost is being open to bias. Given just a few seconds to suggest the answer to '$2 \times 3 \times 4 \times 5 \times 6 \times 7 \times 8 \times 9$', most offer a figure which seems reasonable to them. Yet, if it had been '$9 \times 8 \times 7 \times 6 \times 5 \times 4 \times 3 \times 2$', what seems reasonable is commonly much larger. Similarly, if asked for an estimate of, say, the number of homeless in your country, the figure would probably be biased by your experience of the homeless in your neighbourhood.

Such tendencies can produce conclusions that are not always in accordance with a strict application of formal logic, nor are they always free of error (Garety et al., 2005; Gilhooly, 1996). Nevertheless, even young children can have some ability to reason deductively when the context is meaningful and concrete. For instance, when determining which of two toys is the heavier, they can be aware that if one toy produces the greater effect (perhaps in squashing a cushion), then that toy is the heavier (McGhee, 1997). In similar contexts, they can also reason about what someone does in terms of that person's beliefs and desires (Wellman & Bartsch, 1988). In formal education, therefore, some reasoning ability is likely to be present from a very early age. Furthermore, reasoning in general can be fostered by approaches which help younger children make their thinking conscious by verbalizing and justifying it (Mercer et al., 1999). Older students can benefit similarly by modelling thought processes and scaffolding their thinking along similar lines (Venville & Dawson, 2010).

Moods, emotions and deductive reasoning

Moods and emotions may be incidental to a lesson or caused by something in it. For instance, a student may already feel despondent about some event at home and bring that feeling to the lesson. Other students may arrive to find there is to be a test or an around-the-room question-and-answer session and feel apprehensive about it. Another student, listening to an event in history, may respond emotionally to accounts of people's ill-treatment of others like themselves. Some ways these moods and emotions can affect deductive reasoning will be illustrated. In this kind of purposeful thought, which some consider to be the gold standard of passionless thinking, attention will focus mainly on the interpretation of information and the processing of it to reach a conclusion. Clearly, more than that is involved in deduction, but these other aspects will be described in later chapters in connection with other kinds of productive thought. Equally, there will be times when interpretation and deductive inferencing enter into the other examples of purposeful thought.

Interpreting

Interpretation is what someone does in order to construct meaning from the given information (Blanchette & Richards, 2010). Information is more or less ambiguous and may be interpreted in different ways. A factual statement such as 'There was a fire in the room' can mean very different things, ranging from some cosy, nineteenth-century parlour with a kettle on the hob and bread toasting near a warm, welcoming coal fire, to a raging inferno turning the room into a pile of smouldering ash. This means that 'If there was a fire in the room, then I would ...' could generate very different responses, such as '... then I would go in, sit down and warm my hands' to 'then I would dash outside, call the fire brigade and stand well clear'. The ambiguity here is an obvious one and, in practice, the context or additional information is likely to clarify the matter. Sometimes, however, what clearly means something to one person can clearly mean something else to another, and that difference can stem from how they feel.

The first influence could be from moods brought to the reasoning and which direct attention. In particular, there is a tendency to notice information that reflects or is congruent with the prevailing mood. For instance, someone in a sad mood is more likely to notice a frowning face or depressed language, in effect making the mood an information filter, favouring emotive content which matches the mood (Becker & Leinenger, 2011; Howe & Malone, 2011). At the same time, those who feel anxious have a tendency to interpret ambiguous scenarios in ways that are different from others. In particular, they are more likely to opt for interpretations that reflect threats and risk to themselves, especially when the scenario is of a social situation. Even when interpreting the ambiguous expression on faces in pictures, anxious people are more likely to interpret expressions as fearful and angry than are others (Blanchette & Richards, 2010). This means that happy students are more likely to interpret the fire scenario as welcoming, while sad and anxious students are more likely to interpret it as a hazard.

Anxious children and adults show these biases in their interpretations of information (Richards et al., 2007), but teachers will be relieved to find that a tendency to turn the task they set into a different task through diverse interpretation is not insurmountable; it can be guarded against (when the teacher does not want that diversity) by providing contextual information. The danger is more that a teacher is unaware that prevailing moods and emotions can bias interpretations. This is a minor difficulty in many situations, topics and subjects but could be significant when deductive reasoning is long and complex, so that one conclusion biases the starting point of the next deduction something like the game of Chinese Whispers, when a short sentence is passed around a room via whispers from person to person and is mutated in the process.

Inferencing

The interpretation of the information informs the process of constructing a mental representation of the premises from which an inference by deductive reasoning may follow. Broadly speaking, there is some truth in the suspicion that moods and emotions brought to or generated by the task or topic can impair deductive reasoning, particularly when moods and emotions are intense (Blanchette & Richards, 2010). Emotions like strong anxiety take mental resources from logical thought and tend to make the mental processing of information more difficult, more haphazard and less thorough. The result is that more errors are made. Depression, anger and disgust can similarly reduce reasoning performance (Pham, 2007; Stollstorff et al., 2013). Working memory plays a major part in deductive reasoning and it may be that strong emotions, like euphoria, anxiety or depression, reduce its capacity by filling it with rumination about task-irrelevant events (e.g. Channon & Baker, 1994; Martin &

Kerns, 2011). Very depressed people, for instance, may be torn between two objects of thought: the cause of the depression and the object of study. As their minds wander from the task, they fail to integrate the premises, make an inference and come to a conclusion (Dreisbach & Goschke, 2004; Oaksford et al., 1996; Smallwood et al., 2009). This distraction reduces mental efficiency but, given enough time and encouragement, students could eventually succeed (Eysenck et al., 2005; Hadwin et al., 2005).

Some milder moods and emotions, however, may support logical thought. Sad moods brought to a task, for instance, are known to increase careful and systematic reasoning. When generated within a task, they can also signal that thinking has become unproductive and a more careful or new approach is needed. Positive moods, like feeling happy, tend to decrease deductive reasoning performance possibly because they induce a less detailed or less thorough kind of processing. Happy people also tend to make more moves to solve logical puzzles. They could be less motivated to engage in deduction, choosing instead to enjoy and prolong the prevailing, pleasant mood (Badcock & Allen, 2003; Blanchette & Richards, 2010; Oaksford et al., 1996; Pham, 2007; Radenhausen & Anker, 1988). In social reasoning, 'beliefs, desires, and intentions' are attributed to others, calling for an awareness that others have mental states which shape their behaviour in particular ways. This theory about the minds of others can guide reasoning about what they will do and how they will do it (Converse et al., 2008: 725). Converse and his colleagues found that the likelihood of this theory-of-mind being used was shaped by mood. Happiness tended to lead to its neglect, while sadness increased its use in the kinds of social reasoning problems like those used in classrooms (Badcock & Allen, 2003).

Of course, the content of the topic or task may also be a matter of personal consequence. If the student's emotional appraisal system considers this to be so, then an emotion is likely to follow. 'If a number is even, then it is divisible by two' is probably not a matter of immediate life or death for a student and it may be viewed quite dispassionately. But deductive reasoning can produce conclusions which matter, at least some people. For instance, if the deduction is 'If you use Twitter, then you're a birdbrain', the conversation could be somewhat heated, particularly amongst volatile students. Emotions are not inherently irrational responses to the world: they can be quite rational, given what matters to you; rather, it is what you value which may be maladaptive (Sripada & Stich, 2004). Being logical can be hard when the reasoning has personal consequences. Children find it difficult to put aside their own beliefs and treat an unexpected conclusion with equanimity (Croker & Buchanan, 2011). With older students and adults, the parallel is in finding it difficult to accept conclusions that go against vested interests (Sripada & Stich, 2004). People prefer conclusions that do not contradict their existing beliefs or vested interests, possibly because rejecting such concerns would induce some kind of unease or inconvenience. For instance, if someone has a long commitment to homeopathic remedies, and if they are given evidence that homeopathy has no basis, logic dictates that they should give it up but, instead, they may shy away from that conclusion. Reactions to logical conclusions about smoking, binge drinking and, in the USA, gun control can be similar.

Direct personal experience of emotive situations can also affect thought. War veterans, for instance, were found to reason with more deliberation about emotive aspects of combat (for example, so-called friendly-fire incidents). It was concluded that, where the object is seen as important, more care is taken in reasoning (Blanchette, 2006; Blanchette & Campbell, 2012; Blanchette et al., 2007; Lindström & Bohlin, 2011). Blanchette (2006: 1124) gives as an example a deduction which is likely to be perceived as of consequence, at least by teachers: 'If a child has been abused, then he may suffer from behavioural difficulties.' Both the negative connotations and its practical importance for the teacher could stimulate more deliberation than would have been the case if this had been 'If the meadow is cut, then the grass will not go to seed.'

An illuminating example of task-generated emotions is described by Swain (2013). Two students were engaged in collaborative dialogue in second language learning with the aim of deducing the form of an adjective to agree with a particular noun. In the process, they showed pride, pleasure, admiration, excitement and satisfaction, which arose in and supported the collaborative process, helping to make it successful. This is a reminder that cognition can also have a social dimension (e.g. Vygotsky, 2000) and that emotional effects are both between and within students.

The emotional climate

The emotional climate of the learning environment is the prevailing, background affective tone in which thinking takes place. It is partly determined by the physical surroundings, as when the noise of groundsmen endlessly cutting the grass becomes irritating and distracting, and partly by student and teacher behaviour and interaction, as when a disruptive student stimulates an aggressive response. Although not fixed, its general character may be relatively predicable for a given class, classroom and teacher taken together. In mathematics, for instance, where that climate is one of teacher concern for students and their learning, it can promote academic enjoyment, self-efficacy and effort (Sakiz et al., 2012; Stipeck, 2002). The emotional climate could, therefore, support productive thought both directly, by influencing students' moods and emotions, and indirectly by, for instance, encouraging persistence.

Other classroom practices may similarly affect productive thought. Teachers, keen to make progress, may press for quick responses. Evans (2004) and Kahneman (2012) describe two paths to conclusions, one that is relatively slow and involves deliberate, systematic, analytical thought and the other that is quick, intuitive and relies on prior beliefs and expectations. Goel and Vartanian (2011: 122) argue that analytical thought is much more demanding than intuitive thought and, 'Other things being equal, participants will always choose the less demanding route over the more demanding route.' Even when students are in the mood for analytical thought, care is needed to avoid a default to an intuitive, non-systematic kind of thinking.

Arguers and arguments

Reasoning often has to be justified to others. An argument is a form of communication with the intent of persuading or convincing others of the truth or error of a conclusion (Gilbert, 1995). This might mean, for instance, justifying premises and their interpretation, demonstrating that the conclusion follows from these premises and pointing to the limits of that conclusion. In a sense, an argument says what has been left unsaid in the reasoning and can help someone follow a train of thought. In a classroom, teachers may not take an 'if … then' response without question. Instead, they ask for its justification with questions of the kind, 'And why do you think that?'

The ability to argue and to understand this kind of argument, at least in a rudimentary way, is present before most children attend school, and it develops with age (Stein & Albro, 2001). Having students generate arguments about something which they feel to be worthwhile is a useful pedagogical tool in education, with the potential to help them understand and explore thought and see beyond its superficial features (Matusov & Soslau, 2010). It is important to note, however, that, while formal argument here is deductive and leads to necessary truths, everyday or informal argument often rests on incomplete information, induction and abduction, so has fewer certainties and is 'far more slippery' (Brem, 2003: 148). (Induction and abduction underpin causal understanding and that is the subject of the next chapter.)

To the extent that reasoning involves and is influenced by moods and emotions, then arguments will reflect that. Assertions which threaten values (for example, 'If it is war, then rape is justified') are likely to provoke strong negative emotions and prompt detailed reasoning, with the aim of generating a rebuttal (Goel & Vartanian, 2011). Even reasoning which, on the surface, seems emotion-free, like what to do about climate change, can generate frustration and anger when the deductions seem implausible and hopeless resignation when they seem irrefutable (Lombardi & Sinatra, 2013). The process of argumentation is itself open to emotional effects, as when the arguer has some vested interest in the success of the argument. There may be a defensive response intended to protect self- and public images or it could be that the argument underpins an intended and personally valued course of action. When that is threatened, there can be heated exchanges and anger. Equally, someone who hears an argument can be subject to the same effects or may criticize trivia through a need to persuade others of their intellectual superiority. How people respond to arguments also depends on the culture. In some places in the West, for instance, the norms of behaviour tend to encourage criticism with a less than even-handed negativity (Newton, 2010b).

Seeing the interaction between emotions and reasoning simply in terms of hindering or aiding reason conceals a more fundamental effect on the kind of reasoning induced by moods and emotions. There is evidence that those in a positive mood, perhaps feeling happy, tend to reason in a relatively superficial and heuristic way and their arguments are likely to reflect that. They are influenced less by the strength of an argument than they are by its source. Those in a negative mood, as when feeling sad, tend to be more systematic and analytical in their thinking and root out the deep features of the argument to judge its validity (e.g. Bless & Igou, 2005). In other words, the mood can bring about differences in the nature of that deductive thinking and in how arguments are constructed and considered.

Of course, we are not just moody or emotional; we have a specific mood and a particular emotion, such as sadness, anticipation, joy, pensiveness or apprehension. At this level of detail, some of the generalizations need at least some qualification. For instance, while the positive mood of happiness can lead to more heuristic processing, so can the normally negative mood of anger. Rather than dividing emotions into positive and negative in this context, Tiedens and Linton (2001) suggest that grouping them into those indicating certainty (for example, happiness and anger) and uncertainty (for example, apprehension and anxiety) is useful. In a given context, feelings of certainty signal that detailed processing is unnecessary, while uncertainty signals a need for caution and careful, detailed analysis. This is unlikely to be the full picture, however, as other attributes, such as the intensity of the emotion, also play a part.

Some implications for practice

The popular notion that emotions are bad for you when trying to do some serious thinking has some truth in it, at least for deductive reasoning when the emotions are intense. But there are other times when moods and emotions lend a hand and support it, as when reasoning about emotive situations is backed by personal experience. This illustrates that the ubiquitous exhortation that students should think it through, follow the reasoning and come to a logical conclusion can call for more than the intellect (Gilkey et al., 2010). Reasoning is not a helpless participant in such events and, on occasions, it may make the nature of the threat conscious, stimulate reflection and either accept, discount or generate a way of coping with it (Lazarus, 1991).

The following examples illustrate some ways in which moods and emotions can affect deductive reasoning in practice. A teacher of young children planned a lesson on 'Healthy Eating' and was startled by the effect of vested interests:

The teacher began by asking for examples of 'junk food'. There were heated exchanges as children's favourite food, a matter of personal consequence, was classified as unhealthy. The expected conclusion that: if you eat or drink too much of these things, then you will become unhealthy, was not accepted by the majority. They countered the deduction by reference to healthy parents who had always eaten these things which then brought into play another matter of personal consequence.

A mathematics teacher cultivated a classroom climate which maintained control but inhibited productive thought:

The teacher was always brusque with his students. They fell silent when he strode into the room and, when he asked questions, responses which were not quick and correct were impatiently and sarcastically dismissed. The students avoided catching his attention and relief spread around the room when the lesson was over. Reaching the end of the lesson without being the object of scorn and derision was a matter of some consequence to the students, outweighing the development of deductive reasoning.

Supporting deduction

Many studies of the interaction of moods, emotions and deductive reasoning do not have educational practices as their objective. While bearing this in mind, it is possible to make some suggestions for planning and teaching topics which depend on deductive reasoning.

Students' moods and emotions can be incidental to the activity or content of the topic. Moods and emotions may be brought to a session or generated by something unrelated to what is taught. Whatever the source, they can interact with productive thinking. Managing this interaction can be helped by forethought, action and, to inform future practice, afterthought.

Forethought

Productive thought can be limited by strong emotions. If students are likely to arrive somewhat animated, or if parts of the topic may generate intense emotions, have a calming strategy ready to use. Remove distractions and make the teaching environment organized and calm to set the tone for the session. Teachers routinely moderate emotions ('settle a class down') to achieve their goals. Anticipate negative responses, like boredom, and plan a strategy to avoid them. For example, cast the task in a form in which students have a vested interest or which clearly relates to matters of personal consequence. When tasks are seen as personally relevant or important, students are more likely to think more carefully and analytically. Be sensitive to premises and conclusions that bear upon personal needs, beliefs, values and goals. Emotive content that threatens students' vested interests may generate emotions which prompt the rejection of logical conclusions.

Action

This is where the teaching is in progress. Building and maintaining a supportive emotional climate can have significant advantages for purposeful thought of any kind. The tone can be set by example and the use of a calming activity prior to engaging with the main thinking task. During the task, it helps to show a concern for each student's success in deductive thinking, as this can encourage persistence and a willing engagement. Establish a habit of moderating students' emotions and their expression where these would otherwise take mental resources from the task in hand. Avoid undue pressure for a quick student response; pressure can trigger quick but shallow thinking, instead of deliberate, systematic reasoning. Listening to students is also important (Epley et al., 2004; Everston, 1989). This is particularly so when students already have preconceived ideas or beliefs about the topic. When emotions are present and are likely to affect thinking adversely (as with strong anxiety), more time and less pressure for a response may help. Some students will be able to appreciate that the emotional climate and their part in it is also important in private study, sowing the seeds of self-regulation (Schwartz & Clore, 1983).

While the maintenance of the emotional climate is an ongoing matter, some specific actions are also likely to help students in their deductive reasoning. In particular, check that the interpretation of information is as intended. With older students, practice in interpreting tasks in benign ways has been found to counter the effects of anxiety (Wilson et al., 2006). At the same time, avoid presenting peripheral information in an emotive way, as this may deflect attention from what matters. Listen to and observe students as they collaborate and judge their progress. Not all difficulties are caused by inappropriate moods and emotions; human reasoning is not infallible. At the same time, many moods and emotions are transitory and need attention only if they materially, adversely and persistently affect thought (Swain, 2013). Whatever the source of the difficulty, deductive reasoning is often supported by extending students' mental resources. Even a notepad and a pencil can help the student hold and manipulate ideas when mental resources are threatened by moods and emotions. Students may also think more efficiently without looming deadlines.

Afterthought

When reflecting on the success (or otherwise) of a lesson, also reflect on the quality of the emotional climate. If it was a clear impediment to useful thought, or learning in general, it will need attention. At the same time, students vary and what works with one student may not be so effective with another. If necessary, ask colleagues what they have found to be effective.

In conclusion

So called cold, logical reason is not always as emotionless as some think it is. Interpretation and deductive inferencing were two of the processes that illustrate this. There is some truth in the belief that moods and emotions can be bad for deductive reasoning, particularly when they direct interpretation inappropriately, take up mental resources needed for the task or induce a kind of thinking which does not favour careful, analytical thought. But this is not the entire truth. Some moods may also favour deductive thinking. Fostering these when they are needed could help students make the most of their intellectual abilities.

While making what might be described as 'free-standing' deductions is a common exercise in formal education, it is not everything. However novel a deduced conclusion seems, it was extracted only from what was given. There are no leaps of imagination or sighting of new lands, even dimly. This is for more adventurous kinds of productive thought, where moods and emotions can play a greater role, often with more subtlety. For instance, faced with a big decision, it is tempting to think that deductive reasoning will handle it. In reality, a logical weighing of costs and benefits is rarely, if ever, all it takes. In practice, we compare costs and benefits by recourse to emotions (Mameli, 2004). According to Hume, 'reason is, and only ought to be the slave of the passions, and can never pretend to any other office than to serve and obey them' (Hume, 1739/1978: 462). In other words, reason gets us where the emotions want us to go. Deduction often has a part to play in other kinds of productive thought, so the effects of mood and emotion on it need to be carried forward and added to other effects, still to be described.

Chapter 5

Order from chaos
Constructing causal understandings

While logical deduction, arriving at a valid conclusion, is one kind of reasoning commonly expected in the classroom, constructing a causal understanding is a mental activity which goes further. Whereas deduction squeezes conclusions and consequences from what has been given, causal understanding requires the thinker to note an effect and construct a reasonable cause for it. The mental processes which do this can be oiled by an appropriate emotional climate and by attention to the moods and emotions generated by the topic and the teaching method.

Understanding

Understanding is not something which can be given to students: they have to work at it themselves, relating pieces of information to one another and, importantly, to what they already know to produce a more or less integrated, cohesive whole (e.g. Nickerson, 1985). These cohesive wholes can be seen as mental models of some part of the world or events in it (Halford, 1993; Johnson-Laird, 1983). In reading a story, for instance, the reader constructs a mental model of the situation described and steadily updates it as the story proceeds. Someone may understand the meaning of addition in mathematics through a model commonly known as a number line. A work of art may stimulate or even provoke viewers to make and extend mental structures in ways that may be described as insightful. Understanding is a process of making mental connections and inferring relationships (Newton, 2012a).

Inductive reasoning takes the known and extends the pattern to make a generalization of it. For instance, all the trees someone has seen have green leaves, so the inference is a tentative rule that all trees have green leaves. Abductive reasoning, however, offers explanations of events and observations. For example, someone finds that her computer printer has stopped printing after she cleaned it. Having noted the effect, she speculates that the cause might be a dislodged cable. Abductive reasoning or hypothesis generation enables her to offer a fairly likely, possible explanation (Fischer, 2001; Niiniluoto, 1999; Thagard & Shelley, 1997). Abductive reasoning explains the world by making one event a consequence of another. For example, 'Every time I eat strawberries, I develop a rash. Eating strawberries, therefore, causes the rash.' This causal inference has more or less tentatively tied together two events to answer the question 'Why do I get this rash?' Other elements may eventually be added to the structure to explain why strawberries cause a rash. Such structures render the chaos of incoming information into powerful, organized wholes. These wholes can make engagement with the world feasible, manageable and more or less predictable.

The nature of the causal link in understandings depends on the domain. In physics, the electricity in one wire behaves like electricity in another wire, all else being equal (and that condition is not unduly difficult to meet). In history, antecedent conditions are never identical and consequences never so certain. Understandings of behaviour in the financial world must also allow for the uncertain vagaries of people's behaviour (Kahneman, 2012). Hence, causal understandings can have a different flavour in different learning contexts. Furthermore, we can build mental models which may seem quite sound yet let us down. The child's view of electricity as water flowing through a pipe may make a useful starting point, but if it leads the child to expect that severing a wire lets electricity gush from its ends, she will be disappointed. Similarly, a young student's understanding of human nature is likely to be limited and may produce overly simplistic models of people's behaviour. At the same time, each student's past experience, learning and understanding of human nature may be similar but not identical, so thirty history students could produce thirty different (but, hopefully, overlapping) understandings of some dictator's behaviour.

Not all students, however, routinely construct causal understandings. In what has been called surface learning, some students more or less memorize the information. Generally, a deeper learning which mentally and meaningfully connects cause and effect can be more satisfying, it can facilitate further learning, it tends to be motivating, it is a flexible kind of knowledge which can be applied in new situations and it is durable (Newton, 2012a). Given this, it is not surprising that causal understanding ranks high amongst educational goals. For Piaget (1978), it was paramount as it makes the world more predictable and he was inclined to restrict the term 'understanding' to what enables causal explanation. This includes the use of analogy to explain events. For instance, children familiar with water flowing through a pipe, as in a central heating system, may use it as an analogy for thinking about the flow of electrical current in a wire (Newton & Newton, 1995). Similarly, a young student who understands something of the constraints of household budgets may use this to explain certain events in the financial world.

Yekovich et al. (1991) has described some of the mental processes involved in constructing an understanding: the recall of relevant prior knowledge, giving attention to what matters in the information, and making mental connections within and between the information and prior knowledge. There also needs to be some commitment to the task of constructing a causal understanding. Figure 5.1 summarizes the process.

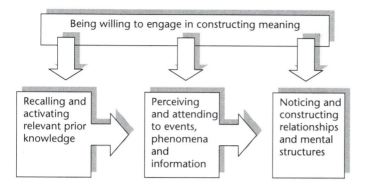

Figure 5.1 Some processes of understanding.

Good teachers seek effective ways of helping students to notice relationships and make mental connections. They may, for instance, use diagrams which structure the information or explanation through an analogy. Or they may try forced prediction (Newton, 2012a). Forced prediction amounts to some form of the question 'What will happen next?' The student is obliged to construct a causal understanding and then articulate it in order to make the required prediction. But understanding can depend on more than just food for the intellect. Each of the steps in Figure 5.1 can entail moods and emotions.

Emotions, moods and understanding

Some interactions of moods and emotions in the elements of Figure 5.1 will now be illustrated.

Engagement

Engagement is a matter of motivation, an outcome of the student's appraisal of matters of personal consequence. People generally engage willingly in an activity if it seems to offer the satisfaction of some personal need or promises to advance some valued goal. If the appraisal, unconscious or otherwise, is positive, the student is likely to be attracted to the activity and show interest. If engagement is rewarding, interest may deepen and extend over time. In other words, engagement is, in essence, an emotional process which depends largely on what the teacher does and offers (Linnenbrink, 2007; Martin & Marsh, 2005; Schutz & Lanehart, 2002). Mestre (2005) has called teachers' exploitation of students' needs, goals and values their pedagogies of engagement. These pedagogies can vary in how effective, systematic and open to reflection they are. Some distinguish between cognitive engagement (thinking and reasoning about the task), behavioural engagement (physical action which relates to the task) and emotional engagement (such as the pleasure which the task engenders) (Connell, 1990; Finn, 1993; Fredricks et al., 2004). In practice, these are not clearly independent and others (e.g. Guthrie & Wigfield, 2000) argue for a more integrated view in which these interact and are mutually supportive. There is, however, evidence of what constitutes a good pedagogy of engagement. It points to the effectiveness of stimulating interest, providing support for understanding, being enthusiastic, providing an encouraging learning environment and helping learners feel emotionally secure (Capie & Tobin, 1981; Darby, 2005; Olitsky, 2007).

Interest focuses and maintains attention on what the learner sees as potentially a matter of consequence. For instance, anything new will attract at least a passing interest while its potential is considered. If the novelty offers, for example, enhanced competence, an understanding of the world, autonomy or affiliation with others, it is more likely to promote engagement (Gläser-Zikuda et al., 2005). The satisfaction of psychological needs such as these is often rewarding, that is, it makes learners feel good (Newton, 1988; Newton & Newton, 2010a). We also come to value some aspects of life more than others. These values, conscious and unconscious, can motivate learners to classify some things as good and others as bad, and to feel positive or negative about proposed events and to favour certain actions. (Values are considered further in Chapter 7 in the context of wise thinking.)

Support for understanding is another element of the pedagogy of engagement. Endlessly learning facts can be tedious, boring and ultimately futile in a rapidly changing world. Never seeing the point can also leave the learner in a world which is chaotic, unpredictable and meaningless. Helping things hang together meaningfully in the learners' minds can add to a feeling of competence, self-efficacy and self-respect and generate a sense of value in learning. Even adult learners still have 'an enduring yearning for wholeness', which includes knowing themselves (Dirkx, 2001: 70). Learning environments which ignore such matters risk students avoiding novelty and, instead, staying with what they know (Turner et al., 2002).

Enthusiasm about the topic is contagious. When a teacher shows it, it increases students' on-task behaviour both during interaction with the teacher and afterwards, in follow-up activity (Bettencourt et al., 1983). It seems likely that enthusiasm attracts others, because it signals that there may be something worthwhile in the task for them. It can, however, be overdone and care is needed to maintain it at a moderate, believable level.

The supportive learning environment refers to what the teacher does to ensure that each learner benefits from a teaching session. Students, young and old, find memorable learning to be associated with a supportive climate and a caring teacher who gives attention to individual students (Dirkx, 2001; Menezes & Campos, 1998). A supportive climate and caring teacher are known to have a worthwhile effect on attainment. A classroom ethos in which learners feel they can make mistakes and ask for support without ridicule contributes to a learning environment which is low in anxiety and emotionally comfortable. There also tend to be other useful outcomes: learners are optimistic about learning and more likely help one another (Waxman & Walberg, 1986; see also 'The emotional climate' in Chapter 4).

A willing engagement with learning and thinking depends on the students' appraisal of the situation. The appraisal results in feelings prompting approach, avoidance or indifference. The appraisal does not stop when engagement begins, but continues to generate emotional progress reports. When there is progress or satisfaction, those reports are likely to sustain interest and maintain engagement. The teacher is also involved in that emotion, not least through her enthusiasm and concern for the students' progress. When success in tests does not call for understanding, some students opt for shallow learning and memorization, but even when understanding would be useful, some still avoid the effort. Trigwell et al. (2012) found that Australian students who express positive emotions about a course (such as feelings of hope or pride) also tend to adopt a deep approach to learning and construct understandings and achieve more. Conversely, those who express negative emotions (such as boredom or anxiety) tend to adopt a surface approach in which information is learned for reproduction without any great concern for constructing an understanding. These students tend to do less well.

Recall from memory

To help someone construct an understanding, relevant prior knowledge and experience must be brought to mind and, if necessary, developed for use in the task in hand. But someone can only recall what, in some form, was once stored. Generally, what a student found to be stirring and emotive is more likely to have been stored than what is bland and dull (Cahill et al., 1996; Laney et al., 2003). Thus, an event involving anger and one involving exhilaration will probably receive preferential access to resources and be quite memorable. For instance, children are likely to remember events in which they were distressed by an injury or excited by a new experience (Laney et al., 2003; Peterson & Whalen, 2001; Phelps, 2006; Lindström & Bohlin, 2011). Autobiographical memories of emotional events tend to be recalled so readily that it led William James to describe them as leaving a scar on the mind (Kensinger, 2009). It seems that they receive a different treatment or are elaborated upon, which makes the memory trace particularly durable and accessible (Morgan, 2010). Indeed, material with strong emotional connotations for the person concerned is generally remembered better than neutral material (e.g. Dolan, 2002; Ferré, 2003). Recall favours emotive events but also tends to overstate emotional experience, particularly when the emotion is negative (Miron-Shatz et al., 2009). Teachers will readily recall an unsuccessful lesson which, for them, will have been a disaster, but they discount and do not bring to mind the many other lessons which were successful. Positive emotions have been found to broaden what is recalled to include peripheral details, while negative emotions may narrow it to what are perceived to be central features (Lench et al., 2011; Talarico et al., 2009). Nevertheless, when positive emotions are intense, they can also narrow recall (Gable & Harmon-Jones, 2010).

Once stored, memories are not set in stone. They may be elaborated, consolidated and related to other mental structures, even during sleep (e.g. LaBar & Phelps, 1998). Over a long period of time, understandings may be quietly and unconsciously updated to reflect new experiences and to maintain their relevance and utility. One consequence is that asking someone how they felt about an event which occurred some time ago may not produce a response which is a true reflection of reality (Holland & Kensinger, 2010). While most emotive information, positive or negative, increases the likelihood that an experience will be stored, the strength of the emotion does make a difference. Low-intensity emotions tend to predispose people to attend to both central and peripheral aspects of an event. As the intensity increases, the focus narrows as though there is a spotlight on central matters. Very intense emotions, however, can be so all-consuming that few details of the event may be stored. For instance, the participants in a traumatic event which generates intense fear may not remember the appearance of those involved (Heath & Erickson, 1998). Similarly, close family mourners at a funeral may be unable to say with certainty who attended.

Recall can similarly depend on moods and emotions. In particular, there is a mood congruence effect in which there is better recall when the current mood matches the mood when the learning took place or the mood in the event (Barry et al., 2004; Bower, 1981). This is a tendency, however, not a certainty (MacLeod et al., 1987); it also depends on what the person sees as emotive or personally relevant. Being in a good mood induces people to believe they have seen things or studied them before, even when they have not. Negative moods predispose people to deny that they have seen things before, even when they have (Holland & Kensinger, 2010; Sergerie et al., 2007). One further role for recall is in remembering to do something in the future. Those who are very anxious or depressed may forget entirely what they should do, while those who are sad remember, but too late (Kliegel et al., 2005).

Forgetting is normal, it is a way of eliminating irrelevant or disturbing memories (Barnier et al., 2004). A tendency to forget or suppress matters tinged with negative emotions increases with age as the ability to regulate emotions increases (Charles et al., 2003; Escobedo & Adolphs, 2010). This makes memories positively biased so that what we do recall are 'the good old days' (Walker et al., 2003). Helping students recall and activate relevant prior knowledge is not a simple, certain event which produces a replica of what was stored, or is limited to what was stored, or even produces the same outcome every time (Kensinger, 2009). Recall can be a selective, reconstructive process, which may itself add to the structure to make it meaningful and, at the same time, is fashioned by moods and emotions (Howe & Malone, 2011; Wessel & Wright, 2004). While emotionally charged information is generally easier to recall than neutral matters, memories laid down in a certain mood may be more difficult to recall in another mood, they may differ in content, they may be more or less focused and they may be false.

Attention

Having helped the learner recall relevant prior knowledge, and bearing in mind its potential shortcomings, the teacher generally presents or has the learner gain new experience and information in some way. Students who are interested or otherwise motivated are likely to attend to what they see as germane to their matters of consequence. Attention, the allocation of mental resources to a situation, is a part of engagement. What matters most is that something important should not pass unnoticed in the contextual detail. For instance, showing children that balls of different colours, sizes and materials all fall at the same rate may be lost in their interest in how high each ball bounces. Generally, teachers try to highlight what matters physically, verbally and by playing down what is irrelevant (Blanchette & Richards, 2010; Meinhardt & Pekrun, 2003).

There can be a tendency for people to notice matters which reflect their current mood, rather like the tendency to recall and interpret information in mood-congruent ways (Becker & Leinenger, 2011). There is a lot of evidence, however, that those in happier moods tend to focus on the general or global features, while those in sad moods focus on detail – the former sees the forest, while the latter sees the trees (Gasper & Clore, 2002). Students feeling sad may give less attention to incidental and contextual information, but what is incidental to them may not be incidental to the teacher. Happy students, on the other hand, may attend more broadly, but, in the effect of gravity on balls which bounce, this is not always helpful (Avramova et al., 2010). When studying a painting, sad students' attending only to its central figures could limit their understanding. Furthermore, those in a negative mood tend to let their minds wander and have more frequent lapses in attention than those in a positive mood. To compound this, those in a negative mood are also less inclined to direct their attention back to the task in hand (Smallwood et al., 2009).

In conclusion, as with recall, emotionally laden materials tends to attract attention and those which generate negative emotions in particular may have a higher priority for mental resources (Anderson, 2005; Eastwood et al., 2001; Meinhardt & Pekrun, 2003). Approaching a task with a positive emotion like amusement or contentment tends to broaden the scope of attention, while negative emotions like anxiety and fear can narrow it (Fredrickson & Branigan, 2005). In some negative moods, attention can also wander.

Building causal mental structures

The next step is to help students relate pieces of information and prior knowledge to construct a causal mental model of the situation in hand. The conscious construction of these representations of the world takes place in the mental 'space' of working memory which, of course, is of limited capacity and is generally biased towards pleasing associations and favours causal constructions which reflect that bias (Halford, 1993; Perlstein et al., 2002). Positive moods and emotions can improve the noticing of coherence and pattern and the application of an understanding in new situations (Clore & Palmer, 2009; Um et al., 2012). One reason seems to be that positive emotions, like happiness, broaden thought and build with it and promote explanation-making (Fredrickson & Branigan, 2005). In addition, when progress towards an understanding is slow, those in a positive mood tend to cast their attention more widely and seek information which may help explain the situation (Gasper & Zawadzki, 2012).

On the other hand, emotions like sadness tend to promote deductive reasoning (Palfai & Salovey, 1993/4). Spatial cognition could benefit from a readiness to see spatial relationships more broadly. Depression can impair spatial cognition, which could obviously hinder the construction of understandings in subjects which call for it, like mathematics and technology (Tucker et al., 1999). Intense anxiety distracts attention and occupies mental resources, so it generally impedes the construction of understanding (Weinstein, 1995).

At the same time, what is to be understood can itself generate emotions. Emotive material is generally more active in working memory and is processed more readily than more neutral information (Lindström & Bohlin, 2011). Similarly, narratives which evoke emotions tend to be given a more cohesive and personally meaningful form than do neutral accounts (Fivush et al., 2008). Empathizing with the emotions of others tends to induce people, even as children, to adopt the characters' goals and can lead to the construction of more causal connections (Ames et al., 2008; Bourg et al., 1993). This temporary adoption of goals of others may increase on-task thought, maintain attention, make events personal and emotionally arousing and, therefore, more memorable (Levine & Edelstein, 2009). Of course, the mental connections in an understanding can, themselves, be emotionally loaded. Sylvester (1994) cites, for instance, understanding why pioneers in the American West settled in particular places. The reasons ('causes') may be partly rational and partly emotional, as when the soil is recognized as good for farming and the landscape feels comfortable.

The focus so far has been on constructing an understanding where there was none, but students may bring causal understandings to the classroom. These understandings can be narrow, overly general, or otherwise deficient, and the teacher's aim is often to help the students enhance or even replace them. Mood can determine whether current conceptions will be maintained or changed (Pimental, 2011). Sometimes, students can be very attached to an understanding, particularly when revising it would mean major mental upheaval or a serious challenge to their beliefs and values. The defensive emotions this stimulates can raise high barriers to change.

The effect of moods and emotions on the mental process of constructing an understanding is complex and not fully understood (e.g. Blanchette & Richards, 2010; Lindström & Bohlin, 2011). Nevertheless, with that caveat, some conclusions with practical implications are possible. When the construction needs mental effort, a positive feeling signals that the situation is not threatening, so the students can give mental resources freely to the task. Positive moods, therefore, favour 'broaden and build' thinking or, at least, serve as a green light or 'Go' indicator for thought (Clore & Huntsinger, 2009; Fredrickson & Branigan, 2005). Emotive content also may attract and receive more in-depth processing, as the emotive element indicates that the content is potentially of personal significance. On this basis, positive moods and emotive content are able to foster the construction of understandings. But, when the emotive content is perceived to threaten existing understandings of personal value, their revision is likely to be resisted. It is also reasonable to expect extremely strong moods and emotions to hamper understanding when they divert mental resources or cause rumination. Given that moods and emotions vary with time, an understanding constructed on one occasion may not be like one constructed on another occasion. Moods and emotions can produce differences in what is recalled, what is attended to and which connections are made. Each understanding, therefore, will bear the stamp of the moment in which it was constructed.

At the same time, students bring moods and emotions with them like baggage, and these can result in disengagement. For instance, most people want to be seen as competent. The act of going into a classroom risks a public display of incompetence; Dirkx (2001) has described the anxieties of mature students who return to learning and find themselves in emotional turmoil. As a consequence, many protect themselves by denying ability at the outset with comments such as 'I've probably missed the point, but ...' Others arrive for sessions they expect to be a waste of time. For instance, teachers sent on an in-service course may anticipate that it will be irrelevant to the 'chalk face'. Their negative frame of mind can make participation minimal, attention transitory and understandings shallow. The precise effect of moods and emotions on thinking can also depend on cultural norms. Koo et al. (2012) argue that the norm for Westerners is to adopt an analytical thinking style while those from Eastern Asia tend to have a more holistic way of thinking. While some positive emotions may promote the construction of a causal understanding, the effect is to adjust thinking relative to these cultural norms rather than to shift both to the same point.

Explainers and explanations

Causal understandings can enable the explanation of an event. Explanations may include arguments but, while arguers are concerned with being convincing and persuasive, explainers generally aim to communicate efficiently and effectively in order to maximize the likelihood that the listener will construct a particular understanding. Teachers often explain in order to help students construct an understanding which has much in common with that of the teacher. For the explanation to be effective, students must engage with it, attend to it, draw on relevant prior knowledge and make the expected inferences. In other words, whatever the quality of the explanation, the students still must construct the understanding themselves, a process open to moods and emotions. Often, teachers will try to make it easier by, for example, including some prerequisite knowledge in their explanations and fleshing out the account with clarifying detail (e.g. Van Merriënboer & Sweller, 2005).

Teachers also ask students for explanations as this can oblige the students to construct an understanding. It also provides information which helps the teacher judge the quality of that understanding. In the classroom, students commonly meet phenomena and events with more than one potential explanation. When constructing explanations involving several potential causes, young children usually prefer to keep it simple and opt for single-cause explanations (a tendency Bonawitz and Lombrozo (2012) describe as applying Occam's rattle). Adults can have a similar tendency although they are more able to take the likelihood of a cause into account and adopt a complex explanation (Lombrozo, 2007).

In applying understandings to events, explanations produced in a sad mood can be of a higher quality and be more persuasive than those constructed in a happy mood, presumably because the application of the understanding is more likely to be systematic in a negative mood (Forgas, 2007). Extending that tendency, when explaining behaviours in social situations, those in happy moods are inclined to be less critical about the participants than when in a negative mood (Forgas & Locke, 2005). Nevertheless, not all moods labelled negative have this effect; anger tends to produce superficial reasoning, although not generosity (Blanchette & Richards, 2010). But even sound explanations may not be welcomed by students. Those which are perceived to threaten vested interests may be rejected by ignoring the explanation or questioning the explainer's motives, a tendency which can, in the extreme, amount to paranoia (Greenberg & Pascual-Leone, 1998).

Some implications for practice

The interdependence of thinking and feeling has been described as a coalition in which emotions and the intellect work together (Pessoa, 2008). The term 'coalition' suggests that there is an intelligent collaboration between the constituents. While there may be no thinking without feeling and the two systems can be mutually supportive, an intelligent collaboration may, at times, be accidental rather than intentional. The aim is to make it intentional, to reduce adverse interactions and promote those which are helpful.

A model of the emotion–cognition interaction

Multimedia learning environments which foster positive emotions also tend to enhance comprehension and transfer of learning, something recognized in the field of 'affective computing', where systems are designed for interaction with people (Pimental, 2011; Um et al., 2012). The interplay of moods, emotions and the intellect in electronic environments is, in some ways, like the interaction with the teacher in the classroom (Daniels & Stupnisky, 2012). This gives a model of the interaction a wide relevance. In essence, the model recognizes that, at times, certain emotions can foster productive thought (here, taken to mean causal understanding) and, at other times, they can lead to unproductive thought (Kapoor et al., 2001; Kort et al., 2001). Figure 5.2 illustrates this. Cognition and emotion are depicted as two dimensions, productive–unproductive and positive emotions–negative emotions, respectively. Curiosity is a moderately positive emotion often associated with productive thought (5.2A). Feeling puzzled, on the other hand, could be perceived as a mildly negative emotion which, nevertheless, could make thought productive, should the student attempt to resolve the puzzle (5.2B). One strategy, instigating cognitive conflict, deliberately places students in this quadrant with the expectation that the combination of interest and anxiety will prompt students to resolve the conflict productively (Lee et al., 2003; Linnenbrink-Garcia et al., 2012). In effect, it places students outside their comfort zone (Schuwirth, 2013), but the balance between interest and anxiety is likely to be crucial; too much anxiety or too little interest could render the approach ineffective. Some negative emotions, like anxiety, can take up mental resources to such an extent that they render thought unproductive (5.2D). A fairly positive feeling of contentment or satisfaction may end further engagement with the task, so relevant thought also ceases (5.2C). Intense positive emotions like euphoria can do the same and could place the student in the unproductive quadrant (5.2C). However, both positive and negative emotions can, at times, lead to productive thought; at other times, the thought becomes unproductive.

From what has been said earlier, it looks like positive moods and emotions are generally good for understanding, while those that are negative are bad for it. This model makes the important point that it depends on the nature of the mood and the emotion. Some moods and emotions commonly described as negative can stimulate useful thought, while some that are positive can impede it. Suppose students begin by being curious and intrigued by a topic. They are likely to be in the positive emotion and potentially productive thought quadrant (5.2A). On closer engagement, however, they may find it confusing or puzzling and difficult to understand and, as a consequence, move to the negative emotion quadrant but still with the potential for productive thought (5.2B). Often, left to themselves or with a little help, many students will rise to the challenge, consciously or otherwise, and construct the necessary connections to make the topic more or less meaningful. Some, however, may become frustrated, despondent or dispirited. This moves them to the negative emotion quadrant with little prospect of relevant productive thought (5.2D). Students may move around Figure 5.2 in a variety of ways, several times in a session. Teachers should be concerned when students are in the unproductive thought quadrants, and especially if they seem to be trapped in the lower left quadrant (5.2D).

Figure 5.2 cannot do complete justice to the complexity of mental events during learning. The usefulness of this model is in the way it depicts purposeful thought as a dynamic process and in the prompts it can offer teachers, but it is not a perfect picture of cognition–emotion interaction. Emotions are not simply positive or negative; they can be activating or deactivating and stimulate approach or avoidance. In other words, additional versions of Figure 5.2 with different emotion axes are possible. At the same time, we can have mixed feelings about something. Figure 5.2, therefore, is only one approximation of reality that can guide planning and action, but there is more to it than is shown and those first thoughts may need to be qualified.

Some teachers intuitively take some of the interactions between emotion and cognition into account, as the following short vignettes show. In the first, involving young children, novelty is relatively easy to call on as a source of interest and engagement.

> In a History lesson, the teacher was aware that the children did not see people from the past as being like those of today. To confront this, she told them of an Egyptian tomb containing the remains of a boy and his toys. The children were curious about the toys (5.2A) and the teacher showed them a wooden crocodile like that from the tomb. The toy generated emotions which motivated engagement while empathy produced feelings probably like those of ancient Egyptian children.

In this snapshot, older students found the topic dull until the teacher engaged their emotions.

> To these students, what floated or sank in water was obvious and boring (5.2C). The teacher asked if the stone and the bottle he held in his hands would float. The students predicted, with indifference, that the stone would sink and the jar would float. But, in water, the stone floated and the jar sank. Indifference became surprise and attention increased (5.2B). Although we may have an innate inclination to try to resolve cognitive conflict, some students give up sooner than others (moving to 5.2C or 5.2D). To prevent this, the teacher showed pleasure at their surprise, invited explanations and responded to them with enthusiasm.

Working with adults does not mean emotions and moods can be ignored.

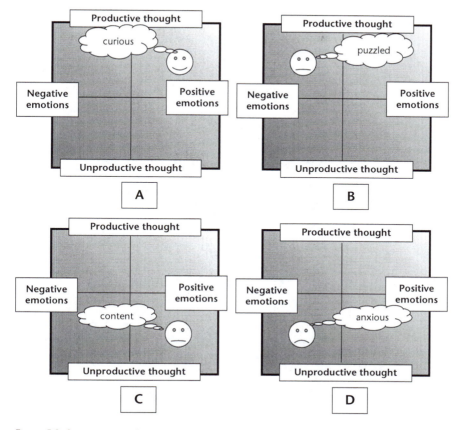

Figure 5.2 Some potential interactions of thought and emotion during learning.

In-service teachers on a course about fostering creativity discussed situations which produce creative behaviours. The instructor mentioned that evil criminals can be very creative. One teacher heatedly rejected the possibility that creativity and evil could co-exist in one person (placing him in 5.2D). The instructor gave some examples; the aim was to move the teacher to 5.2B and, ultimately, to 5.2A. The teacher, however, had nailed his colours to the mast. On reflection, the instructor regretted not beginning with examples.

These again illustrate that there is more to teaching and learning than just the intellect and, in practice, the two systems, emotion and the intellect, may be inseparable (Duncan & Barrett, 2007). Many acknowledge this but ignore it. Witness the well-known practice of Physical Education teachers who have the best two players select their teams from the rest of the class, regardless of how the rejects feel.

Supporting causal understanding

Some of what applies here has relevance in supporting deductive reasoning. Given that constructing a causal understanding can also involve deductive reasoning (e.g. Kell & Oliver, 2003), what has been said about that also applies here. As before, forethought, putting plans into action and afterthought contribute to support for understanding.

Forethought

When planning a topic, identify what it is that students will see as relevant to their interests. This does not always lie in the topic's practical utility. For instance, students like novelty, opportunities to develop competence, and some autonomy. Make it a priority to tell the students early in a lesson what is in it for them. Sometimes, topics have to be taught which do not immediately attract interest or which must be taught in order to open the door to important themes. Weigh carefully the pros and cons of inducing engagement via supplementary entertainment or whizz-bang activities. Their emotive nature can make the entertainment memorable, while the lesson's target remains boring and is lost. Nevertheless, such activities can generate positive moods and emotions, induce engagement and could put students in a frame of mind that broadens their thinking. If carefully planned so that they highlight the targeted cause–effect connection, they could make the learning memorable. When students are likely to arrive with an inappropriate causal understanding, consider a cognitive conflict approach.

Check for content likely to be perceived as a threat to values, goals or beliefs, and decide how to neutralize the threat. Also anticipate possible negative reactions to the approach or teaching method, as this risks students moving into an unproductive quadrant, perhaps undetected. A change in activity can raise spirits; positive (good-natured) humour can also alleviate negative emotions (Samson & Gross, 2012). When students have to formulate careful explanations, it can be hampered by some positive moods, like overexcitement, so plan a cooling period, supported by your example (see also Chapter 4).

Action

The establishment and maintenance of an appropriate emotional climate may be necessary. Cultivate relationships which reflect a concern for each student's understanding and discourage classroom atmospheres which lack mutual respect. Aim for an ethos in which students feel they can express ideas or ask for help without ridicule, and model what is expected of their interpersonal behaviour.

Such an emotional climate is likely to foster engagement and positive moods that can favour the construction of causal understandings (e.g. Darby, 2005; Fredrickson & Branigan, 2005). A culture of student optimism about learning and teacher enthusiasm for learning adds to a constructive climate. Highlighting success and progress may help to foster optimism and hope. Enthusiasm is contagious and can change students' states of minds without them noticing it. Optimism and enthusiasm both support cognitive and emotional engagement and a positive frame of mind and, hence, understanding. Nevertheless, avoid overacting enthusiasm; an excess reduces its effect and can make the teacher look silly. A grim, gloomy demeanour is another mood which can be caught. While theoretically useful for certain kinds of systematic, analytical thought, it may not support causal understanding. As with other kinds of productive thought, strong moods and emotions tend to distract attention, interfere with recall and occupy mental resources. Similarly, guard against the development of strong anxiety, as it can trigger a surface approach to learning with an emphasis on memorization. Music has been found effective in changing adolescents' moods but may not be appropriate in a classroom setting (Saavikallio & Erkkilä, 2007).

When using cognitive conflict to stimulate productive thought, it is wise to monitor the levels of interest and anxiety. The approach depends on some negative emotion to motivate thought to resolve the conflict, so intervention would negate the effect. However, ensure that the approach does not become counterproductive when interest is low, anxiety is high or students lack persistence or show helplessness. Having constructed an understanding, students should be encouraged to think of any personal significance in it, as this could make it more memorable.

There is a lot to do and think about when teaching, so it is probably better to avoid the temptation to intervene frequently; it is possible to make an acceptable mood or emotion worse. A minimalist approach commensurate with maintaining a constructive emotional climate seems advisable. Older students and adults can, when prompted, often adjust their own moods temporarily (see also Chapter 10).

Afterthought

When reflecting on a lesson intended to develop causal understandings, remember that understandings, once constructed, are not inert. They can develop and change over time as they are used and as experience adds to them. At the same time, an understanding constructed on one occasion may not be quite the same as that constructed on another. Students and their states of mind vary from day to day.

In conclusion

Causal understanding goes beyond the given and produces tentative causes for observed effects and events. In the classroom, this often means constructing mental models which incorporate and function with the causes commonly accepted as appropriate for the effect in question. In other words, other people's explanations (abductive inferences) are reconstructed and applied. This occurs in partnership with moods and emotions which, ideally, oil the process. In general, positive moods and emotions seem to put students in a productive frame of mind, but that also depends on the precise nature of the task and on how the student appraises the situation. Here, the emphasis has been on the reconstruction of targeted or accepted understandings. There are times when these do not exist or are withheld and the teacher expects students to construct their own. The next chapter addresses creative thinking and problem solving of this kind.

Chapter 6

The inventive mind
Creative thinking and problem solving

Constructing a particular understanding with the help of a teacher is one thing but arriving at your own understanding largely unaided takes it further. It is not a case of trying to reconstruct someone else's mental representation of the world with a teacher highlighting what is relevant and correcting unwanted inferences; instead, students, to a large extent, go it alone to produce something that is, at least, new to them and meets the needs of the situation. In a small way, the students are 'world making' (Fischer, 2001), constructing their own tentative hypotheses and conjectures and taking new perspectives. In a sense, the question changes from 'Why?' to 'What if?' but answering it still needs abductive reasoning and, often, deductive or inductive reasoning to support it. Creative behaviour is a diverse activity and a highly valued one.

Creative thinking

Thinking has a variety of goals and some are highly valued for what they can do for the thinker and for others (Craft, 1999; Pink, 2005; Shaheen, 2010; Sharp & Le Métais, 2000). Creative thought, or world making, is one of them. The ability to create something new stretches back at least 40,000 years, when, with the help of language, our ancestors showed they could construct mental representations and manipulate them to improve their lot and develop and express ideas. This creative ability showed itself in, for instance, our ancestors' remarkably expressive art and the artefacts they left behind (Carruthers, 2002; Perlovsky & Levine, 2010). While some people have shown themselves to be more creative than others, most of us are not helpless and can respond to a need with some imagination and creativity (Boden, 2004).

Western governments, and others, see economic potential in creativity and urge teachers at all levels of education to cultivate it in their students (e.g. DfES, 2003; Milne, 2007; Newton & Newton, 2010b; Park et al., 2006; QCA, 2005; Sharp & Le Métais, 2000; Tan, 2000). This is not without its critics who argue that an endless supply of novel products will make life emotionally disturbing and unstable (Cropley et al., 2010; Osborne, 2003). At the individual level, however, some creativity and an inclination to use it can be an asset, as it has the potential to help people meet new needs and changing demands; that is, it can be a valuable asset in life. But creativity is easily neglected if a school is judged only by the acquisition of accepted knowledge and it can be stifled by teachers who do not welcome the unexpected question or answer (Averill et al., 2001; Craft, 2002; Garner, 2007). It can also be different in cultures that have other notions of creativity.

Popularly, creativity may be seen as something rather mystical and ineffable that, if you are lucky, you are born with (Osborne, 2003; Sternberg, 2006). According to Carruthers (2002: 226), 'anyone who is imagining how things could be other than they are will be thinking creatively'. This 'What if?' thinking requires the student to make mental connections and relationships to produce something more or less new to the student and to do it largely unaided. Novel ideas alone are not sufficient; they must also be appropriate. This means they must be plausible, meet a need, function as intended, or otherwise show some rightness-of-fit in the eyes of others (Amabile, 1996; Csikszentmihalyi, 1996; Newton, 2010b; Siegesmund, 1998). What counts as appropriate depends on the domain: for an architect, it is function, for an historian, plausibility, and for an artist, it is rightness-of-fit. Which is more important, novelty or being appropriate depends on the domain and the culture. For example, novelty is less important in architecture and, in East Asia, novelty can be less important generally (Al-Karasneh & Saleh, 2010; Glück et al. 2002; Newton & Donkin, 2011; Niu, 2009; Sofowara, 2007).

Novelty and being appropriate are not everything. Creativity is valued more if it produces an impression of cleverness, elegance, well-craftedness, simplicity or economy (Glück et al., 2002; O'Quin & Besemer, 1989). Again, what makes an impression also depends on the domain. There may also be a need to consider the ethics and wisdom of introducing a product, creative or otherwise (Craft, 2008; Cropley, 2001). In all cases, however, creativity involves choices and decisions, some large and some small (Sternberg, 2006). Matisse, for instance, appeared to paint quickly and smoothly but slow-motion film shows instances of hesitation as he decided what to do (Merleau-Ponty, 1964).

There is also a tendency to associate creativity with the arts. Creativity in other domains is popularly seen as doubtful, less worthy of the name or somehow deficient (Newton, 2010b). This may be due to narrow conceptions of thinking in different domains and to the terms used: we have the 'creative arts' but not the 'creative sciences'. Constructing a scientific explanation of some event is more likely to be described as problem solving. But problem solving is a creative activity which calls for 'What if?' thinking. For instance, in archaeology, the skull of a long-extinct hominid was found with two score marks at the back. Leopards were known to live at the same time as these hominids and their bones were found in the same place. The reasoning (here, an abductive inference) was: What if these marks were made by a leopard's canine teeth? The marks were consistent with a leopard's dentition and with the assemblage of bones. This hypothesis amounted to a new understanding which was scientifically plausible in that it explained the observations well, and was economical or parsimonious (Thagard & Shelley, 1997). In other words, it was a creative and satisfying solution to a puzzling problem. On the other hand, a composer, faced with the problem of producing a piece of music which was right for a particular occasion, would commonly be described as creative. Jonathan Harvey is such a composer and he prefers to think of composing as problem solving (Newton & Newton, 2006). Other activities commonly described as creative, like textile design, can similarly be seen as problem solving (Maiden et al., 2004).

Fostering the creative processes could begin with problem finding. Having students find problems can be as simple as asking them what they are curious about or what puzzles them in a specific context. Young children often ask questions reflecting curiosity and puzzlement but, broadly speaking, domain-specific problem generation increases with age and subject knowledge (Hu et al., 2010). Older students may be given fairly open tasks or projects in which they identify, explore and solve a problem themselves (LaBanca & Ritchie, 2011). The nature of the curriculum and the resource demands of open projects can, however, limit their use in favour of defined problems which suit available resources.

Those who wish to nurture creativity and problem solving may try various approaches. Understanding the problem is often what students find particularly difficult, so a teacher may set the problem and, with the students, explore how it can be interpreted, perhaps by constructing a mind map. Bowkett (2007), for example, offers a collection of simple approaches like this. More systematic is de Bono's Cognitive Research Trust programme with its well-known Six Thinking Hats strategy (de Bono, 1995). Hats of different colours are used to indicate when a particular kind of thinking is needed. The White Hat, for instance, directs attention to the need for more information. Generally, students enjoy the approach and it has been found effective for those with Special Educational Needs (Moseley et al., 2005). More formal is Hurson's (2008) Productive Thinking by Design. This sets out the design process in a sequence of steps, each one supplemented with ideas to support thinking. Highly systematic and intended for older students and adults is the Theory of Inventive Problem Solving (Altshuller, 2000). Creativity is not, of course, just about producing ideas; the ideas have to be appropriate. Evaluating ideas for appropriateness is likely to be a continuous, partly unconscious process which can lead to their acceptance, change or rejection (Stanko-Kaczmarek, 2012). Some of these approaches try to make it more conscious at some point, but it is likely that less formal evaluations will continue to be made before a formal appraisal.

Where some approaches mention moods or emotions, they do so only in a general way. For instance, de Bono's Red Hat allows students to say how they feel about ideas in the belief that emotions alter the brain's chemistry, which enables the production of new ideas (de Bono, 1987). There is, however, a need to discriminate between emotions – some may block new ideas. In Hurson's approach, discontent with the present is used as a motivating emotion (cognitive conflict; see Chapter 5). However, more than discontent can be motivating and emotions can do more than motivate. The fostering of creativity needs to take into account the different effects of moods and emotions and consider the stream of affective and cognitive experience in creative activity. While there is no strategy, formula, algorithm or list of instructions that guarantees success for creative thinking, students could benefit from a look at the changing interaction between mood, emotion and cognition in creative thought.

Moods, emotions and creative thinking

There can be parallels between constructing an understanding and creative thinking which makes the emotion–cognition partnership in the context of understanding relevant here. World making, producing new ideas and solving problems, however, is a powerful capability which attracts the interest of researchers, particularly in what makes people engage in it and the mental processes they employ. Popularly, emotions are seen as bad for thinking, but an exception is made for creativity: the work of artists, writers and poets, for instance, is seen as better for the emotional suffering and torment which motivated it (Averill et al., 2001; Gino et al., 2009; Ragozinno et al., 2003; Russ, 1996; Sternberg, 1985). The motivation to be creative and the mental processes involved are, indeed, subject to moods and emotions, but not usually in this extreme way. Some useful studies of motivation and the interaction of moods and emotions with creative thinking processes have been made.

Motivation and the nature of creative engagement

As might be expected, moods and emotions determine motivation and whether there will even be a willing, creative engagement with the task. This makes how a task is presented important, as it can shape how students feel about it. Adler and Obstfeld (2007) emphasize fun, enjoyment and interest to set a positive mood that draws students in. Should framing the task in that way be difficult or artificial or if the prevailing mood is negative, they recommend that the students' attention is drawn to the importance of the task and the need for an outcome of quality. Trying to use competition to motivate can be counterproductive if it is likely to be a distraction or a source of anxiety. Showing some high quality, creative products or solutions might be expected to motivate students, but the effect can stifle ideas and increase copying of the models, especially with those students who are in a positive mood and so could have let their imaginations broaden and range more widely. On the other hand, beginning with a weak example of a product can keep the advantages of a broaden-and-build, positive mood open (Rook & van Knippenberg, 2011). Interest has been found to promote creativity and those in a positive mood tend to find their satisfaction in the task's intrinsic interest, agreeableness and the production of several potential solutions. At the outset, cheerful students are likely to appraise the task with these in mind and, if the opportunities are absent, may interpret it in ways which provide them (Hirt et al., 2008; Stanko-Kaczmarek, 2012). Motivating students with external rewards, such as a promise of a longer break or less homework, can make the task tedious and induce negative states of mind. Gloomy students, however, may find satisfaction in the esteem and reward they judge will come with success (e.g. Gasper, 2004a; George & Zhou, 2002; Kaufmann, 2003; Kaufmann & Vosburg, 1997; Vosburg, 1998).

Thinking creatively

As far as problem finding is concerned, people in a negative mood are commonly noted for their ability to find fault, impediment and obstruction and to point to difficulties. Their ill-humour may, on occasions, prompt them to find solutions themselves but it could just as easily prompt the view that someone else should do something about it. In the classroom, problem finding can be an idiosyncratic, iterative and drawn-out activity. It can also involve heightened emotions probably stemming from the personal investment a student has to make in the work. Identifying intellectual problems in a particular field, such as physics or history, can produce intense emotional experiences, like excitement. This may be due, in part, to recognizing an opportunity for enhanced public and self-esteem (Liggett, 1991; Lubart & Getz, 1998; Ritchie et al., 2011).

Positive moods often seem to encourage creative thought and problem solving (e.g. Fredrickson, 2004; Hirt et al., 2008; Isen et al., 1985, 1987; Kaufmann, 2003; Vosburg, 1998). These moods indicate that the situation is benign and safe to explore and play with ideas. Concerns about being assessed can suppress creativity as it makes people respond more cautiously, but positive moods may lessen those concerns by indicating that the situation as a whole is not threatening. Because positive moods tend to broaden attention and make thinking more flexible and divergent, the variety of ideas can be greater (e.g. Clore et al., 2001; Fiedler, 1988; Fredrickson, 2001; Grawitch & Munz, 2005; Kaufmann, 2003; Schwartz, 2002; Schwartz & Clore, 2003). This effect does, however, decline over time.

This sounds like negative moods will be bad for creative thought, but that is not always so. Those in a negative mood have been found to give more attention to collecting information to use in solving a problem than those in a positive mood (Spering et al., 2005). In certain circumstances, there is more creativity in a negative mood. For instance, feelings of social rejection can increase the creativity of artists, a finding not far from the popular view of the role of emotions in the arts (Akinola & Mendes, 2008). In a given task, as might be expected, those in a neutral or negative mood produce fewer ideas than those in a positive mood. When the task is long, however, and the number of ideas is declining, most of them tend to be produced by those in a neutral or negative mood (Kaufmann & Vosburg, 2002). Positive moods can also predispose people to accept mediocre solutions - they may stop at the first one which works, while those in a neutral or negative mood are more inclined to search for the best solution they can produce (George & Zhou, 2002; Vosburg, 1998). The outcome can be the production of more complex solutions because the strategies are generally more analytical and systematic than those encouraged by positive moods. Negative moods tend to produce a cautious, thoughtful persistence, which can lead to well-constructed ideas (e.g. Fredrickson, 2004; Gasper, 2004a; George & Zhou, 2002; Kaufmann, 2003; Martin & Stoner, 1996; Schwartz, 2002; Schwartz & Clore, 2003). This caution can also make students produce (or express) fewer ideas overall than those in a positive mood, but it may be reduced simply by reminding them that all ideas are acceptable (Gasper, 2004b). It is often not how many ideas are produced but the quality of those ideas which counts, and that may be where those in negative moods can make a significant contribution. In short, creativity is not necessarily denied to those in negative moods, but how they arrive at a product or solution may be different and the nature of the solution could reflect that (Spering et al., 2005).

Regarding the effect of specific emotions on creativity, anxiety and fear tend to block idea production in group brainstorming so group work is not always productive for all students at all times. Surprise, guilt and pride can encourage people to engage with a task but shame tends to make them withdraw from it. Hope, on the other hand, encourages perseverance (Rank & Frese, 2008). As with moods, moderately positive emotions are better suited to idea generation, at least in the short term, while neutral emotions seem better suited to the evaluation of those ideas (e.g. Isen, 2008).

These observations are supported by a synthesis of many studies of creative thinking but they are not hard and fast rules; people do not always behave as expected. At times, it can be useful to see the effects from other perspectives (Baas et al., 2008; Davis, 2009). For example, one of these looks at the effect of mental arousal or level of activation. The capacity for complex thought increases as the level of mental arousal increases but only up to a point. Beyond that, strong arousal takes mental resources away from the task in order to attend to the source of arousal. For instance, someone who is cheerful is more likely to engage in task-related productive thought than someone who is ecstatic and has her mental resources otherwise engaged. At some optimum level of mental arousal, the potential for creative thought is at its greatest (De Dreu et al., 2008; Russ & Grossman-McKee, 1990). This adds a caveat to what has been observed: the strength of the mood or emotion also matters; a low level of an emotion may foster creative thought but a high level of the same emotion may hinder it. Similarly, happiness tends to make people inclined to engage with a task (i.e. it is promotion-focused) and, at the same time, is activating. This has the potential to be productive and make good use of a widening of attention and increased flexibility of thought. Sadness, on the other hand, is deactivating so that engagement with the task is, at best, reluctant. Anxiety, although activating, is associated with avoidance (i.e. it is prevention-focused). As a result, there is little worthwhile engagement. This illustrates the potential complexity of the interaction between moods, emotions and the intellect. Students are likely to be pulled in different ways by their emotions and it is these combined forces that determine the outcome.

The stream of affective experience

Being creative often takes time. The problem or task has to be interpreted, ideas generated and evaluated, possibly rejected and replaced by new ideas which may be adopted and adapted further, and so it goes on. Many years ago, Wallas (1926) described the creative process as one involving preparation (understanding the task, developing relevant knowledge), incubation (in which the task and the knowledge are related and viewed from different perspectives), illumination (in which an idea emerges, sometimes quite suddenly) and verification (where the idea is examined, checked and refined). The first half of the process calls for divergent thinking, and the second, for convergent thinking, but this seemingly neat sequence can be fragmented and iterative. Whatever the sequence of events in practice, moods and emotions will form, grow, fade and be replaced by others in a stream or flow of affective experience (Lazarus, 1991; Vandekerckhone & Panskepp, 2009; Watson, 2000). The excitement of a promising idea is motivating but turns to disappointment with failure, perhaps followed by a gloomy interlude without ideas, then growing hope as one with promise begins to form, and so it goes on. Positive feelings provide a 'Go' signal indicating that thinking is promising and worth pursuing; negative feelings provide a 'Stop' signal and warn that things are not going well and a change of direction may be needed. But, at times, the mood may not be the best one for the current need (e.g. Kröper, Fay et al., 2011). For instance, generating promising solutions may be exhilarating, but such excitement is not conducive to the careful evaluation these promising solutions now need. Similarly, the gloom of a failed idea can be deactivating and there is the danger that the student will give up. Some can change or moderate their moods themselves (Averill et al., 2001; Phelps, 2006). In the workplace, group leaders may manage events to sustain purposeful thought. For instance, accepting that creativity is never certain, and treating colleagues with respect and dignity (referred to as interactional justice) promotes expansive thought and risk taking (George, 2007). At the same time, a group leader, noting a change in mood, may switch to a part of the task which benefits from that mood and return to the other part as the mood changes. Making the reasons for the switch explicit in the form of a review of progress or through feedback can help people make the most of their current state of mind. In the stream of affect, it is not a matter of good and bad emotional states but of one being better suited than another to a particular stage of the creative process.

Inventors and inventions

'Inventions' and 'inventors' are terms used here in their broadest sense and include the unsupported construction of explanations. What was said in Chapter 5 about explainers and explanations is also relevant here.

Consider first an inventor presenting her invention – material or intellectual – for evaluation. The initial appraisal is likely to be made intuitively and heuristically, using the emotions as a filter to select what looks, feels or sounds right and reject what does not (Djamasbi et al., 2010). A justification of the decision tends to be constructed after the event, which makes the appraisal process appear more rational than it is. Two attributes of the creative product, appropriateness and impression, can lend themselves to debate more than does novelty. Neither appropriateness nor impression are dichotomous notions (Yes or No/Good or Bad) but moods can shift the judgment towards one side or the other. Those in a positive mood are likely to be more optimistic and less critical (Forgas & Locke, 2005). Those in a negative mood can be inclined to judge ideas as simply good or bad, perhaps more often bad. (Those who have to judge innovative ideas are advised to consider them in different states of mind (Rank & Frese, 2008).)

As for the inventor, perhaps more than anything else, a material invention generally has a lot of time, effort and even money invested in it. The inventor can be firmly committed to it and is likely to find criticism to be a threat which provokes quite negative moods and responses. Positive moods and emotions, on the other hand, can contribute to persuasiveness, perhaps by a contagious lowering of the critical faculties of listeners (Baron, 2008).

Some implications for practice

There is a lot of interest in the creativity of adults in the workplace and studies tend to reflect this. At the same time, interest may be biased towards successful creativity and away from failed creativity and the role of emotions in it (Adler & Obstfeld, 2007). Nevertheless, studies of students' creative thinking do suggest that the observed effects are generally like those seen in adults, allowing for age, experience and the change of context (Rader & Hughes, 2005). This makes such observations useful, particularly in relation to older students and especially when the approach is to offer them 'authentic', real world learning situations.

Any exercising of creativity takes place within a pedagogical framework which, at its widest, includes the institution's goals and the teacher's goals and beliefs about what constitutes creativity in a particular context and how it might be achieved. What counts as creativity in a classroom activity is generally very different from what counts as creativity in a psychology laboratory. For instance, in the latter, there may be a task to make as many different paper birds as possible (Fischer et al., 2007), while what counts in the classroom can be one, clever, apt idea. Some teachers can have misconceptions and narrow, undifferentiated notions of creativity and lack a regard for what is appropriate, and this can shape the creative opportunities they provide (Newton, L.D., 2012). Equally, some may find unexpected responses unwelcome and dislike student autonomy in creative activities (Beghetto, 2007). Creativity, however, can be stifled by detailed direction, an oppressive management of learning, pressure for quick solutions and an unrelenting concern for information acquisition (Adler & Obstfeld, 2007; Avey et al., 2012).

Students may enter this pedagogical structure with a mood or emotion generated in someone else's lesson. They could arrive discontented, bored or frustrated if it was a dull lesson or uncontrollably elated from one that was physically active or badly managed. These starting points can determine whether or not students engage with a task and how they respond to it. For instance, expecting students to work together productively can depend on moods for its success: happy people are usually more cooperative than unhappy people (Hom & Arbuckle, 1988). Of course, happiness can quickly change to unhappiness if the group finds its ideas are inadequate so, conceivably, cooperation declines at the very time when it may be needed. A teacher may use enthusiasm to motivate students or adjust their mood, but students can pass their own moods on to others. Apathy, for instance, can be contagious and make students' thought unproductive (Hood, 2008). Of course, not all students are happy working in a group and while being obliged to do so may help to develop the capacity for collaborative activity, they may not be in a state of mind which maximizes their creativity. In practice, a mixture of group and independent activity could enable discourse when it is helpful.

The emotion–cognition interplay can sometimes support creativity and sometimes hinder it. The aim is to make the interaction a productive partnership which maximizes the likelihood that there will be creative thought. Given that there is likely to be a stream of affective experience as students work on a task, the partnership, left to itself, could form and dissolve several times during a session. In general, the teacher should monitor the stream of experience and compensate for an out-of-joint partnership by, for instance, redirecting the students' mental effort to parts of a task which could benefit from a particular mood. There may be times, however, when moods or emotions need to be moderated or changed in order to make a session productive. Often, this may not need a direct, mood-changing strategy but, instead, could come from a judicious, 'What if?' hint from the teacher.

Supporting creative thinking

Even very young children find and solve problems creatively when the tasks allow for their age and experience. A successful outcome can be rewarding and can strengthen feelings of self-efficacy, as in the following event.

One young child wanted to write that she was four-and-a-half years old. She could write the four but not the half but she solved the problem by depicting a half of a figure four next to the first four and was proud of her solution (Worthington & Carruthers, 2003). The child began with a puzzling problem and, without help, found a satisfying solution.

Some older children were engaged in reading, thinking about and writing poems. The work was extended by a confident teacher, who took the risk that the stream of affect might go in an unproductive direction.

The teacher had in mind the interpretation of poems constructed by chance (e.g. Padgett, 1994). He had the children half-fill a small bucket with words cut from newspapers. Each group took out six at random and placed them in line in the order in which they were retrieved. Another line was added under the first. The children read the 'couplets' aloud. Some said it was 'silly' but one or two protested that their words 'nearly' made sense. Others vehemently objected that the couplets did not rhyme. The teacher sowed seeds of doubt by asking if poetry had to rhyme. Attention moved to 'missing' words, like 'the' and 'of'. One suggested that they could supply such words. Another retorted hotly that it would still be 'rubbish'. The teacher suggested that they should try it. Some said it still made no sense so the teacher had them exchange their couplets with the 'senseless' ones of others. A show of hands now showed that more made sense. How could some now make sense when, before, they were 'rubbish'? The children concluded that what makes no sense to one person might make sense to another. Somewhat relieved, the teacher asked why that might be.

Some teachers unwittingly establish and reinforce an emotional response in students which can endure. The next student spent a lot of time in the negative emotion/unproductive thought zone (paralleling Figure 5.2D), an experience she would probably remember for a long time.

She found high school practical science 'terrifying' and felt under pressure to get the 'right' answer and to do so quickly. Emotions like anxiety hindered recall so that potentially creative tasks were fruitless, dreaded exercises and the teacher did nothing to alleviate the feelings. The student contrasted her experience with that provided by another teacher. This teacher accepted 'mistakes' as normal and allowed time for more unhurried thought (Roy, 2007). Creativity does not thrive on anxiety, fear of failure and pressure (Adler & Obstfeld, 2007). Some teachers develop habitual ways of teaching which inhibit creativity while others intuitively support an emotion–cognition partnership.

In the normal course of classroom events, strong emotions may be less evident than moods, dispositions and traits (Mumford, 2003; Newton, 2013). Given that being creative calls for some form of understanding and may involve deductive reasoning, support for these may also contribute to creative thinking. Some suggestions based on studies of creative thinking are summarized below.

Forethought

First and foremost, there is a need to be clear about what does and does not count as creativity in a given subject. In science, for example, a teacher needs to know that classroom opportunities for exercising creativity include generating explanations of events that are new to the student and constructing practical tests of them. The same teacher should also know that making a model of the solar system using detailed instructions generally involves little creativity on the part of the student (Newton & Newton, 2009a). Similarly, in Art, a teacher should be aware that simply throwing paint around is generally not enough, some right-ness-of-fit with intentions is usually expected (Newton & Donkin, 2011).

Creativity is both a product and a process and the aim is to foster and develop the process in order to increase the likelihood that it will lead to a successful product. Products can be both mental (such as a plan of action, a new way of thinking about an event, a solution to a problem) and material (such as a picture, an object to satisfy a need, something to make a device work better) (Newton, L.D., 2012). The task needs to be framed carefully. A creative task puts the onus on the students to take responsibility for their thinking. If it is framed badly, it risks publicly exposing intellectual weaknesses. This can induce apprehension and anxiety, suppress creativity, confirm those weaknesses, and generate image-preserving behaviours which can distract and disrupt others. For instance, having students write poems and read them to the class could lead to prevarication or deliberately writing nonsense in order to avoid the risk of ridicule (Thompson & Perry, 2005). The task needs to be seen as interesting, potentially enjoyable or otherwise relevant. Interest can take the threat from a situation, broaden thinking and prepare learners for generating ideas (Willis, 2007). It may also be of particular benefit for those students who tend to be less creative, at least in the arts (Stanko-Kaczmarek, 2012). With younger students, the opportunity for increased competence in some valued way can also catch their interest (Asleitner, 2000; Baas et al., 2008; Newton, 1988). As might be expected, allowing some autonomy or freedom of thought and action also fosters creative thinking (Ritchie et al., 2011). Take care with the examples you show. Very good examples of creative products risk discouraging students and can reduce their creativity. Also consider how the students should work on the task. If it is to be in groups, think about the group composition and the traits of individuals, bearing in mind the tendency for moods to be contagious. Creativity can be unpredictable, which, for teachers used to more controlled instruction, may be unsettling. The danger is that this feeling may lead you to curtail or over-manage the task.

Action

Note the students' state of mind on arrival. Working more formally with the whole class, perhaps on a mind map to interpret the task, can reduce strong emotions to a more productive level. If the prevailing mood is positive, it could help to broaden and build ideas, but, if not, some expression of enthusiasm could pick the mood up. Otherwise, and if appropriate, remind students that all ideas are welcome and acceptable at this stage. Do not assume that a negative mood precludes creative thought. It may plough a different furrow from that produced in a positive mood but it could still be productive. Incentives for good performance can be counterproductive; they tend to narrow thinking and can curtail idea generation (De Dreu et al., 2011). Competition can have a similar effect through adding pressure, even anxiety, to the task. To begin with, tasks are likely to put the students outside their comfort zone (as in Figure 5.2B), which can be effective if they rise to the challenge. If not, they may need a hint or two to move them on. For students whose moods could be described as moderately negative, emphasizing the importance of the task and the need for a considered solution is potentially useful.

Tasks intended to practise creative thought can extend over a relatively long period of time, particularly if it also involves problem finding. Over that time, moods and emotions will rise and fall in a stream of affect. Monitoring that stream is important to maintain progress. Avoid letting the students languish in the negative mood/unproductive thought zone, as remotivation can be difficult. Try 'What if?' suggestions to re-establish optimism and maintain the flow. Alternatively, students may be directed to another part of the task where the mood could be supportive, as in collecting further information to inform idea generation or clarifying what the outcome should be. Treat students' ideas considerately so that students feel safe enough to take risks with their thinking. Highlight the enjoyment and interest for those in a positive mood and point to imminent success and boost the self-esteem of those in a negative mood. False praise, however, is patronizing and is readily detected and rejected. Avoid time pressure. Few things narrow and curtail thought's quiet explorations more than the clock. Monitor group work. Collaborative problem solving is a useful skill which calls for some form of cooperative working. Positive moods support collaboration; negative moods, however, are contagious, particularly if expressed by a dominant group member. A disengaged student can also elicit annoyance from the teacher, which reinforces the disengagement (Skinner & Belmont, 1993; Sutton & Wheatley, 2003). To counteract contagion, the teacher might join the group temporarily as its dominant member and show some enthusiasm for the students' ideas. Group work is not always effective, particularly if students see it as a way of replacing the task with more rewarding interpersonal activity (see also Chapter 10).

Use activity to refresh stale thought. Creative thinking can fail when the mind is unable to break away from an unproductive train of thought. Activities that may help include a short period of exercise, tidying and non-competitive play. Deep breathing, having a short break or taking two minutes of quiet time can also change a mood. Thinking about a past or future happy event and imagining the feelings can have a similar effect, as can distraction with another task (e.g. Augustine & Hemenover, 2009; Carthy et al., 2010; Davis et al., 2010; Parkinson & Totterdell, 1999; Schnall & Laird, 2003; van Goethem & Sloboda, 2011). Even helpful moods do not last for ever and may need to be refreshed by a short break or change of activity. Teachers should use their own powers of persuasion through example – moods are catching (Bettencourt et al., 1983; Mackintosh & Mathews, 2003; Willis, 2007).

The stream of affect in lengthy tasks will, inevitably, take many turns. Students should learn that this is normal; what is important is that they should show persistence and work through them. To this end, it would be of benefit to foster resilience in students (Pooley & Cohen, 2010). In this context, resilience means a tendency to respond to an obstacle to productive thought with resourcefulness in order to overcome the setback. Those who are normally happy may have an advantage here (Forgeard, 2011). Older students may learn to see these turns as information that thought and action are going well or need a change of direction. Some older students have learned to regulate their emotions to some extent and drawing their attention to the need for a change can be effective and may encourage self-initiated regulation in the future (Forgas & Vargas, 2000).

Afterthought

Being creative can be emotionally rewarding but demanding. It can be easier to give up and wait for someone to give instructions. Tasks need careful matching to students' interests and predilections. It could be worthwhile to consider how a task might be improved and reflect on the stream of affect it generated.

Few people are free from the neglect of the role of emotions in learning and work. For instance, research in universities is, by definition, a creative process of long-standing, often held in high regard. Nevertheless, research managers have often not learned that emotions both sustain and destroy it. On the one hand, people commonly do research for its emotional rewards and the personal needs it satisfies. But they often have to do it in a climate of target setting and short-term performance measurement, which, of course, can produce emotions inimical to creative thought, innovation and invention (Goodall, 2012).

In conclusion

Teachers are widely expected to foster creative thinking in their students. This needs an understanding of creativity in specific curriculum contexts, how it can be affected by moods and emotions and what teachers might do about it. Although there are broad tendencies which shape creative thinking, underlying these can be specific factors which raise, lower or otherwise determine the responses of particular groups of students. For instance, some argue that brain development affects creative behaviour in teenagers. They point to teenagers' impulsiveness, their tendency to take risks, to seek intense sensation and to press for autonomy, which marks them off from both younger and older students (Giedd, 2008; Payne, 2010; Sercombe, 2010). Seeking and generating intense sensations could prove to be obstacles to task-related attention and productive, divergent thinking. On the other hand, a craving for autonomy could be used to advantage in setting a task that supplies it. Whether or not these stem from brain development, or the lack of it, matters less here than that the teacher recognizes and allows for these tendencies in their practices. Differences in the quality of support, resources, the physical environment, and the frequency and nature of competing distractions can also make a difference to the performance of students in different situations. Differences due to mental disorders, however, do not necessarily impede creativity – it depends on the nature of the disorder and the nature of the creativity; some disorders might even heighten it, as in art (see also Chapter 10). At the same time, some things known to support creativity are not ethically acceptable. Social rejection, for instance, may promote creativity in art but would not be appropriate in the classroom. Before considering matters of this kind, however, the next chapter looks at the more comprehensive thinking needed for wisdom.

Chapter 7

Wise thoughts in action
Hearts and minds in harmony

Education can easily become little more than acquiring information when what is needed is wisdom in using it (Gregorian, 2007; Kuhn & Udell, 2001; Sternberg, 2001). Wise thinking produces a sufficiently comprehensive understanding of a specific situation to point to acceptable actions. The process recognizes uncertainty, considers information offered by the emotional system and makes principled decisions about actions. The aim of this chapter is to present some views of wisdom and, in the light of these, describe certain distinctive aspects of wise thought which make emotion fundamental to its processes. It then considers and illustrates what contribution formal education might make to the development of a capacity for wise thinking.

Wise thinking

Wisdom has long been valued and the wise venerated. In Ancient Egypt, administrators, scribes and temple initiates were taught to be wise with the help of maxims. In Greece, the Delphic Oracle declared Socrates to be the wisest man alive and his wisdom was disseminated in Plato's Academy. In Ancient China, the sage was the ideal person, renowned for thoughtful listening. The great Confucian scholar Dong Zhongsu considered wisdom to be one of the great virtues which listening could produce (Kwok, 1989). Wisdom had a high status amongst medieval Anglo-Saxons who condensed it into proverbs and believed that 'a man ... must adorn himself with wise learning' (Kramer, 2009: 71). The writings of wise people were collected and stored in the House of Wisdom in Baghdad until its destruction in the thirteenth century (Birren & Svensson, 2005; Brugman, 2006; Clements, 2008; Curnow, 2010; Hollon, 1971; Hua, 2012; Meri & Bacharach, 2006). Always considered to be the pinnacle of achievement and a cardinal virtue (Baltes & Staudinger, 2000; Carr, 2010), wisdom has diverse meanings. It can, for instance, refer to strict religious observance, insightful understandings of the world or the human condition, or an ability to act prudently or profitably (e.g. Duvall & Hays, 2005; Ozoliņš, 2013; Zuck, 1991). Wisdom has been studied mainly in theology, philosophy and psychology [although psychologists generally avoided it until late in the twentieth century (Jeste et al., 2010)]. It has also attracted some attention from time to time in education (Lehtinen, 2010).

Theology and wisdom

Some religions distinguish between secular and divine wisdom. Secular wisdom generally refers to those understandings offered by, for instance, physics, botany or history and is constructed by experts in those fields. Divine wisdom, on the other hand, refers to understandings revealed by, for example, the study of religious texts. This revealed understanding can supply a worldview with values, a meaning for life and what constitutes appropriate conduct in preparation for the next life. Secular wisdom, limited by the human mind, unable to address the purpose of life and potentially producing an overweening vanity, is seen as the lesser of the two wisdoms (e.g. Hattaway, 1968; Kołakowski, 1972; Kunau, 2011; Scott, 1961; Signer, 2008). Nevertheless, a division between secular and divine wisdom is absent in some religions. Everything is connected in Native American spirituality; a wise person feels that connection and lives in harmony with the world (Garrett & Wilbur, 1999). In the Confucian tradition, a wise person brings peace and harmony to home and society (Yang, 2001). Without accepting the need for a divine entity, the atheist or agnostic may, nevertheless, have a world-view and values (Taylor, 2007). For instance, a concern for the Earth's ability to sustain life, expressed more poetically by Lovelock (2006) as the Gaia theory, could underpin beliefs about how people should interact with the animate and inanimate environment. This points to an ethical pluralism in some societies, as values derive from different views of reality and change with them (Baum, 2010).

Philosophy and wisdom

In philosophy, Aristotle distinguished between theoretical wisdom, associated with extensive, coherent knowledge, and practical wisdom, approximating to knowing how to live a good life in relation to others. While acknowledging the value of practical wisdom, for Aristotle theoretical wisdom was supreme, as it brought mankind nearer to the gods (Ross et al., 1980). According to Giddy (2012), the African sage sees wise people as having convincing answers to fundamental questions about the world and the human condition. Ryan (1999: 124, 131), however, argues that 'a wise person does wise things' and that takes more than just knowledge. Ryan concluded that wisdom is appreciating the value of, and knowing how to live well in, specific contexts. This could be described as a practical wisdom, which calls for values, principles, judgments and decisions. The Russian philosopher Sadovnichiy (2006) describes wisdom as 'the wide experience of many generations, collected and checked over the millennia', accompanied by an ability to use it. Academic erudition alone is not enough: wisdom is the informed, successful, deliberate and principled navigation of life's affairs (Schollmeier, 1989). The British philosopher Nicholas Maxwell (1984) has argued cogently for an urgent change in emphasis in academic enquiry, from acquiring knowledge to promoting wisdom, on the grounds that our knowledge has outstripped our ability to use it wisely. Using (or deciding not to use) knowledge often involves choices and decisions and Kierkegaard has highlighted the role of seemingly inconsequential decisions in determining life's trajectory (Kaufman, 2009; Milbank, 1996).

Psychology and wisdom

Psychologists generally recognize wisdom's cognitive and affective dimensions although some tend to focus on its more accessible or measurable cognitive competencies (Marchand, 2003). Baltes and Staudinger (1993, 2000: 122; Baltes & Smith, 2008: 56), for instance, describe wisdom as expertise in 'the fundamental pragmatics of life' which entails 'good judgment and actions that contribute to living well ... despite the uncertainties of human life'. Sternberg (2001) offers a balance theory of wisdom in which tacit procedural knowledge is applied to life's problems to achieve a common good. This calls for a balancing of intra-, inter- and extrapersonal interests. Clearly, philosophical notions relating to applied or practical wisdom are evident in the psychological concept (Brugman, 2006). Brown (2006) considers that wisdom calls for self-knowledge, altruism, judgment, life knowledge, life skills and the management of emotions, while Pascual-Leone (1990) saw a necessary role of emotions in being able to gain an empathetic understanding of others. All this wise thinking was labelled 'post-formal', to signify that it was beyond Piaget's 'final', formal stage of cognitive development (Piaget, 1972), being underpinned by the mental processes of, for example, recall, reflection, reasoning, understanding, critical and creative thinking (Labouvie-Vief, 1990). This complex thought is applied to life's ill-defined problems to facilitate personal decisions, advising others, managing society and reviewing the direction of one's life (Kramer, 1990). Staudinger and Glück (2011) divide it into general wisdom (in which thought is about the situations of others) and personal wisdom (when thought is applied to one's own circumstances). Given the potential difficulties of dealing with one's own emotional attachments, they argue that general wisdom tends to be the easier of the two. Few may reach the peaks of wisdom according to psychological tests but at least some adolescents are known to become wiser with time (Marchand, 2003). Wisdom is not an all-or-nothing matter; there are shades of wisdom and someone can be wise in one situation and unwise in another (Jeste et al., 2010). According to Marchand, the first level of wisdom is characterized by narrow perspectives, a dichotomous view of right and wrong, and certainty; the second, by idiosyncratic decisions, a recognition of context, priorities and people's goals; the third, by thought involving multiple hypotheses, a comparison of options, and a willingness to compromise.

Some might argue that wisdom is what it is commonly believed to be. In the merchant class in medieval Holland, for instance, a wise man was described as civilized, sensible, self-reliant, prudent in his affairs and God-fearing, a view which evolved into 'the cunning necessary to amass as much money as possible' (Pleij, 2002: 700). Recent notions or folk theories of wisdom have been collected. For instance, in Canada, wise people have been seen as knowledgeable, educated, intellectually able, thoughtful, skilled in everyday affairs and exceptional. They can see through to essentials, they understand the self and others, they are unobtrusive, respectful, tolerant and have good judgment (Holliday & Chandler, 1986). US citizens generally associate reasoning ability, learning from experience, judgment and perspicacity with wisdom (Sternberg, 1985), while in Austria notions include the wise as able, insightful, reflective, compassionate, moderate and having a desire to help others (Bluck and Glück 2004; Glück & Bluck 2011). These notions have much in common with those of philosophers and psychologists. Yang (2011) has pointed out, however, that notions of wisdom are acquired in a particular culture, so different conceptions can arise in and be maintained by different cultural groups. For instance, in contrast to Sternberg's study, Hispanic people in the USA have tended to associate spirituality, a willingness to learn and being involved in doing good works with wisdom (Valdez, 1993). A wise person in Taiwan must be knowledgeable, competent, benevolent, compassionate, modest and open-minded and, to be judged wise, must show it consistently through his or her actions (Ardelt & Oh, 2010; Takahashi, 2000; Yang, 2011). Similarities in notions across cultural and temporal boundaries, however, have led some to propose universal features of wisdom, such as self-knowledge, detachment, integrated thinking and self-transcendence (Curnow, 1999). Nevertheless, just because societies value a particular kind of wisdom does not mean they value it for the same reason; Christopher and Hickinbottom (2008) warn against assuming an identity of purpose. In parts of the West, wisdom promotes individuality and autonomy, while in parts of the East, it furthers group interests and supports filial duty.

Wisdom has, amongst other things, meant having a broad and deep understanding of the world, following rules of conduct, living a virtuous life, having religious faith, being sceptical, and managing the uncertainties of life (Brugman, 2006). Aristotle's concept of practical wisdom, however, bears some resemblance to a notion of wisdom seen as particularly relevant today. Practical wisdom as the construction of broadly contextualized understandings of specific situations, potential actions and likely consequences, and the choosing of acceptable actions for the good of the self and others, is generally what is meant now by the process of wise thinking (e.g. Hollon, 1971; Jump, 2012; Schollmeier, 1989). While such thinking strives to construct wise products, just how wise they are depends on their success, although others may have views on the proposed course of action. In what follows, wisdom means thought for the purpose of constructing a more or less comprehensive understanding of a specific situation with possible courses of action, considering likely consequences of those actions, and the choosing of an action on a principled basis. What is an acceptable action in a particular context calls for values, moral judgments and decisions. Education, on the other hand, has tended to focus on the development of knowledge which, at its best, may amount to a theoretical wisdom, albeit satisfying but potentially inert.

Education and wisdom

'Education' is an ambiguous and vague term, which can be interpreted in different ways at different times and in different contexts (Harðarson, 2012; Katz, 2009). Practical wisdom does not have to be fostered in the classroom but, given the regard for it, it is not surprising that it has been described as the most valuable of possible educational goals, potentially providing the basis for 'living well' (Gregory, 2009: 117). White (2007), for instance, sees school education as opening the way to personal fulfilment, involvement, work and wisdom. Ferrari (2009: 1099) believes that fostering wisdom prepares people for a 'responsible and happy life'. In the USA, Hollon (1971) argued that higher education should also be the pursuit of wisdom, and more recently the vice-chancellor of Macquarie University has maintained that education was and is to help people become wiser and, in so doing, make the world a better place (Schwartz, 2012). Similar views are expressed in the UK. Carr (2010), for example, expresses concerns about the erosion of higher education by utilitarian, narrow, vocational concerns, and Pring (2010: 91) argues for a wider vision of learning which supports 'the intelligent management of life' (see also Jump, 2012). Practical wisdom is also seen as a 'new direction' for adult education (Bassett, 2011: 35).

Some argue, however, that wisdom is not teachable and that what is needed is knowledge from which wisdom springs (Woodhead, 2012). Nevertheless, there are people who are very knowledgeable and yet unwise: knowledge alone is not enough. Practical wisdom calls for the construction of context-specific and fairly comprehensive understandings of situations, potential actions, consequential inferencing and informed judgments about what is acceptable (Ardelt, 2004). Evolution saw to an ability to think but not to some of the personal attributes, attitudes, dispositions and practice that shape it. Experience may teach some of these, but the way may be prepared in school. Studies of the effect of thinking skills programmes on achievement find them to be generally worthwhile (Higgins et al., 2005). More specifically, wisdom-related thinking can be enhanced by teaching certain knowledge-search strategies and activating wisdom-related resources (Böhmig-Krumhaar et al., 2002; Staudinger & Glück, 2011). Nevertheless, some may argue that fostering practical wisdom is desirable but futile for most students, as it requires 'post-formal' thought. But wise thinking, like understanding, is spread along a continuum (Ardelt, 2004; Baltes & Staudinger, 2000; Bassett, 2011). In contexts that are meaningful and matter to the learner, thinking for action may usefully be practised even when it is rudimentary by adult standards. Some might argue that simplifying situations to bring them within the grasp of such students renders them trivial, but what matters here is the progressive development of personal attributes and expertise in the processes relevant to wise thinking. While accepting that maturation and experience matter, wisdom is underpinned by attributes and elements that could benefit from practice and that lay a foundation for future wise thinking (Lehtinen, 2010).

Given that wisdom is intended to be benevolent, supporting the 'good life' and the 'common good', Paris (2001) has asked how 'good' is to be identified. This is an important point (Grayling, 2003). What is good or bad is determined by values. Generally, family, society and formal education transmit and reinforce some of these values that help the learner function in a given culture (Stipeck, 2002). Nevertheless, cultures are rarely homogenous and while subcultures share values, they may also have their own. Increasing globalization and migration add to the diversity. As described earlier, Schwartz (1994) found values overlap in a wide variety of cultures and these provide some common ground for deciding what might be good, but a teacher will also need to recognize that a shared value may not always mean that it refers to the same ends in different cultures. Learners, even adults, are unlikely to arrive with complete and coherent world-views, even when these are provided for them through, for instance, transmitted religious beliefs. While education may be partly about the common values of the overarching society, teachers will need to recognize that there is variation and that values change with time. What counts as 'fundamental' and 'good' is culture-dependent and there is generally some loose consensus about it in a given community (Staudinger & Glück, 2011). In the West, for instance, it can centre on the individual and autonomy; in the East, it may focus on the collective and filial duty (Christopher & Hickinbottom, 2008). While some of what one person sees as 'good' is likely to be seen similarly by others, agreement is unlikely to be entire or fixed.

Jeste et al. (2010) collected the views of fifty-seven 'international wisdom experts'. These experts tended to believe that wisdom is a uniquely human quality, it is not synonymous with intelligence and the process of wise thinking can be learned. In short, it is not an all-or-nothing concept and, even at its best, it approaches perfection only asymptotically (Pascual-Leone, 1990). On balance, fostering practical wisdom – or, at least, fostering what underpins it – is a worthwhile goal. Just because it is not done does not mean it cannot be done. But, what might teaching do?

At least in the West, emotions have been seen as bad for thought (Haidt, 2001), but from an evolutionary perspective they may help, not hinder, personal and social decision making and commitment to action (Buss, 2001; Haselton & Ketelaar, 2006). In wise thinking, it is not simply a matter of emotions shaping thought: affect is at its core and dispassionate thought alone could produce unwise actions.

Moods, emotions and wise thinking

Moods and emotions prompt behaviour in an attempt to support what matters to someone (Damasio, 2000; Oatley & Jenkins, 1996). Given that wisdom involves various kinds of thought, including constructing relatively comprehensive understandings, creating alternative courses of action and inferring their consequences (Sternberg, 2003), it has the potential to interact with moods and emotions to the same extent as its constituents. For example, depressed people tend to recall sad events more than others and may not see the wood for the trees when trying to construct an understanding. In creative thinking, those in a happy mood feel secure enough to engage in broad, flexible thinking which promotes the construction of alternative courses of action. Intensely activating emotions, like elation, may take mental resources from purposeful thought. When making principled decisions – the purpose of practical wisdom – people tend not to know that their choices can be shaped for good or ill by what are often fleeting emotions, yet these choices can have long-term implications (Andrade & Ariely, 2009; Bower, 1981; De Dreu et al., 2008; Fredrickson, 2004; Grawitch & Munz, 2005; Hirt et al., 2008). Even if such interactions are ignored, practical wisdom seeks decisions and it is the emotional system that often evaluates the alternatives and indicates the personally preferred option (Hullett, 2005). As Immordino-Yang and Damasio (2007: 3) put it, emotion-related processes provide a 'rudder to guide judgment and action'. Our concerns, some of which are held unconsciously, enter into our decisions, and the emotional system is well placed to weigh the options against these. Objective reasoning may advise that working for a big company offers more opportunities than exist in a small business, but this ignores a lot of what matters to the applicant – the emotional system is quick to point that out. While intelligence may help, it is not sufficient; values, moral sensitivities and personal qualities also play a part.

Values

Values are beliefs of broad application which lead us to favour certain behaviours and outcomes in life. Schwartz (1994) has demonstrated that they operate as a system in which some values have priority. They motivate us to seek action and help to gain what is preferred. Values may be held and applied without conscious thought, so, at times, they may not be evident, even to ourselves. Schwartz (1994) found evidence for ten types of value relating to:

> Power (e.g. social status, control of people)
> Achievement (e.g. success, ambition)
> Hedonism (e.g. pleasure seeking)
> Stimulation (e.g. excitement, risk-taking)
> Self-direction (e.g. freedom, creativity)

Universalism (e.g. equality, tolerance)
Benevolence (e.g. helpfulness, honesty)
Tradition (e.g. respect, devoutness)
Conformity (e.g. politeness, normative behaviour), and
Security (e.g. safety, stability).

He divided these into two dimensions: Self-Enhancement (e.g. Achievement and power) versus Self-Transcendence (e.g. Benevolence and Universalism), and Openness to Change (e.g. Stimulation and Self-direction) versus Conservation (e.g. Security and Conformity) and found these dimensions to be 'very nearly universal' across a wide variety of cultures, although particular values and priorities are not always identical (Schwartz, 1994: 42). (Tradition is a part of Conservation but hedonism can be part of Openness to Change and Self-Enhancement.) People develop or acquire such values from basic needs, interaction with carers, experience, society, ready-packaged world-views and their own reason (Freeman, 2000).

The role of values in practical wisdom is recognized in the attributes commonly associated with the wise. For example, a study of Taiwanese conceptions of wisdom found them to include competence, benevolence, compassion and openness, corresponding to Schwartz's Achievement, Benevolence and Universalism (Yang, 2001). In other words, wise people have guiding values which determine behaviour. Other values commonly associated with wisdom include being respectful, fair, empathetic, mindful, conscientious, and showing humanity, tolerance, integrity moderation, consideration for others, and being open to ideas and alternatives. The common problems of social life have probably produced similar values in many societies; hence the commonalities observed by Schwartz. Nevertheless, different solutions to those problems may produce different values or priorities in and between cultures.

Moral judgments and decisions

Values determine what someone sees as good or bad and may motivate a desire for some state of affairs. Practical wisdom seeks to achieve that state of affairs through actions. Negotiating a way to that state can call for moral judgments and decisions. Moral judgments determine which actions are right and which are wrong. (Evolutionary psychologists suggest that there are also some innate moral emotions, such as caring and sympathy for others (e.g. Hauser, 2006). If this is so, they may come from innate values.) For many years, making moral judgments was considered to be a purely rational exercise. Kant (1785/2002) argued that morality was a matter for reason and, more recently, Harris (2011) does something similar. Psychology also focused on reason until recently, when it found that moral judgment is more a matter of intuition and emotional response than conscious reasoning (Greene & Haidt, 2002; Pham, 2007).

Haidt's social-intuitionist theory describes moral judgments as made in quick, affect-laden, automatic evaluations which answer the question 'How do I feel about it?' The valence of the feeling (positive or negative) indicates the outcome. Making judgments in this way takes unconscious values into account, it is fast and it enables the weighing of dissimilar elements and complex situations (Greene & Haidt, 2002; Haidt, 2001; Peters et al., 2006). Haidt adds that we tend to justify these emotional judgments rationally afterwards, if we do so at all.

The point is that decisions are often taken intuitively with a lot of direction from the emotional system. A classic example is the rail trolley problem. A runaway trolley is en route to kill five people, but a quick throw of the switch can send it down another track where it would kill only one person. Would you throw the switch? Most say they would. In another scenario, the only way to stop the trolley is to push someone in front of it. Would you do that? The outcome would be the same but most feel this direct action to be repugnant, presumably because it contravenes a moral precept, innate or otherwise. However, if their moods are made positive beforehand, they are more likely to agree to push the bystander to his death, demonstrating that it is an emotional balance (Valdesolo & DeSteno, 2006). The philosopher David Hume (1739/1978) was exceptional in considering 'sentiment' to determine moral judgments, something which has found favour only more recently.

On this basis, the emotional system facilitates judgments and decision making and helps us commit to and persevere with actions (Haselton & Ketelaar, 2006). It is not, however, a perfect weighing machine. Schnall et al. (2008c) had participants make moral judgments about scenarios involving sexual relations, marriage, car use, and a morally controversial film, while inducing disgust in participants using an unpleasant odour. Those subject to the odour were more severe in their judgments than those who were not. Schnall (2011) concluded that what is dirty or disgusting is felt to be wrong and this feeling generalizes to intuitive moral decision making. Conversely, cleanliness reduces the severity of moral judgments (Schnall et al., 2008b). Tests of moral reasoning amongst college students in Canada also indicate that elated students take longer and offer more simplistic, minimalist solutions than those who are mildly depressed (Zarinpoush et al., 2000). There is one further effect that should be mentioned. Some people tend not to act in accordance with their values when they also value what others think of them. In effect, their emotional system tells them to do what they believe others expect.

Spellman and Schnall (2009) go beyond emotional effects and argue for embodied cognition in which other bodily states also contribute to the intuitive responses described by Haidt (2001). For instance, holding a warm drink in the hands inclines people to judge others as warm-natured. This wider view seems plausible, but does not entirely rule out the possibility that bodily states may also have their effect through the affect they generate.

Personal prerequisites of wisdom

Wise thinking is not always easy. For instance, chemical and physical changes in adolescents' brains may be responsible for their increased tendency to be impulsive, rash and seek sensation and risk. The heady mix of underdeveloped values, impulse and thrill seeking is likely to bear strongly upon moral judgment and decision making (Albert & Steinberg, 2011). At the same time, it is easy to be mentally lazy and disregard others. There needs to be an inclination and a readiness to take principled decisions about actions. This calls for attitudes, habits of mind and ways of thinking which support, amongst other things, understanding matters in broad contexts, taking other perspectives, identifying consequences, recognizing the limits of knowledge and certainty, weighing alternatives and controlling impulses (Bassett, 2011; Haidt, 2002; Staudinger & Glück, 2011). Many of the personal qualities believed to support practical wisdom are cultivated in a variety of societies (Jeste & Harris, 2010).

To sum up, practical wisdom can draw on a variety of kinds of thinking which are, themselves, potentially subject to interaction with moods and emotions. There is also an inextricable connection between the intellect and the emotions in wise thinking when it makes decisions of personal consequence. This is not to say that the emotional rudder will always keep the ship away from the rocks – it may serve vested interests which are irrelevant, inappropriate, false or unachievable. For instance, the values of another age may be admirable but irrelevant today. In wise thinking at its best, however, there is a constructive interaction between objective and subjective mental processes which integrates affect, cognition and experience while recognizing the rights and sensitivities of others to produce advice worthy of consideration (Sternberg, 2005).

Wise thinkers and wisdom

Those with knowledge and experience may develop some ability to make choices which turn out to be wise, but those with little opportunity for extended interaction with others seem less likely to do so. Given that this experience comes from more than formal education and continues after it, wisdom may develop over time, giving some foundation to the popular belief in 'older and wiser'. Age is not, however, a guarantee of wisdom; people need to be willing and able to learn from that experience and use their mental abilities to produce wise actions. If they do, there is some evidence that wisdom produces, or at least is associated with, increased feelings of well-being and life-satisfaction (Sternberg, 2005). General wisdom, giving wise council, has been described as easier than personal wisdom which applies to one's own actions. Giving wise council on matters of general concern is, of course, subject to the mood and emotional effects involved in arguing, explaining and creating. A wise person will probably be cautious about advising others; people are different and what is right for one can be wrong for another. Instead, wise thinking could be fostered by helping others make their vested interests conscious and reflect on their validity and relevance in the context concerned. Can formal education make a useful contribution?

Some implications for practice

The opportunity to develop a capacity for wisdom may be amongst the best offerings of formal education, but education has its own exigencies and short-term goals. A teacher under pressure can often achieve such goals without a concern for matters of wisdom. Attempts at fostering wisdom in higher education may even be subverted by the students themselves. Hollon (1971), in the USA, highlighted the way that developing wisdom can be sidelined by students who favour the development of knowledge and skills for monetary advantage. Hollon was not against the making of money — the necessities of life require it — but he saw a great loss to the lives of his students in such a narrow view.

Fostering practical wisdom

Reznitskaya et al. (2009) have described the use of stories with 10- and 11-year-olds to stimulate dialogue about right and wrong and wise behaviour. One such story is about a rescued wild goose, nursed to health by a young girl (*Amy's Goose*; Holmes, 1977). The children discuss whether it is right or wrong to keep the goose as a pet and consider questions, such as 'Do animals deserve a good life?' *Rain Forest* (Cowcher, 1988) describes what the destruction of a forest does to its animals and can be used similarly. There was evidence that a tendency to take multiple perspectives spread amongst the children during such discussions. History is a subject which comprises plausible stories of people pursuing their own interests, sometimes in conjunction with what they see as the good of others. These stories have been seen as a resource for fostering wisdom in classrooms (Brown, 2006; Sternberg, 2001; Wineburg & Wilson, 1991). For example, the teacher presents the framework for some specific issue, such as the Boston Tea Party. The class (in groups) research the topic and its underlying issues (e.g. British taxation of its colonies) and debate it, focusing on right and wrong as seen from both sides and on the wisdom of particular actions. Roca (2008) has described teaching for practical wisdom in business studies in a university programme. He argues for the analysis of 'stories' about predatory businesses and a 'wise' reconstruction of those stories by the students. With undergraduates in the USA, Havlick and Hourdequin (2005) aimed to foster practical wisdom in environmental studies. Working to the principle that practical wisdom is highly contextualized and needs the application of knowledge, they argue for taking students out of the classroom and into the field where they can be engaged with real world problems in physical, intellectual and emotional ways. Bassett (2007), when working with older adults, has them note wise and foolish actions described in the media and turn those seen as foolish into wise actions. These examples illustrate that 'stories' of one form or another are widely seen as useful ways of presenting specific contexts to stimulate consideration of values, make moral judgments, take decisions and exercise thinking perspectives, such as taking another's point of view. Such 'stories' could be presented using information technology, which allows the learner to interact with it privately, at a comfortable pace (Lehtinen, 2010). Staudinger and Glück (2011) describe proverbs as cultural crystallizations of wisdom. Understanding and evaluating such proverbs has been suggested as a way of fostering wise thinking (Bleyl, 2007).

Ardelt (2004) warns against only developing 'wisdom related knowledge' that is 'theoretical, abstract, and detached' when in reality wisdom is personal, concrete and applied. Gregory (2009) adds that fostering wise thinking is appropriate at all stages provided it is not an exercise in solving personally remote quandaries. Ideally, the potential for relevant and personal action should be drawn from students' concerns. Kuhn and Udell (2001: 261) argue that children acquire dispositions, awareness and 'tools for wisdom' by reflecting on issues from their own experiences, an ability which can develop with age (Marchand, 2003).

Preparing students for and practising principled decision making

Such studies are useful, as they suggest how practical wisdom might be fostered at a given stage of education. Given the nature of wisdom, fostering what underpins it needs a long-term perspective. How learners develop, emotionally and cognitively, is also important, as it places limits on what is possible. For example, children's conceptions of moral behaviour develop with time (Kohlberg et al., 1983) and the interaction of emotions and cognition continues to change through adolescence and into adulthood (Albert & Steinberg, 2011). Nevertheless, even very young children can have some grasp of what wisdom entails, even though rudimentary. For instance, notions of wisdom and the wise person amongst Austrian children (Grades 1 to 4, roughly 6–9 years old) included attributes such as intelligence, social ability and some recognition of the need for values; one response described a wise person as someone who 'knows what is good and bad' (Glück et al., 2012).

Taking all together, a framework for progressively developing the necessities of wise thinking is suggested in Figure 7.1. On the left is forethought, being careful, thinking ahead and choosing actions with prudence and caution. Here, situations are relatively simple. On the right is practical wisdom – the generation and principled selection of ideas for achieving particular goals. These generally involve more complex situations. Thinking about the situations calls for certain personal qualities and attributes. For those on the left, there is a willingness to consider consequences, a readiness to reflect on experience, to feel sympathy, and have values like harmony and fairness, qualities within the grasp of younger students. Towards the right, these become progressively more

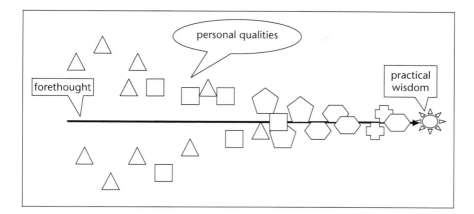

Figure 7.1 A progressive model for fostering personal qualities and attributes which contribute to wise thinking.

demanding or develop later. For instance, they might include an allowance for uncertainty. In this way, younger students engage in prudent thinking and show forethought about consequences, while older students engage in principled thought about actions in more complex situations. In the early stages, qualities and attributes may be developed and used in isolation, as indicated by their distance from the line of progress. Over time, they are increasingly brought together, orchestrated and applied in situations calling for principled decision making, recognizing that 'wisdom is an emergent property of integrated brain functioning' (Jeste & Harris, 2010: 1603).

Given that wise thinking can involve, amongst other things, deductions, causal understandings and creative thoughts, what has been said about forethought, action and afterthought in connection with each of these also applies to fostering wise thinking and need not be reiterated. But, in addition, emotions do not simply interact with wise thinking but are an integral part of its decision making in matters of consequence for the self and for others. This is where logic is potentially useful, but is not everything. Decision making in such situations is supported by various personal qualities and may be practised at different levels. To illustrate this with learners of different ages, some exemplification follows. (Readers will appreciate that concrete exemplification necessitates assuming certain values, such as that people have value *sui generis* and there is a necessity to live together successfully (Ozoliņš, 2013). Prescription is not intended.)

Elementary/primary school

This would focus on the left side of Figure 7.1 to develop personal qualities (e.g. empathy and sympathy), values such as those associated with universalism (e.g. fairness, reciprocity, protecting the environment) and benevolence (e.g. being helpful, kind, considerate) to apply in forethought and decision making. Children as young as 5 years old can see emotions as having an important role in deciding what is good or bad behaviour (Danovitch & Keil, 2008). As they develop the ability to take other perspectives, some practice at self-transcendence could be included. Classroom and playground events might be used to teach the 'Golden Rule' ('Don't do to others what you don't want them to do to you'). Adults necessarily take decisions for children, but there are many opportunities for children to see the value of forethought and that consequences follow decisions. Even choosing a book to read may entail giving up the chance to read a different book. The basis of such decisions may be unconscious and intuitive, but, as Haidt (2001) has pointed out, intuitive decisions are not to be dismissed out of hand but may need scrutiny. These embryonic qualities and habits may be integrated progressively through stories and events which present dilemmas or predicaments for children to discuss 'What should s/he do?' Teachers of younger children generally teach a variety of subjects and this can facilitate wide-ranging thought, a feature of wise thinking.

Middle/secondary school

Moving to the middle of Figure 7.1, additional qualities may be fostered (e.g. a willingness to compromise, a recognition that knowledge has limits, actions can have unanticipated consequences, outcomes can be uncertain). Values would be more open to reflection in generating relatively simple advice for others (general wisdom) and themselves (personal wisdom). A study of the notions of wisdom amongst adolescents in a variety of countries found them to see wise people as charismatic, unconventional and purposeful thinkers who were rarely poor, pessimistic or naïve (Sánchez-Escobedo, 2013). Notions of wisdom can be more open to development after about 14 years of age (Staudinger & Glück, 2011). Students could also begin to recognize that decisions are rarely entirely conscious, intellectual exercises but involve unconscious values often signalled by feelings. Particularly relevant here is the need to draw attention to impulsiveness, as awareness of it can reduce it (Lehrer, 2009). In subjects like History, students see the consequences of decisions and may consider how they would handle such situations themselves. Although subjects like Technology often concern themselves with the inanimate, they affect lives and present us with alternatives, each with consequences. Proverbs as neatly packaged (but limited) guides to wise action may sometimes complement such activities (e.g. 'You need the wit to know what to say and the wisdom not to say it. It is better to limp slowly along the right path than to stride quickly along the wrong one. When elephants fight, the grass is crushed' (Giddy, 2012).) A systematic 'ABC' approach may guide students' thought:

- *Assess,* understand and clarify the situation and the desired outcome, explore how it impinges on lives, values, beliefs and goals.
- *Build* actions which might produce the desired outcome, recognizing that nothing is certain and compromise may be necessary.
- *Choose* an action with morally acceptable consequences.

This ABC approach may be practised on situations of personal consequence for the students. Lacking experience, students have been found to learn from those with it (Jeste & Harris, 2010). Older students are often taught by a variety of subject specialists and that can result in compartmentalized teaching and learning. This is not insurmountable: the International Baccalaureate programme, for instance, has students explore a complex problem in a cross-curricular way (Wells, 2011).

Senior school and beyond

Towards the right side of Figure 7.1, what has been practised earlier would be extended with increasing expectations of self-regulated thinking. By this stage, values may be strongly held and discussion may be perceived as threatening. Older students may be in higher education where wisdom is supposed to be a significant goal. The development of wise thinking, however, can take second place to the transmission of information. Reasoning and logic matter, but – when it comes to motivation, life goals and working with others – so can emotion. By this stage, students should appreciate that life's decisions are not matters for the intellect or the emotions alone, but for both in partnership (Webster, 2010: 164). As students usually specialize narrowly at this stage, they might consider dilemmas and moral and ethical problems in their fields of study. In Geography, for example, problems of population growth may be explored, the aim being to research the complexity of the problem and make choices (e.g. Repetto & Holmes, 1983). What is involved goes beyond the concerns of Geography and students need to show that they recognize this. Ethical decisions, however, are probably easier than ethical actions (Sternberg, 2013). Older students may develop some capacity for wisdom in action by mentoring others (Smith et al., 1994). While students may not reach the wise end of Figure 7.1, they should have the means to continue the journey.

Some teachers may already concern themselves with some of these ideas. For instance, relevant personal attributes may be developed by programmes which give attention to 'personhood' ('someone who thinks and feels about what she is doing') (Gregory, 2009: 112). Lipman (2003) argues for critical, creative and caring thinking. All have a role in wise thinking, and the associated dispositions (e.g. being sensitive to context, imaginative and empathetic) would make a useful, even essential, contribution. Such personal attributes are potentially helpful. Indeed the long-term goal of developing a capacity for wise thinking and an inclination to use it could be a unifying concept for what are often worthy but isolated attributes.

In conclusion

Wisdom is underpinned by certain mental attributes and tendencies, which may be developed so that they contribute increasingly to principled decision making. Preparing students for wise thinking may be amongst the most testing tasks a teacher faces, and often lacks the rewards of seeing it come to fruition during formal education. Equally, the teacher is expected to be a model of wise behaviour, progressing as a novice from rigid lesson plans to flexible plans that take into account the students' points of view (Arlin, 1993).

The process of wise thinking is characterized badly if it is seen as a matter only for the intellect. Motivated by emotions, subject to them and having them deeply embedded in it, practical wisdom is a partnership of heart and mind. Here, the emotional system provides us with information, draws our attention to matters of consequence, weighs alternatives, recommends one or two of them and prompts action (Peters et al., 2006). When successful, the partnership widens the definition of what it means to be rational (Stanovich, 2010). It is not, however, infallible and, for a successful partnership with the intellect, its recommendations may need scrutiny or critical thought. That is the subject of the next chapter.

Chapter 8

Quality control
Critical thinking

Critical thinking is described as evaluating thought for the purpose of improving its quality or for judging its trustworthiness. Two actualizations are summarized, one being a part of productive thought in action and largely serving the first purpose, the other being applied to that thought after the event and often serving the second purpose. These are not mutually exclusive: thought may be evaluated by the thinker and others as it is produced and then checked afterwards by anyone so minded. As with other kinds of purposeful thought, critical thinking is open to error, bias and the influence of moods and emotions. Furthermore, what can be a fruitful emotion–cognition partnership for certain kinds of purposeful thought may not be the best one for critical thinking, potentially giving rise to tensions when they operate together. Some interactions and possible tensions are described, and implications for practice considered.

Critical thinking

Critical thinking means different things to different people (Abrami et al., 2008). For instance, it can be synonymous with 'good' thinking (Pithers & Soden, 2000), a vigilant, careful, sceptical frame of mind routinely applied to products of thought to judge and respond to their quality. From this point of view, any kind of purposeful thought performed by a mind with this inclination could benefit and qualify as good thinking. On this basis, critical thinking should pervade all forms of purposeful thought if it is to be productive in a worthwhile way. Accordingly, some would call any good, purposeful thinking 'critical thinking' whether it is directed at deduction, causal understanding, creative or wise thoughts (e.g. Halpern, 1997, 2001; Siegel, 2010). People may not have a natural tendency to think critically (van Gelder, 2005) but, if developed, it could empower them to avoid manipulation and exploitation. For that reason, fostering a critical disposition (and a creative one) may also have the aim of supporting and disseminating Western democratic principles (Arum & Roksa, 2011; Brookfield, 2013). Lipman (1973), well known for his *Philosophy for Children* project and communities of enquiry concept, aims to encourage sound thinking, a combination of critical, creative and caring thinking (see also Chapter 7). He sees creative and critical thinking as forms of enquiry – the former constructs new ideas, while the latter makes them more precise. Problem solving calls for creative and critical thinking and is seen by some as an antidote to teaching by information transmission and learning, which amounts to information accumulation. As a consequence, some accounts of classroom thinking focus on creative and critical thinking (e.g. Erickson, 2007).

As an evaluative judgment, critical thinking may also be applied to a product after the event, detached from the thought and action which generated the product. For instance, someone else's thought may produce certain beliefs, and thinking critically about those beliefs as presented to us could determine how well founded they are. Equally, someone may return to their own thoughts and, seeing them in a new light, accept, reject or improve them. Hence, McGregor (2007: 209) describes critical thinking as 'the mental act of reviewing, evaluating or appraising something (including a picture, play, information, evidence, or opinion) in an attempt to make judgements, inferences or meaning about that something in a rational, reasoned way'. In this actualization, critical thinking is a distinct form of purposeful thought applied to other kinds of purposeful thought. Critical thinking of this kind, applied to given materials, can be an examination subject in its own right. For instance, Thinking Skills, a syllabus for 17- and 18-year-olds, aims to encourage 'free and open debate, critical and investigative thinking, and informed and disciplined reasoning' (Cambridge International Examinations, 2013).

The two perspectives, one integral and one detached, are not mutually exclusive: someone may construct a novel explanation with a critical mind and consider it to be sound. Critical thought applied to it after the event may or may not agree. (Figure 2.1 illustrated this dual actualization of critical thinking.) There are, however, dangers in using the term as a catch-all for various kinds of productive thought, or in allowing creative and critical thinking to lose their separate identities. First, while it may direct attention to the need for soundness, it may also lead to the neglect of particular kinds of productive thought in the classroom (see e.g. Newton & Newton, 2000). Second, while its broad intent might be the same in different contexts, critical thinking varies with kinds of productive thought and context. Brookfield (1997) has pointed out that while some aspects of critical thinking are of wide application, others tend to be context-specific or tied more or less firmly to particular academic domains or subsets of those domains (see also Bissell & Lemons, 2006; Jones, 2007, 2009; Mok et al., 2008; Perkins 1993). Third, and particularly important here, it ignores the different interactions of moods and emotions with the various kinds of purposeful thought and the tensions these introduce when critical thinking and other kinds of purposeful thought are rolled into one. At times, instead of improving that thought, critical thinking may impede or even terminate it. Useful critical thinking may, at times, be better as an intermittent application of critical reflection, but more of this later. Maintaining the distinction is practically useful in teaching and learning – it directs teachers' attention to the exercising of kinds of thought for particular purposes, it facilitates the development of notions of that thought and the act of suspending critical thinking temporarily (or, at least, that sceptical part of it) has a ready meaning. For these reasons, the distinction is maintained here.

Students' critical thinking has evaluation at its heart (Facione, 2011; Moseley et al., 2005; Pithers & Soden, 2000), often with the intention of producing a better understanding of the world (Donnelly & Hogan, 2013). In the classroom, students may be encouraged to detect and correct sloppy thinking as their attempts at productive thought proceed. At the conclusion of what is meant to be their best attempt, the products may be open to wider scrutiny. At other times, instances of reasoning from a wide range of sources, including literature and the media, may be presented to students for critical evaluation. Mason (2008), summing up the perspectives of several philosophers, found that some see critical thinking as calling for certain thinking skills, while others see dispositions and attitudes to thinking as more important. Some see knowledge of critical thinking concepts to be important, while others emphasize knowledge of the domain in which the thought takes place. Mason (2000) has suggested that these might be integrated into:

1. knowledge of the domain under scrutiny (e.g. physics, art, a political debate, a managerial policy)
2. knowledge of concepts in critical thinking (e.g. bias, credibility, egocentricity, ethnocentricity, unwarranted assumption, vested interest, and worldview) (e.g. Rudinow & Barry, 1999)
3. a critical attitude (e.g. being reasonably sceptical, having a tolerance of ambiguity, an attachment to reason, being open-minded and willing to reconsider) and a moral orientation (such as, honesty, unselfishness, fair-mindedness) (e.g. Facione, 2011)
4. critical reasoning skills (e.g. analysing, evaluating, and forming well-founded judgments; not all agree with calling these 'skills', but there appear to be abilities which can be developed) (Black, 2012; Black et al., 2008; Siegel, 2010).

It follows from this that critical thinkers have knowledge, certain mental skills and a tendency to orchestrate and apply them to evaluate the thinking of themselves and others. When successful, this gives the thinker (who wants to 'get it right', do what is best, avoid self-deception and being duped) a certain autonomy and independence of thought. As a means of evaluating what bears on us in life, such as politicians' promises, events, sales talk and advertisements, it has evident value. But it also adds to the trust someone can have in their own mental products by making them well founded.

There are other terms and notions which relate to critical thinking. For instance, critical reflection is, as the term suggests, about considering experience after the event, often to see what can be learned from it (Burns, 2002). It, too, can be a form of critical thinking, bearing upon how thought and action might be improved in the future. Popularly, critical thinking is often seen as being negative about the thinking and beliefs of others. 'Constructive thinking' is a term coined in an attempt to avoid the negative connotations associated with the word 'critical' (Manz & Neck, 1991; Thayer-Bacon, 1998). There is also metacognition, 'thinking about one's own thinking' for the purpose of, for example, planning a thinking strategy, monitoring its effectiveness and, if necessary, adopting a more productive approach (Black, 2012: 108; Colman, 2003; McGregor, 2007). Metacognition can make thinking more efficient, effective and productive (Higgins et al., 2005; Marzano et al., 2001; Watkins, 2001). Its monitoring role could amount to a more or less continuous appraisal of the progress of thought. Although it may occur automatically and unconsciously in some circumstances, bringing it to bear as needed to regulate controllable mental processes could enhance reasoning and productive thought. Consequently, the deliberate self-regulation of thought has attracted interest (see, for example, Schunk, 2012). In general day-to-day affairs, however, people tend not to monitor and regulate their thinking. It has been suggested that, when the quick and intuitive system fails, the metacognitive feelings of difficulty trigger the slower, analytical, deliberate and often conscious self-regulatory system (Alter et al., 2007).

Supporting critical thinking

Support for critical thinking ranges from specific advice to comprehensive teaching programmes. For example, contrastive teaching is recommended in which topics are compared, one with another (e.g. Johnson & Johnson, 1993). Students are helped to make their thinking explicit and explain it to others to stimulate reflection (e.g. Bereiter & Scardamalia, 1989; Fisher, 2001) and critical thinking is rewarded in tests and examinations to show that it is valued (see, e.g., Brookfield, 1997). Amongst the programmes are the materials of the Philosophy for Children movement, used across the world and adapted for students of all ages, the 'tools' of de Bono's Cognitive Research Trust programme, such as the Six Thinking Hats, used in various contexts, and the strategies of Quellmalz's Multicultural Reading and Thinking programme, intended to promote reflective reading and enhance the ability to test beliefs (for reviews, see McGregor, 2007; Moseley et al., 2005; Trickey & Topping, 2004). Some programmes are tailored to particular academic subjects, such as mathematics or science [e.g. Cognitive Acceleration in Mathematics/Science Education (Adey and Yates, 1989; Adhami et al., 1998)]. Others, such as having students draw pictures to represent their notions of concepts and events, have a wider application. Groups of students share and explain their drawings (which are not intended to have artistic merit) and, hence, gain new insights and perspectives (Donnelly & Hogan, 2013).

Generally, a mixed approach to fostering critical thinking has been found to be useful (Abrami et al., 2008). This amounts to exploring critical thinking outside a specific discipline, then practising it in specific subject-related topics. It works particularly well when teachers have had some training and know what critical thinking means and how to do it. For example, they might use 'thought encouraging questions' such as 'What are some questions about ...?' 'What do you mean by ...?' 'What conclusions can we draw ...?' and 'What do we need to do next ...?' Or they might have students discuss ideas in a 'community of critical thinkers' where the teacher fosters student dialogue and has students formulate thought-encouraging questions themselves (Golding, 2011: 362).

This advice, although surely useful, often overlooks the interaction of moods and emotions with cognition or makes reference only to the generation or avoidance of emotions. For example, the effective picture drawing approach of Donnelly and Hogan (2013) was found to generate laughter, humility and rapport, and Ennis (2001) mentioned the need to respect and be sensitive to the feelings of others and recognize their dignity and worth by, for example, couching criticism as rhetorical, alternative views. Moods and emotions can bear upon critical thinking and, conversely, it can bear on them.

Critical thinking and emotions

While we might hope that critical thinking will detect the adverse effects of emotions on the products of thought, critical thinking is itself subject to moods and emotions and is neither 'bloodless, solemn [nor] dispassionate' (Wade, 1995: 24). This is well known in the retail trade; while we think we are discerning and careful in our choices, packaging, displays and staff training are designed to induce moods which make customers less critical (e.g. Aylesworth & MacKenzie, 1998; Gardner, 1985). The same applies to the evaluation of mental products: the meta-cognitive appraisal of inferencing in productive thought can be less critical in a positive mood (Strain et al., 2012). Conversely, moderately negative moods generate more self-criticism and less self-confidence (Efklides & Petkaki, 2005), but a strong negative mood, such as a deep depression, can obstruct the self-monitoring of thought (Slife & Weaver, 1992). When evaluating someone else's mental products, they may generate moods and emotions. Responses to those products can reflect appraisals of how they bear upon matters of personal consequence and vested interests and critics may respond in ways that bias their evaluations. As a result, criticism can show signs of egocentricity, ethnocentricity, conformism, self-deception and wishful thinking, perversity and appeals to emotion.

For example, we care about our how we see ourselves and how others see us. Self-interest can bias arguments, judgments and actions so that we favour our vested interests. If we have an idea and proudly tell people about it, it is hard to be a dispassionate and unbiased critic of someone else's idea that contradicts or competes with our own. When something affects us directly, detachment – looking at it as though it did not affect us – is not easy. We are also creatures of our cultures. From an early age, certain values and beliefs have been absorbed, lying unexamined and taken for granted in the background of our minds. Ideas or behaviours which challenge them may be routinely, even indignantly, dismissed. Witness, for instance, someone's reaction to criticism about her close family, regardless of the warrant for that criticism. Being open-minded can be emotionally difficult, as when someone of one religious faith is faced with evaluating some aspect of a different faith. Ethnocentric behaviour can also include a tendency to agree with the thinking of members of our own group and to conform to the majority view (Lönnqvist et al., 2006). Some objects of thought can be emotionally difficult to handle. For instance, on seeing the mutilation of young children in wars, feelings may propel reasoning in one direction rather than another. Sometimes, reasoning can become a comforting fantasy and lack realism (Carver & Connor-Smith, 2010; Vosgerau, 2010). Evidence which makes the critical thinker feel comfortable by support-ing what he or she values may be afforded greater credence than contrary evidence [a variant of Heider's confirmatory bias theory in which discordant information is rejected (Lindzey & Byrne, 1968)]. Discordant information can be threatening to beliefs, so we feel uncomfortable with it and play it down. Some feel a need to convince others of their ability and will perversely oppose any argument which is not their own (Brehms & Brehms, 1966). While biases are often unconscious and unintentional, some are deliberate attempts to persuade others to a point of view. Appeals to emotion, for instance, attempt to persuade others by eliciting fear or envy. The argument against a proposed supermarket may conclude with 'Once they get their toe in the door, where will it end?' (Rudinow & Barry, 1999). Objective evaluations are likely to be particularly difficult on occasions when vested interests are felt to be threat-ened. The emotions generated urge critical thinkers to protect or further those interests. Ignoring this urge can call for considerable conscious effort.

It looks as though the critical thinker should suppress all emotion and become the ultimate rational machine. While there may be a tendency to see the effects of moods and emotions on critical thinking as bad (Vince, 2006), this is not always so. Unconscious metacognition, for instance, can generate feelings about the progress and effectiveness of thought and provide informa-tion which can curtail or redirect mental activity, although not always appro-priately (Efklides & Petkaki, 2005; Spada et al., 2008). Beyond that, exposing and evaluating assumptions is a central task in critical thinking which, amongst other things, calls for interpretation, analysis, inference and, of course, evalua-tion. Careful analysis, for instance, can benefit from moods that are subdued and calm, even sad (what Andrews and Thomson (2009: 620) describe as 'analytical rumination' or 'the bright side of being blue'). Such moods can serve to reduce distraction and sustain on-task engagement. People in a happy mood tend to be more generous and helpful than those who feel sad (Clore & Palmer, 2009; Gasper & Zawadzski, 2012; Isen et al., 1973). But the emotional needs of 'good' critical thinking are a potential problem for some kinds of productive thought.

Critical thinking seems better served by a calm, careful, neutral or slightly negative frame of mind. Deductive reasoning is similar in this respect and there may be some synergy between these two kinds of productive thought. Creative thinking, however, benefits from a more positive frame, one which induces a feeling of safety and allows the mind to engage more readily in broaden-and-build activity. The mood is not conducive to simultaneous, 'good' critical thinking, so, in the absence of an overly sceptical frame of mind, ideas may form and develop. But a premature insistence on firm, critical thinking is likely to change the mood, suppress emerging ideas, curtail the creative process and render it fruitless. This applies, more or less, to those kinds of purposeful thought which go beyond the given. In other words, there are tensions between critical and abductive reasoning which may directly constrain and stifle constructive thought at its outset or change the frame of mind with the same effect. In a perfect world, the would-be critic would reserve judgment until it can support productivity.

The critical thinker is open to help and hindrance from moods and emotions. Elder (1996: 35) has pointed out that no one is 'a disembodied intellect functioning in an emotional wasteland, but a deeply committed mindful person, full of passion and high values' (and, sometimes, it should be said, low values). Caring about rational and fair argument can predispose someone to engage in critical thinking. The satisfaction of successfully evaluating the products of one's own thoughts and improving them can be rewarding. Without such motivation, critical thinking may not happen. At times, however, critical thinking may have to take a back seat until there is something to evaluate.

Critics and criticism

Not everyone, even the older student, is aware of what being a critical thinker means (Stedman & Adams, 2012, but see Beasley & Cao, 2012). Critical thinking involves certain personal attributes, such as a concern for the quality of thinking and for honesty (Ennis, 2011). These values motivate the critical thinker to evaluate thought and see the task as worthwhile. But would-be critics sometimes mistake the task for a process of hostile fault-finding when it is meant to be a fair and balanced evaluation of the processes and products of productive thought. This hostility is particularly evident in the West, where there tends to be a culture of negativism in the judgment of other people's mental products (Newton, 2010b). It must also be recognized that critical thinking is not infallible and may itself be subject to bias and weak thinking. Does this mean that there should be a higher level of critical thought to monitor its probity? In practice, any evaluation should itself be open to appraisal and, potentially, rejection. People commonly invest more than mere time and effort in their attempts at productive thought and, predictably, criticism can be perceived as a threat to the self and public image. For this reason, Ennis (2011) added concern for others as a desirable attribute for the critical thinker.

When fostering critical thinking, there may be a need to counter its excesses. Scepticism can be taken to such an extreme that it rejects everything, good and bad, and freezes thought. Not every little assumption, argument and belief can be interrogated in the hope that certainty will emerge; only taxes and death are certain. Extreme scepticism, amounting to the peremptory dismissal of careful thought, is likely to be unreasonable, possibly stemming from a need to bolster one's self or public image as a great thinker. Not everything needs critical analysis, nor is every scrap of weak thinking worth pursuing relentlessly. Sometimes it is important that weak thought is corrected: at other times, it is of little consequence. The clergyman and wit Sydney Smith (1771–1845) knew an historian, Henry Hallam (1777–1859), who was notorious for negating everyone's beliefs but his own. Someone said, 'Without fear of contradiction', at which Smith gently interrupted with, 'Are you acquainted, Sir, with Mr Hallam?' (Pearson, 1977). We probably all know a Mr Hallam.

On occasions, critical thinking can be untimely and too quick to reject ideas. Some people in a group seem unable to suspend judgment and so reject the embryonic ideas of others before they have been adequately explored (Bailin, 2006; White & Robinson, 2001). This is not to say that there is no place for critical thinking in constructive thought, but there is a need to recognize when and how to apply it. Critics may also lean in the other direction. Some adults, rather than confess that they felt someone's exposition was meaningless, are quick to agree that it was particularly erudite. Admiration for prominent people also tends to make would-be critics inclined to agree with those people's views. Ultimately, in striving for fairness, critics must question their own motives and assumptions (Newton, 2010b).

There can be a price to pay for productive thought, sound knowledge and the autonomy it offers. As Benson (1983: 16) put it, 'If autonomy calls for a supple mind it also calls for a stiff neck.' Brookfield (1994), studying the responses of North American adults to engaging in critical thinking, found powerful and ambivalent emotional responses to it that made them uneasy yet attracted them to it. For instance, there was a feeling of 'impostership' in which the participants found themselves to be uncomfortably audacious in evaluating the work of others ('Who am I to criticize the experts?'). There was also nervousness about exposing and evaluating assumptions underpinning beliefs which could alienate them from their families and friends and attract hostility: no one likes a Socrates at a party. To offset that, these students now felt less frustrated by a lack of certainty and ambiguity.

Some implications for practice

Mental processes are shaped for better or worse by the pressures on them, so critical thinking has a worthwhile, essential purpose in evaluating thought. Nevertheless, critical thinking is not always supported, whatever the level of

education, and there can be little difference between graduates and school leav-
ers in their critical thinking abilities. For instance, both groups tend to make
assertions without justification (Pithers & Soden, 2000). Strategies for supporting critical thinking can work, but their effects may only be moderate, at least
in the short term (Niu, 2013). Support for critical thinking which mixes
awareness and knowledge of critical thinking concepts with practice in specific,
subject-related contexts seems a prudent approach (Anderson et al., 1997;
McGregor & Gunter, 2006). In this respect, Mason's (2000) list of the essentials
of critical thinking is a useful guide, and more so if it is interpreted to include
the various influences of moods and emotions.

Fostering critical thinking

In general, the raising of students' awareness of sources of bias in critical thinking is likely to be a useful role for the teacher. Modelling his or her thinking
aloud to exemplify critical thinking may also help the students become
conscious of mood effects and vested interests. It would, of course, be worthless
if students habitually leave critical thinking to the teacher. To make it a matter
for the students, the teacher may scaffold students' critical thinking using
thought-encouraging questions (Abrami et al., 2008). For example, when self-
interest has biased critical thought, the question might be 'What makes you say
that?' The ultimate goal is for students to ask themselves such questions, so this
scaffolding process has to be progressively withdrawn. This is more likely to be
successful if students are aware of the concepts and have the language to use
them, perhaps practising their use in groups or 'thinking communities'. It has
to be remembered, however, that exposing thoughts to others can make
students anxious, which turns to feelings of annoyance or humiliation if those
thoughts are found wanting. When the same students evaluate their own
thoughts or those of others, their evaluation may depend on what mood they
are in: positive moods inducing generous appraisals and negative moods
producing lists of faults and nitpicking. Being aware of the role of critical
thinking and how it can go awry is likely to be of help to the student.

When fostering critical thinking, it is wise to bear in mind that critical
thinking itself is not immune from the pressures that influence other kinds of
productive thought – it is not necessarily cold, high reason. At the same time,
there can be tensions between the emotion–cognition partnership which
favours critical thinking and that which favours some other kinds of productive
thought. And, while critical thinking benefits from a sceptical disposition, an
overly assiduous application of it at the wrong time can render adventurous
kinds of thinking fruitless. There will be occasions when these tensions need
forethought and management.

Teachers are not always sympathetic when critical thinking is directed at
their own thoughts.

In a Physical Geography lesson, the terminal moraine at the front edge of an advancing glacier was described as being produced by the leading edge pushing rocks and soil in front of it. One student suggested that most of the debris was probably produced by the glacier's conveyor belt action carrying material on its surface to the leading edge. This constructive critical thought was dismissed with some amusement.

On the other hand, some can find imaginative and considerate ways of making a point.

In an Art project, a student chose to explore the life and work of an artist he greatly admired. This admiration made him blind to the artist's weaknesses. The teacher took an artist who the student knew the teacher admired and modelled his evaluation, making explicit resistance to the temptation to overlook weaknesses and overplay strengths. The student revisited his own work and identified those parts where the partnership between emotion and cognition had biased the account.

Sometimes, the generation of emotion is not anticipated.

In Modern World History, a teacher talked of the Cold War. Her students tended to see it from one side, their side, and became indignant at her presentation of another perspective. She modelled her thinking about an imaginary dispute between two families and used this to illustrate the value of trying to see another's point of view. The students took the point (some more than others) and re-engaged with the topic.

Finally, the quality of thought can simply be weak:

After the third piece of bad news, someone in the staffroom complained, 'Bad things happen in threes. I should have expected it: it stands to reason!' To which, the (unsympathetic) colleague, replied, 'What reason?'

Things to consider when planning to foster good purposeful thought

In Mason's (2000) list, young students will generally have less domain knowledge, their grasp of concepts like ethnocentricity is likely to be incomplete, they may be habitually uncritical and their capacity for reasoning may be limited. Nevertheless, they should be able to engage in critical ways with some kinds of unfair judgment, erroneous thought and bias and begin to develop a habit of critical thinking where it matters. Again, the teacher may make such students aware of simple versions of the concepts through modelling and by scaffolding their thought. Some students may have developed the expectation that teachers evaluate their thinking for them, so requiring that students do it themselves could break the habit. They may also practise testing their thoughts through discussion. Some may find criticism difficult to accept, while others may tend towards negativism regardless of the quality of an idea. Over time, the aim is to implant a desire for fair, valid argument, made considerately, and a pleasure in and respect for 'good' thinking. Although this is a long-term endeavour, Lipman (2003; Lipman et al., 1980) is of the view that we underestimate younger children's ability to reflect upon their thinking.

As they become older, an awareness of critical thinking can be extended to include sources of bias stemming from perceived threats to needs, goals, values and other vested interests. At some point, students recognize that selfishness and self-interest shape ideas, conclusions, decisions and actions. However, adolescents seem, by their nature, to be impulsive thinkers who jump to conclusions and overgeneralize and can be satisfied by an overly simplistic answer (Albert & Steinberg, 2011). Knowledge of sources of bias in thinking should be extended to include, for example, reactions to emotional subject content, the liking of evidence which supports preconceptions, conformity in thought and the uncritical attitude (see, for instance, Lau, 2009). They may also be encouraged to use willing peers as critical mirrors. Individually, they should be helped to review their effective and ineffective thinking in specific subjects so that they see the value of self-reflection. From time to time, students may be given tasks which predominantly require critical thinking skills. In many respects, deductive reasoning and critical thinking respond similarly to moods and emotions, so what was said about support for the former applies more or less to the latter and will not be repeated here.

When thinking critically is expected during other constructive kinds of purposeful thought, the possibility of certain tensions should be considered. It helps to know how, when and where critical thinking is to be applied. Critical thinking also has to have a place in constructive thinking to ensure that, for example, it fulfils its purpose or is otherwise appropriate, but some students may have to learn to moderate early, strong criticism and, at times, suspend disbelief. At the same time, the teacher may have to plan for changes in frames of mind to facilitate the move from creative thought to evaluative thought and back to creative thought when that is needed.

Conclusion

Here, critical thinking has been described as an evaluation of the quality of thought to judge or improve it. Good thought can benefit from some form of critical thinking but critical thinking is, itself, open to bias, sometimes from moods and emotions and sometimes from emotions arising from vested interests. Some of these influences have already been described in the context of various kinds of productive thought, and they apply here, too. Students may construct their thoughts for particular purposes more or less uncritically and some critical thinking could improve them. There may be times, however, when there is a tension between critical thought and some other kinds of purposeful thought. Someone who is too ready to reject an embryonic idea, for instance, may never solve a problem. Applied to the mental constructs of others, critical thinking is a tool for countering manipulation and exploitation and fostering critical thinking can have ideological motives. But it can also be of daily benefit in someone's life in helping to make their thinking better, more reliable and more satisfying.

Chapter 9

Testing times
Emotional performance

Performance can be stressful. Anxiety associated with tests and with learning a second language has been studied for some time, probably because of the evident adverse effects it can have on performance. This is where an emotion really does throw sand in the works. While a little anxiety may support productive thinking, an excess is likely to impede it and reduce performance. Not all students are affected equally, but those who are affected are unlikely to achieve as much as they might or demonstrate fully what they can achieve.

Performances that matter

There are various situations where performance matters. The obvious one is in the assessment of capability or attainment where the outcome is a matter of personal consequence for the student. At the informal and less conspicuous end of the scale, teachers routinely judge students' thinking by asking questions, engaging in dialogue and observing their work. This is a part of normal student-teacher interaction, often used to guide support, and it may pass unnoticed by the students. More conspicuous is the written, class test of capability, the outcome of which may be public and passed on to parents or carers. Potentially of more concern is the formal, high-stakes, public examination which may open or close doors to career aspirations. Often unconsciously, students appraise such situations, gauge the threat to their goals, ego and their public image, and they feel anxious. Test anxiety, as it is known, has received some attention, probably because of its clear potential to interfere with performance.

Another such situation is when students are called on to respond in public. Performance of this kind, often oral, can also be anxiety inducing. For instance, being called on in class to answer a question can be like a public, oral test. Some will recall the increasing dread felt when a teacher used a round of questioning in class and, turn by turn, your public performance came nearer and nearer. Performance of this kind has received particular attention in the context of modern foreign language or second language learning, where oral interaction is used to develop spoken language proficiency. The risk that inadequacies will be revealed to others (and confirmed to the performing student) is, as in tests, likely to be perceived as a threat to goals, ego and public image and can generate an incapacitating anxiety. The effect has been described as an affective filter, which impedes information in two directions: the teacher's instruction has difficulty passing through it, and the student has difficulty responding. It seems probable that the effect is of wider significance than its original context.

Neither an anxious temperament nor a calm disposition predisposes or precludes the experience of performance anxiety, but they may make it more or less easy to instigate. What matters is the students' appraisal of the particular context, their perceptions of threats in it, and the extent to which they feel they can cope (McDonald, 2001). More recent studies of the interaction of emotions and cognition have led to a better understanding of test anxiety and affective filters.

Tests of productive thought

Assessments of thinking competence should clearly reflect the purpose of the kind of productive thought expected. In deductive reasoning, for instance, students might be asked, 'If I throw two, six-sided dice, then what is the chance they will both come to rest with the same side uppermost?' Causal understanding enables explanation and, in some domains, prediction and application of knowledge in new contexts. For example, 'Why does an apple float but a tomato sink in a bowl of water?' (Explanation); 'If I cut this strange fruit in half, what would you expect to see?' (Prediction); 'Make a model house and fit its rooms with lights using torch bulbs, batteries and switches' (Application). Creative thought and problem solving require the student to go beyond the given, to produce something which is more or less novel to the student, appropriate and in some way satisfying (the terms vary with the subject). The process could begin with problem finding. For example, 'Suppose that the electricity supply in your district went off for several weeks. What problems would this create? Choose one, explore it and suggest a solution.' Problems are also presented for solution: 'A visitor is coming to see you. Can you tell her something about yourself with a picture? Think carefully about yourself, then draw and paint a picture which will tell the visitor what kind of person you are.' In wise thinking, the acquisition of its contributory elements could be tested. For example, 'Amy loved the wild goose and nursed it back to health, so why did she let it go?' More demanding would be a response to the following scenario: 'A particular herbicide kills bracken (an invasive fern found on moors and heaths). Farmers use this herbicide to control bracken so other plants will grow and feed the birds and animals from which farmers make their living. This herbicide has been banned because it harms the growing of spinach. But farmers now have nothing to help them manage moorland where spinach is not grown. How would you solve the problem?' Critical thinking is a careful, sceptical way of thinking, which can make itself evident in the quality of the various kinds of productive thought we expect of students. Proficiency in evaluating the thinking of others may be assessed directly. For example, 'James has just told me that he had an awful time having a tooth out at the dentist's. Dentists are so incompetent nowadays! Evaluate this judgment.'

It is in preparing for and responding to such questions that students may become anxious. A little anxiety, however, is not necessarily a bad thing; it can make the student alert and attentive, but, in excess, performance declines.

Test anxiety

Anxious responses to test-like situations may have their origins in parenting behaviours: unrealistic expectations, continual criticism, blame and punishment, tight control of behaviour, and frequent expressions of annoyance and anger (Stipeck, 2002). Frequent anxiety experienced in school, the classroom's emotional climate and public testing can make it a habitual response (Pekrun, 2006). The effect is that those who have or could develop what it takes to perform successfully do not do themselves justice (Connors et al., 2009; McDonald, 2001; Pintrich & De Groot, 1990; Putwain, 2009). Test anxiety can show itself early, and increasingly as students become older, some experiencing anxiety to the point of dread in one or more subjects, leading them to drop out of school as soon as they can (Segool et al., 2013; Wachelka & Katz, 1999).

Pekrun et al. (2009) offer a fuller picture of the emotional event in which learning activities progress from less stressful classroom lessons, to examination preparation on the part of the student and teacher, and to the examination itself (Figure 9.1). After, there is likely to be a more or less anxious wait for the result and then the emotions that follow from that. Emotions felt during this sequence may affect well-being, but obviously those before and during the event bear directly upon examination success. Students often have strategies intended to help them learn and cope with emotions, although these can be

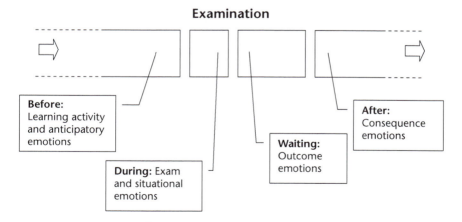

Figure 9.1 The sequence of events potentially producing test-related emotions.

inefficient and maladaptive. For instance, some engage in comfort eating, prevarication or try to elicit unwarranted reassurance from friends.

Two dimensions of anxiety are *worry* and *emotionality* (Spielberger & Vagg, 1995). Worry refers to thoughts about the assessment, such as concerns about self-worth and image amongst classmates, the reactions of parents and material consequences of failure (e.g. Bonaccio & Reeve, 2010). Such thought may also inflate or 'catastrophize' consequences and thereby amplify anxiety (Putwain et al., 2010). Emotionality refers to physiological effects which, in the extreme, can be trembling, nausea, loss of bladder control and a panic attack. Assuming that the physiological responses are not so strong that they physically preclude engagement with the test, performance declines only if the worry component is high. This suggests that thoughts about the potential consequences of a test play a more central role in performance than the physiological effects. The thought associated with worry intrudes on, interferes with or displaces examination-related thought, taking mental resources from the task in hand. Strong anticipatory worry (Figure 9.1) can interfere with preparation for the test, while situational worry during the test can affect recall, processing, and expression of knowledge and ideas.

This interference view of test anxiety suggests that the examination is not attended to properly so that cues are missed and, hence, questions are not fully understood. Even recall of relevant information may be difficult (King et al., 1991). The lack of mental resources would also mean fewer are available for conscious processing in working memory so that connections, relationships, causes and reasons are missed and complex tasks like problem solving could be adversely affected (Dowens & Calvo, 2003; Eysenck, 1997). Anxious children tend to find it harder to complete thinking tasks, take longer over them and make more errors, although, given more time, they can do better (Eysenck & Payne, 2005; Hadwin et al., 2005; Stipeck, 2002). This indicates that some mental resources are being used for other purposes in anxious students so they are less efficient in their thinking than those who feel little anxiety. Given that at least some of these effects stem from the distraction of worry, it indicates that working memory, which deals with attention, is being affected (Eysenck & Calvo, 1992; Putwain et al., 2011). The effect on metacognitive processes, which might otherwise detect thinking deficiencies, is likely to be limited when attention is elsewhere (Cassady & Johnson, 2002; Hembree, 1988). Many students could benefit from help which, when provided, can help them improve their performance, sometimes remarkably (Stipeck, 2002; Wachelka & Katz, 1999; Weems et al., 2010; Zeidner et al., 2012).

Affective filters

For some students, public performance of almost any kind can trigger emotional responses which affect their thinking. One of these is shyness. Being the focus of attention, as when called on to respond orally or simply being watched, can generate strong anxiety, resulting in lower school grades (Crozier & Hostettler, 2003). As might be expected, shy students feel particularly anxious or embarrassed when they have to speak in class. They may, for instance, have difficulty generating rhymes, alliterations and people's names, but the disadvantage they experience can be broader and tends to spread over a wide range of situations.

In second language learning, Swain (2013) describes an 8-year-old, fluent in Greek and proficient in English, excitedly responding to a question in class. She did not know the English word for 'cucumber' and, as her answer poured out, she unconsciously used Greek. Everyone laughed and she was embarrassed and cried. At 50 years old, she still remembered her mortification. In Hong Kong, many students learning English feel nervous, anxious, embarrassed and uncomfortable when they have to speak English in the presence of others. As might be expected, anxieties are also generated by tests, some of which are likely to be oral (Du, 2009). This situation-specific anxiety, first noted in the 1980s, seems to occur wherever second languages are learned and is not unlike stage fright (Horwitz, 2010). Like stage fright and test anxiety, it can be a serious impediment to learning and performance. A pioneer in this work (Krashen, 1988) noted that the emotion can also affect motivation. This can be in either direction: the 8-year-old went to the supermarket to find the word 'cucumber', but others might avoid further contact with the second language. It depends on the student, the situation, his appraisal of the threat and ability to cope with it.

Fraught thought

Pekrun (2006) has offered a useful framework which can predict emotions in tests and can be extended to include those in second language learning. It hinges on how students read the situation. First, there is the perceived value of the outcome. For instance, many value their self-image and how others perceive them. Their appraisal of the situation may suggest to them that their lack of proficiency is a threat to what others will think of them and to their career prospects (He, 2013). Students often have aspirations or goals, which depend on examination success, and failure threatens these (Pekrun et al., 2009). Then there is the matter of control of the situation. Given an approaching performance, how will the student cope, what can be done to ensure success and how feasible is it? Similarly, does the student have a strategy for coping with, for instance, the need to communicate orally in a second language? The appraisal of such matters generates an emotional response. As Pekrun (2006) has illustrated, this appraisal can lead to a variety of emotions. For instance, a student who believes he knows the subject and has the ability to perform at the expected level is likely to feel in control and unthreatened. At worst, his emotion may be neutral and it could be one of pleasurable anticipation. Someone who knows the subject reasonably well and believes she can cope may even feel pleasantly hopeful. On the other hand, a student with little confidence or who believes he lacks ability is likely to feel, at best, sad, and even hopeless. But one who unconsciously appraises the situation and finds threats and uncertainties about being able to control or cope with it is likely to feel anxious. Pekrun (2006) suggests that a typical appraisal might proceed from 'How will I perform?' to 'If my performance is poor, does it matter?' to 'If yes, can I do anything about it?' If students feel there is something constructive they can do, there may be a feeling of relief, pleasant anticipation and motivation. If there is uncertainty, there is likely to be anxiety and, to cope with it, disengagement and avoidance. If it is clear that nothing can be done, there could be hopelessness and resignation (Miceli & Castelfranchi, 2005).

Given that performance generally does matter, some anxiety is not uncommon, particularly amongst those who put success down to ability rather than effort. But we also vary in how much anxiety we feel. For instance, some people are more disposed to feel anxious than others (e.g. Onyeizugbo, 2010) and women are more likely to feel (or admit to) anxiety than men (Stipeck, 2002). Those for whom the test language is not their first language also tend to feel more anxious than native speakers (McDonald, 2001). But a little anxiety is not necessarily bad, as it can improve performance. Samuel Johnson said in the eighteenth century that, 'when a man knows he is to be hanged in a fortnight, it concentrates his mind wonderfully' (James Boswell's *Life of Samuel Johnson*, 1791). That, however, might be just too much anxiety.

Some teachers tend to see tests and examinations as being less stressful than their students do (McDonald, 2001) and the potentially adverse effects of anxiety may not be recognized or alleviated. In He's Hong Kong study, the teachers tended to overestimate the likely embarrassment, nervousness and anxiety and underestimate the impact of public image and the student's lack of confidence in knowledge (He, 2013). Teachers' judgments of emotional effects caused by tests, language learning and similar situations may vary with context but seem unlikely to be accurate.

Far and wide

Some anxiety is probably to be found wherever performance is expected and it matters. Lowe and Ang (2012), for instance, found it in Singaporean and North American students, Ndirangu et al. (2009) found it in Kenyan schools and Andrade and Williams (2009) record its frequent incidence in Japan in foreign language learning, where it also contributes to students' reluctance to participate in discussions. But this does not mean that the sources of anxiety or the specific nature of their effects are the same in all cultures. Matters of personal consequence and the extent to which a student feels in control may be different. Nevertheless, once performance anxiety has been activated it is likely to result in some distraction from the task in hand and can reduce productive thought. Learners with diverse backgrounds may show anxiety effects, but for different reasons.

In constructing a causal understanding of an event in order to explain it, for instance, attention must be given to the details and a mental model constructed in working memory. Making a prediction requires that this mental model be articulated to produce an outcome under new conditions. Recalling an understanding for application in a new situation can similarly require mental transformation and manipulation. These processes call upon memory, attention, mental capacity and manipulation. Creative thinking as the construction of something novel and appropriate draws on resources that, in an anxious person, are limited. Strong negative emotions can narrow thought and fragment the flow of thought ('lose the thread'). Critical and wise thinking also draw on such processes. And, of course, the effect is not confined to pencil and paper tests. For instance, being called on in class to answer a question can, for a brief time, amount to a public, oral test. Some students avoid eye contact in the hope that the question will not be directed at them, even when they have an answer. What might be done to alleviate the problem?

Some implications for practice

Although the problem may be described as performance anxiety, its nature varies with the student and the context. In test anxiety, anticipatory anxiety gets the better of some students and they fail to prepare adequately. Other students may have good study habits but situational anxiety overcomes them (Figure 9.1). In second language learning, anxious students may make their condition worse by trying to avoid mistakes, yet mistakes do not seem to distract other students (Gregersen & Horwitz, 2002). Whether any of these feel anxious and worry about mistakes probably depends on what matters to them and how much it matters. This can mean that what works for one is not always the same as what works for another. To be effective, actions need to be tailored to the cause (Stipeck, 2002). These actions may come from several directions: the school, the teacher, and parents.

What the school might do

Performance anxiety may not figure highly in the concerns of a school as a whole. Unlike student disruption or bullying, it can be a private experience for the student and rarely attracts the attention of school managers, even though they are likely to be concerned about their school's examination successes. Nevertheless, when attention is given to it, it can make a difference.

In the USA, for instance, some older high school students were taught to manage their emotions in stressful conditions. They showed less test anxiety and their test performance improved (Bradley et al., 2010). Also in the USA, some high school and college students with learning disabilities practised relaxation techniques, challenged their irrational beliefs, imagined test situations while using relaxation techniques, were taught strategies for test preparation and given training in test procedures and test taking. When compared with a group of similar students who did none of these, the effect on performance was very positive (Wachelka & Katz, 1999). Broad-ranging strategies of this kind have been found to offer hope to test-anxious students in general (Embse et al., 2013). Popular beliefs in the comforting feel of furry animals also seem to have some foundation; before examinations, students in some universities can spend time handling dogs which are being socialized for guide dog work (BBC, 2013). Nevertheless, it seems that there is a risk in eliminating anxiety entirely, as it might reduce the test performance of those who are not anxious, perhaps by making them complacent (Stipeck, 2002).

Anxious performance in a second language may have its origins in the student's reaction to public speaking, the teacher's expectations, the student's beliefs about those expectations, the classroom procedures and the consequences of performing badly (Young, 1991). Each of these may be susceptible to a different strategy. For instance, desensitization by frequent practice in public may weaken students' reactions to public speaking, but if teachers and students believe that an extensive vocabulary and grammatical perfection is essential, problems are likely to persist for those students who are afraid of error or are perfectionists. Making students aware that facility in communication develops with learning and practice and allowing the use of some compensatory strategies, such as using mime, approximation and circumlocution, can help, provided that the teacher also moderates error correction (Asuncion, 2010; Young, 1991). Classroom procedures that make the performing student the sole centre of attention, for instance, can raise emotional barriers. Making performance less formal and exposed by having students give collaborative presentations to small groups, by engaging in freer, 'round-table' discussions, and by playing games using the target language can lower anxieties (Varga & Stulrajterova, 2008). Distancing the public by using e-learning environments can, as might be expected, also reduce anxiety (Huang & Hwang, 2013). One such approach had students plan, record, edit and listen to their presentation using online radio (Tello, 2010). However, sight of the ultimate goal – that students should talk directly with people – should not be lost. When anxiety comes from beliefs about the consequences of performing badly, strategies used to reduce test anxiety are likely to be relevant.

Students who are severely handicapped by anxiety are likely to benefit more from the help of specialists and should be referred to these (Benor et al., 2009). Overall, this points to the value of support which is tailored to the particular needs of the student, recognizing also the student's cultural background.

What the teacher might do

There may be some students with a tendency to be anxious or even helpless in any activity involving their performance. They may have habits of mind that are maladaptive and need to be changed (Pekrun, 2006). In general, however, it is unlikely that students will be equally affected in all areas of the curriculum. Some teachers have a tendency to generalize and assume that their students respond similarly in all contexts when reactions may be specific to a subject or some activity in it, like oral work (Goetz et al., 2007). How matters of test anxiety are addressed will depend on the age of the learner and on the nature of the problem. Bearing this in mind, a teacher may help students in various ways.

Anticipatory anxiety

Knowing the cause of performance anxiety can inform what a teacher does about it and it may help to talk with students about it (He, 2013). Making students aware that others feel the same anxiety as they do may be a way of starting a conversation about performance anxiety but it is unlikely, by itself, to alleviate the problem (Pekrun et al., 2009). Self efficacy is belief in one's capacity to organize and execute the courses of action required to manage prospective situations (Bandura, 1997). As self-efficacy increases, test anxiety decreases (Onyeizugbo, 2010). Making students aware of the emotional benefits of taking control and working to a plan sets the scene, but students need specific goals, priorities, study skills and a timetable (e.g. Cismas, 2009). There are many books on study skills that offer such strategies. Mind maps, for instance, can be succinct, memorable devices, which can show relationships (e.g. Buzan & Buzan, 2006; Svantesson, 1989). Students often want to avoid unpleasant tasks and those who experience anticipatory anxiety are likely to be amongst them. Organizing the workplace and removing distractions may help. At the end of the day, Benjamin Franklin used to prepare for the next day's tasks, a practice which he found to be productive. Similarly, having a short break when a task has been successfully completed may encourage refreshed engagement later. Well in advance of an examination, questioning individual students about their study activities and giving feedback on them may also help (Pekrun, 2006).

Situational anxiety

Providing information that reduces uncertainty can lower anxiety. This refers to both the level of thinking expected ('This is a good answer because ...') and to the format and mechanics of the activity (Stipeck, 2002). In the case of oral activity in second language performance, students could be told that the plan is to work in small groups rather than as a whole class, and that imperfection is normal (Young, 1990, 1991). Activities that generate more hope and less anxiety, such as continuous assessment rather than an all-or-nothing examination, put less at stake. Frequent tests and oral work may also desensitize some students to them. Other ways of testing students can be less threatening, but do not always work out as expected. For instance, normally anxious students can be less anxious about online tests than they are about formal, pencil-and-paper examinations. But students who are not normally anxious can become more anxious doing such tests (Stowell & Bennett, 2010). Of course, if the latter were not unduly affected by the increase in anxiety, the gains could still be worthwhile. Information technology allows more complex forms of testing. For example, adaptive testing selects and presents questions with a 50–50 probability of success. The test can be completed with fewer questions. Adaptive tests of reasoning, however, have been found to disadvantage those with high levels of anxiety, possibly because of the immediate, resource-demanding challenge (Ortner & Caspers, 2011). Showing students what to do if anxiety gets the better of them may help. They might try sitting well on the chair, breathing deeply and in a controlled way, or tensing the muscles of the body and consciously relaxing each part. Reducing time pressure can also improve test performance, but this is unlikely to help oral activity if it results in long periods of inarticulate, public exposure (Hadwin et al., 2005). Some teacher modelling to illustrate how to cope with going blank in an assessment of oral language skills, followed by practice, could also help (Young, 1991).

Outcome and consequence emotions

The immediate end of the performance offers only a temporary respite. Rumination, dread and worry about the next performance will begin sooner or later. Correct any tendency to inflate, dramatize or catastrophize consequences of errors and omissions (Putwain et al., 2010). It may help to ask, 'What is the worst that could happen?' or 'Would that be the end of the world?', and discourage rumination about performance outcomes and consequences. Similarly, discourage students blaming their shortcomings on anxiety when that is not the cause. Instead, have students reflect on what they might do differently in preparation for the next performance. When it is the cause, have them reflect on progress in past performance to build confidence (Young, 1991).

Nevertheless, it is probably better not to promise that all will be well; old habits die hard, so maintain a sense of realism. Avoid taking full responsibility for test preparation. It is meant to be a joint enterprise and, ultimately, one that students need to learn to manage for themselves. Do not attempt to deal with very severe emotional problems alone. Professional counselling is more likely to be effective (Bonaccio & Reeve, 2010). Finally, not all problems are easily solved.

What parents might do

Parents are seen as laying the foundations for at least some of what becomes test anxiety. In particular, children come to fear the consequences of failing to meet parents' academic expectations. From a teacher's point of view, it helps to have parents who care how their children perform, but not when it becomes counterproductive. It may be possible to let parents know that praising their children for success matters but that it is better to attribute it to effort than to ability. Attributing success to effort reinforces the value of preparation and strategy use. Ability is beyond the students' control so failing a test is perceived as simply confirming their innate and unalterable deficiencies (McDonald, 2001).

The effects of performance emotions can start early, as this instance illustrates:

> The school gave formal reading tests to all seven-year-olds. Those who failed were withdrawn from normal classroom activities and given remedial support. One child, found to be a very competent reader by her teacher, was so nervous and apprehensive that she failed the test and, despite the protestations of her teacher, was labelled 'in need of remedial support'.

For some students, the teacher's approach makes their emotional responses worse.

> A student was competent in reading French but failed miserably in oral communication. He also found it difficult to listen to a recording of himself attempting to talk in French (or in his first language, for that matter). The teacher waited for a response and corrected each error as it was spoken. Progress in spoken French was minimal. In the next year, another teacher took a different approach. His conversations were more casual, less critical and often one-to-one. The student's confidence increased and his talk become less halting. Of course, this approach alone was not enough to eliminate the problem and progress was probably fragile, but it was something to build on.

And it does not always go away with age.

> A trainee teacher knew he had taught a lesson badly. The supervising teacher's judgment counted a lot in awarding qualified teacher status and so had significant consequences. On receiving this teacher's report, the trainee was very defensive, challenged every criticism, and became quite aggressive, even in the face of overwhelming evidence. When he was asked to recall the other, successful lessons he had taught during that week, he subsided and felt the threat recede.

In conclusion

Performance is a complex matter which depends on many things, and reducing anxiety may not always improve it or affect male and female performance equally (e.g. Chapell et al., 2005). Similarly, reducing it for oral activity or an examination is unlikely to improve attainment if the preparation has been inadequate. Learners also vary in emotional resilience (Connors et al., 2009). Hembree (1988) concluded that the effect of anxiety on performance depends on age, reaching a peak between US Grades 7 and 10 (roughly 12–15 years old) and declines in undergraduate years. Presumably, competitive university entry would tend to favour those with coping strategies, so the observed decline may be partly due that. But, even with younger children and older students, anxiety can be disabling or, at least, limiting. For instance, the shy child and even the postgraduate in an oral examination may be adversely affected, even reduced to trembling and tears, by it. There is evidence that systematic and comprehensive programmes to prevent emotions becoming maladaptive can work (e.g. Benor et al., 2009; Evans et al., 2008; Maxwell & Melnyk, 2000; Weems et al., 2010) and recent studies of the effects of reducing performance anxiety confirm that they can produce improvements in attainment (e.g. Bradley et al., 2010; Kaviani et al., 2011).

Chapter 10

Different strokes for different folks

Nature and nurture

A class waited for the teacher to announce the test results. The first student felt a surge of apprehension and then came his mark: 39 per cent. His apprehension became resentment and he sulked most of the morning. The second student also felt apprehensive: 30 per cent. She looked down and swallowed hard, disappointed. Later, she stoically engaged in the lesson, just as she always did. A third student listened with composure: 50 per cent. He grimaced briefly and continued to play with a pencil. His subsequent participation was half-hearted. A fourth student was pleased to find that her mark was 50 per cent, and her boisterous response did not meet with approval. Just four students, but they had four different responses. Some of their inclinations are written in their genes, not in a specific way but as broad tendencies. Nevertheless, whatever the innate tendencies, the environment moulded and added to them. Amongst other things, they had different goals and aspirations, so the test mark was of more consequence to some than to others.

Genes and the environment

Temperament contributes significantly to what makes people different. Rothbart (2012: 13) defines temperament as 'individual differences in reactivity and self-regulation'. Reactivity refers to how readily attention, emotions and physical activity are aroused. For instance, some people are quick to anger, while little disturbs the equanimity of others. Similarly, some students approach and others retreat from a task, in the way that a street disturbance attracts some spectators while others shy away. Self-regulation refers to the voluntary control of attention, emotions and activity. More formally, it is the ability to monitor and modify 'cognition, emotion and behaviour [and] adapt to [the] demands of specific situations' to facilitate purposeful thought (Berger et al., 2007: 257). Some seem able to focus attention and concentrate readily and some make more effort to change a reaction or substitute another in its place. Temperamental tendencies show themselves early and Rothbart and her colleagues have described their main features. Surgency reflects a tendency to feel positive emotions, approach new situations optimistically and show high activity levels.

Another tendency is associated with withdrawal and feeling fearful and sad and low levels of physical activity. A third includes a tendency to notice detail and maintain attention, to find pleasure in low levels of stimulation and to show effortful self-control (Rothbart, 2012). Temperamental traits develop or differentiate, adding, for example, a tendency to affiliate with others, show empathy, perceptiveness and emotional sensitivity (Evans & Rothbart, 2007). The voluntary control of attention also develops in the early years of schooling (Rueda et al., 2005). Rothbart (2012) argues that such traits have a homeostatic property that returns each of us to our behavioural home base. We can move away from that base but, sooner or later, we are brought back to our normal state of being. Broad temperamental tendencies remain with us throughout life. Eisenberg et al. (2010), however, remind us that genetics are not everything: heredity biases us towards certain responses, but those biases are shaped by our interaction with the world.

The influence of the environment also begins early. Parents and carers encourage and discourage behaviours in children. The children also learn by watching adults (Florez, 2011). For instance, a young child will often observe an adult's behaviour and then look to her mother for a response. The response marks out behavioural norms in her world. Similarly, values held by the family are made evident by example and, when they are not upheld by the child, by disapproval. The child grows and interacts with the wider world, adding to and adjusting those values and beliefs as her personality develops. Personality, a more or less consistent pattern of thought, emotion and behaviour, including values and beliefs, encompasses temperamental tendencies and is influenced by them. The personality trait of extraversion, for instance, has much in common with surgency; conscientiousness can call for effortful self-control; neuroticism can be associated with fearfulness and sadness and agreeableness with affiliation. Such traits are, in part, shaped by the environment (e.g. Blair, 2010; Lupien et al., 2009). The family, the values and experiences it provides, and the culture and its behavioural expectations, all contribute to that learning environment. But traits can also determine that environment. For instance, someone who tends to approach new experiences increases their variety and opportunities for learning (Rothbart, 2012). Similarly, a tendency to experience positive emotions may be reduced by an environment which offers perpetual failure and discouragement.

This is a reminder that those in different cultures and subcultures may have similar temperaments but the local social environment shapes them in different ways, so that what counts as appropriate behaviours and adaptive responses varies (Gross & Thompson, 2007; Southam-Gerow & Kendall, 2002). Those in some Eastern societies, for instance, have been described as reserved (Chon et al., 2000; Hahn et al., 1999) but so have some people in certain subcultures in the West, and we should not assume that such differences are permanent or universal. As Averill et al. (2001) have pointed out, the prevailing norms of a society and the processes of enculturation shape what people perceive to be a threat to their well-being, how they respond to it, and what counts as an acceptable expression of how they feel. Such behaviours vary with time and place.

When the child becomes a student, she develops goals that are often like those of similar-minded people around her. But, one of these goals is likely to include feeling good. A lesson which lacks interest or self-evident relevance, or where interaction is intimidating is likely to make her feel negative. To return to a more comfortable state of mind, she may seek ways of entertaining herself, either alone or through affiliation with others. Adolescents may also have a more specific goal of feeling good by looking good in the eyes of others, usually their classmates. Teachers want the foremost goal to be to learn and increase mental resources (Boekaerts & Corno, 2005). When the student's priorities are not those of the teacher, there is the potential for behavioural problems and conflict. To the student, behaviours such as clowning, showing off, inattention and aggression directed at the teacher are well suited to meet her goals. To the teacher, they are major impediments to a successful lesson. The teacher is also likely to have a need for respect. A student who achieves her ends by being disrespectful risks angry responses from the teacher. This may, of course, add to the student's status in the eyes of her friends so it reinforces her behaviour.

Some young people have mental disorders or conditions which affect their productive thought (Hadwin et al. 2005). Schizophrenia, for example, is one for which thoughts and feelings do not work well together. The symptoms include, amongst other things, disorganized, irrational thought, possibly caused by an inability to maintain attention for more than a short while (Andreasen, 1995). Bipolar and unipolar disorders relate to mood problems. In the former, mania and depression alternate; in the latter, there may be an unrelenting depression (e.g. Moldin et al., 1991). Autism involves difficulties with social interaction, possibly associated with an inability to form a theory of mind, that is, a failure to understand or be aware of the mental states of others (Frith et al., 1991). More generally, severe learning disability can be associated with (but not necessarily caused by) difficulties in understanding emotions. There are anxiety disorders involving panic attacks, obsessions and phobias, which can swamp people's ability to manage the interaction of their emotions and cognition (Weissman et al., 1995). There are also the effects of brain injury, as in the well-known case of the railway worker Phineas Gage. In 1848, an explosion blew an iron bar into Gage's forebrain. He survived, but changed from a capable, reliable and organized worker to an impulsive, unrestrained drifter. Damasio (1994) describes Elliot, who had a tumour removed from the front of his brain. He recovered physically but became easily distracted and unable to make sound decisions, even when they were in his own interest. It should not be assumed, however, that all mental disabilities are inimical to productive thought. Van Gogh, for instance, spent a lot of time in mental institutions but he was, nonetheless, famously expressive in his art. Creativity has been popularly associated with mental disturbance, with some small justification. Studies in various Western countries have found that those with schizophrenia, bipolar disorder and depression are overrepresented in artistic occupations and creative activity (Simeonova et al., 2005). It may be that being creative gives these people a feeling of well-being (Galvez et al., 2009; Kyaga et al., 2011).

Differences in students' responses, therefore, have their origins, like many things human, in nature and nurture. When those test scores were announced, some reacted strongly and with little restraint; others showed more self-control. Different students may also respond differently to the same teaching. Introverts, for instance, tend to prefer a structure to their learning while extroverts generally like it to be freer, but may be less able to sustain engagement with implications for tasks which have to be completed unsupervised (Eysenck & Eysenck, 1985). A student who tends to react with negative emotions can develop fearful inhibitions, phobias, panic disorders and anxiety, which get in the way of productive thought. Some may turn their negative emotions outwards in anger and this can produce angry responses from parents and teachers that reinforce the behaviour. While the students are angry, their minds are not productively engaged in the task. Those students who tend to be more sociable seem susceptible to depression when they experience social loss, and that depression can reduce motivation. When these behaviours threaten learning and well-being, they are maladaptive (Barkley, 2006). Beyond immediate considerations, they can also impede success in adult life. Nevertheless, not all students have difficulty in managing the emotion–cognition partnership to suit the needs of the classroom. In particular, those who have some facility in effortful self-control have fewer problems and are more resilient than those without it (Rothbart, 2012).

Developing self-regulation

For those without useful self-regulation (from a teacher's point of view), maladaptive behaviours can be changed, particularly if addressed early. Equally, those without self-regulation strategies can be taught them (e.g. Tugade & Fredrickson, 2007). For instance, a preschool programme in the USA, Early HeartSmarts®, aims to help young children recognize and regulate emotions using 'emotion shifting tools' such as redirecting attention to more pleasant matters and sensations (Bradley, 2009). Another programme aimed to make teachers and parents of young children aware of temperaments and ways of responding to them while, at the same time, the children were taught the same with the help of puppets. The programme reduced the children's disruptive behaviours and helped them benefit from the teaching (McClowry et al., 2005). Some children have a tendency to be inattentive or have attention that jumps rapidly between objects. A five-day training programme using specially designed computer games calling for increasing levels of attention has been found to improve such children's ability to control their attention (Rueda et al., 2005). Again in the USA, Wyman et al. (2010) noted that students with aggressive behaviour, social difficulties and low levels of engagement in class activities risk low academic achievement, social isolation, substance abuse and mental health disorders in later life. They identified such students in elementary schools and taught them to monitor emotion in themselves and others, to moderate emotions (with the help of, for example, a metaphorical 'feelings thermometer' using 'mental muscles' to avoid the 'hot zone'), through modelling self-regulation, and prompting and reinforcing self-regulatory behaviours. As a result, there were significant reductions in behavioural problems. Even simple devices, such as 'reading' spectacles without lenses used in a play-like way, provide effective training for sustaining attention. Bodrova and Leong (2007) had young children wear these spectacles to be like 'real' writers and found it increased on-task behaviour. (Adults also use devices and rituals to help them engage with a task. The writer Honoré de Balzac is said to have worn a gown like a monk's habit for that purpose (Sand, 1876).)

Taken together, this indicates that weak control of emotion has the potential to impede productive thought and, conversely, regulation has the potential to support it. This regulation may be by the teacher, the student, or both. Strategies for self-regulating emotions develop early. For instance, young children may moderate an emotion by thumb-sucking, nail-biting, gaze avoidance, finger-tapping or rocking. Usually, students do not arrive helpless but bring strategies, good and bad, with them. Young children, when faced with an anxious situation, sometimes announce, 'I'm going home now.' Mark Haddon's *The Curious Incident of the Dog in the Night-Time* (2004, Jonathan Cape) is a vivid account of how the world appears to an adolescent boy with Asperger's syndrome. The intensity of sensory experience often overwhelmed him, so he pushed the world into the background with repetitive, mental tasks, like doubling 2 in his head until he reached 33,553,432 and felt calmer. With such strategies and rituals, and tools taught by his teacher, he coped with the clatter of everyday life. While it can be more effective to provide self-regulation tools early, those who fail to acquire them are unlikely to make the most of their thinking potential.

Nevertheless, it should not be forgotten that the interaction between cognition and emotion is two-way. A failure to process information, for example, can generate negative emotions like frustration, which, in turn, makes the task more difficult (Webster-Stratton, 1995). Cognition is itself open to self-regulation to increase the likelihood that it will be successful. Strategies can be as simple as rereading text or constructing a map of relationships described in it. Some strategies have to be taught and practised, such as the *IDEAL* approach to problem solving [*I*, Identify the problem; *D*, Define it meaningfully; *E*, Explore potential solutions; *A*, take Action; *L*, Look back and review (Bransford & Stein, 1984)]. *I* ensures that students grasp what they are to do, while *D* can involve putting circles around key words and exploring their meaning. When students begin to do this unprompted, it is evidence of some self-regulation of thought. Another strategy, Self-Explanation, supports the understanding of text. Instructional text leaves a lot of relationships unspecified. Supplying them would make the text long and tedious. Consequently, the reader has to infer connections that bridge steps in an argument. Chi et al. (1994) found that if students (about 13 years old in their study) explained to themselves at regular intervals what the text was telling them (in their case, at the end of each sentence), there were substantial gains in understanding. Predicting what will happen next is another way of forcing the reader to construct a mental model and articulate it to suggest a probable outcome (Newton, 2012a). Winne et al. (2006) have produced software to support the understanding of instructional text. As the student works at the text, they can use the software to make notes, create a glossary, label and index content and construct graphic organizers. Winne and his colleagues suggest that this is helpful and it also teaches students to deploy such activities routinely. When supporting online study, setting deadlines, having students prepare glosses and engaging in self-reflection also helps them become more self-regulated (Fisher & Baird, 2005). Perry et al. (2002) have demonstrated that even young children learning to read are capable of acquiring and using self-regulation strategies to support their comprehension. For example, if a child does not recognize a word, he is taught to build it phonetically, and, if that fails, seek assistance. The strategies more likely to endure are probably those that are simple, memorable and useful (Newton, 2012a).

This highlights the value of knowing about student differences and strategies which overcome obstacles to productive thought. There is evidence that helping students to manage emotions and cognition can allow attention and working memory to function more productively. Nevertheless, it does not mean it is always quick or easy: it calls for persistence and an acceptance that none of us is perfect (Eisenberg et al., 2010).

Some implications for practice

Fostering self-regulation in students takes some of the burden off the teacher, just as fostering adherence to the rules of conventional behaviour does for class management. But, in the long run, it also gives students coping skills and a sense of competence of broad benefit in life by supporting mental and physical health, relationships and work performance (Baumeister & Vohs, 2007; Grazziano et al., 2007; Immordino-Yang & Damasio, 2007; Koole, 2009). Self-regulation can be conscious and unconscious but, as it is brought into consciousness, it is open to control, adaptation and improvement. This makes conscious self-regulation potentially potent. How much students contribute, however, is partly determined by their innate tendencies, socialization and cultural differences (e.g. Gross & Thompson, 2007; Jones & Wheatley, 2006).

Appraising self-regulation skills

Self-regulation involves forethought (preparation for the task), performance control (actions taken while working on the task) and self-reflection (responses to working on the task) (Cleary & Zimmerman, 2004). The Plan–Do–Review sequence used with children reflects these behaviours in a simple way (e.g. Vogel, 2001). How do we know if students' self-regulation is useful?

In formal studies of academic self-regulation, students may be asked to recall their thoughts, describe them as they work, submit products for inspection or keep a diary of thinking habits (Boekaerts & Corno, 2005). Each could offer clues about the students' management of emotion and cognition and some are what teachers do routinely. For instance, teachers commonly ask students to explain how they arrived at an answer to find the point at which thinking took a wrong turn. Observations of students at work singly and together can also point to behaviour that bears upon productive thought. With that starting point, the teacher may reflect further on students' tendencies by asking themselves some questions. For example,

- Is the student's thinking often unproductive? Productive thought can be demanding, so expectations must be reasonable and there must have been opportunities for the kind of productive thought in question.
  - *If the answer is 'No', then going further may be unnecessary, at least as far as this aspect of academic performance is concerned.*
  - *If the answer is 'Yes', then further enquiry is needed.*
- Is there evidence that the lack of productivity stems from weak self-regulation of moods and emotions? For example,
  - *Does the student tend to be highly reactive in this context, perhaps showing an unwarranted elation, overconfidence, impulsiveness, anxiety, pessimism or frustration?*
  - *Does the student lack sustained attention, perseverance, concentration or is easily distracted?*
  - *How well does the student moderate or control strong reactions that are impeding potentially productive thought?*
  - *Is the student aware of the potential impact of moods and emotions on thinking?*
  - *Can the student adjust a mood or emotion to suit the needs of the situation?*
- Is there evidence that the lack of productivity stems largely from a weak self-regulation of cognition? For example,
  - *Does the student begin a task without forethought or subdivision of the task into manageable parts, or without an orderly approach?*
  - *Does the student unreasonably persist with an unproductive line of thought, lacking flexibility?*
  - *Does the student lack persistence with a potentially productive line of thought?*

○   *Does the student seek to identify the cause of failure (e.g. lack of knowledge, lack of knowhow, ineffective strategies) and remedy it (e.g. by changing the way of working)?*

○   *Does the student check that the product is fit for purpose and, if not, do something about it?*

What these questions mean depends on the context. At the same time, the division of questions into thinking and feeling is artificial as one can influence the other. For instance, a student may regulate disappointment and frustration by looking for a fault in reasoning. The division simply serves to ensure that both receive attention. Thinking about students' emotion–cognition partnerships in this way, however, should not be seen as a way of labelling students permanently with their self-regulatory difficulties. Students change through what they learn and because they mature and acquire more experience. Assessments of this nature are not one-off tasks. But, having arrived at a view that a student lacks a certain self-regulation skill, the next step is to test the belief and, if necessary, support the student in developing that skill. Where there are more serious learning difficulties, a specialist's help in diagnosis and advice should be sought.

Fostering the self-regulation of the emotion–cognition partnership

Cleary & Zimmerman (2004) present a sequence of events in self-regulation: forethought, performance control, self-reflection. Gross (1998, 2001, 2002) offers a parallel sequence for emotions generated when anticipating an event, during the event and looking back on the event. Studies of self-regulation have described some of the things that students do (or could do) during the course of these events, largely to manage thinking, (e.g. Ley & Young, 2001; Parkinson & Totterdell, 1999; Pintrich, 1999; Saarikallio, 2009; Schraw et al., 2006; Thayer et al., 1994; Wolters, 1998; Zimmerman, 2008; Zimmerman & Martinez-Pons, 1986). Merging and supplementing these produces an illustrative account of the thinking–feeling partnership in purposeful thought (see Table 10.1). Particular emotions may be more common at some points than at others but they are not tied to any one part of the process. For instance, boredom or frustration may have to be addressed at any time. At the same time, actions taken to support thinking can generate emotions, some of which may be supportive (such as interest or a moderate level of excitement), while others may hinder it (such as anxiety or frustration). Equally, those actions taken to regulate emotions may bear upon thought, as when intense anxiety is moderated, allowing task-relevant thinking to take place.

To illustrate, consider a task in which students have to write a story or essay. Forethought could relate to overcoming apprehension or boredom. The former might be dealt with by taking some deep breaths and starting the task;

the latter might be eliminated by looking for personal relevance in the task. Younger students may then recall that such writing has to be like a sandwich with a top, middle and bottom. Older students may use a funnel approach in which the account begins with the broader context and narrows to the specific problem in hand. Performance control in this case may call for a management of that sinking feeling when the information seems overwhelming. A short break could distance the task, reduce the feeling and enable re-engagement with an additional strategy, such as collating the information according to groups identified in a mind map. Constructive self-reflection may be something students neglect: having 'finished' the task, they hand it in. Some may find that checking their work is boring. A 'pair and share' strategy in which students pass their essay to another student for appraisal (an exercise in critical thinking; see Chapter 8) could allow some affiliation and overcome boredom. A concluding action would be for students to reflect on the process and feel satisfaction with it. Teachers should avoid destroying that satisfaction and any growing confidence in self-regulation by their response to the submitted work. Where appropriate, feedback should include further advice on self-regulation (e.g. Perels et al., 2005).

Some strategies may work better for some students than for others. For instance, while music may calm the troubled breast of an introvert, a hobby may do it better for an extrovert (Thayer et al., 1994). There can also be cultural differences in strategy use. For example, Purdie and Hattie (1996) found that, although Japanese and Australian students used a similar range of strategies, such as structuring the environment and checking work on completion, Japanese students placed more emphasis on memory strategies. Nevertheless, there is the problem of having students use strategies unprompted. Whipp and Chiavelli (2004) found that success in their use on a web-based course maintained motivation. Perhaps in other contexts, early and evident success in using a strategy could make it more likely it will be used again.

Fostering self-regulation of the emotion–cognition partnership does not call for new teaching skills. Modelling and scaffolding are not uncommon but need to go beyond support for cognition to include emotion and the partnership between cognition and emotion.

Challenges

Some students find it difficult to manage their emotions and thoughts because of particular conditions. For instance, they may show an excessive reactivity to emotion-arousing events, have difficulty in sustaining attention or communication or have mental processing disabilities (e.g. Bylsma et al., 2008). Such students can benefit from self-regulation if ways are found which make it a habit (Montague, 2008). A combination of organized, orderly teaching supported by diagrams depicting important information, and with instruction on a simple, self-regulation strategy, offers some promise of

Table 10.1 Illustrative examples of the self-regulation of the emotion–cognition partnership in a temporal sequence

	Emotion	*Cognition*
Forethought: Preparing for the task	Overcoming procrastination, apprehension, anxiety (e.g. adjusting the frame of mind through exercise or music) Removing distractions Initiating self-motivation (e.g. preparing a checklist, seeking personal relevance)	Understanding the task (e.g. identifying key words) Subdividing the task into discrete units Planning, sequencing, goal setting Selecting strategies to apply to the discrete units of the task
Performance control: Engaging with the task	Establishing a feeling of control, a feeling of being effective Maintaining motivation (e.g. keeping a record of progress) Overcoming frustration (e.g. exercising, then trying a different approach)	Applying strategies (e.g. self-explaining, predicting, sorting, mind mapping, drafting, summarizing) Noting dead-ends and changing strategy as needed
Self-reflection: Afterthoughts	Establishing a feeling of satisfaction, reinforcing confidence in self-efficacy (e.g. by noting achievements) Self-rewarding (e.g. by taking a break) Avoiding rumination (e.g. addressing the cause of negative feelings)	Evaluating outcomes (e.g. judging the match between the goals and the outcomes, making good any deficiencies) Evaluating processes (e.g. considering time management, the effectiveness of the strategies, changes for future tasks)

success with these students. Montague (2008) points out that these students can find it difficult to give up on a strategy which is going nowhere and try another. They can also be slow to use a known, effective strategy in new situations. To illustrate a successful mathematics problem-solving strategy, she describes her seven-step model, which involves: a careful reading of the problem, a student rendition of it, a diagram of it, a plan of action, an estimate of what the solution might be, then the application of the plan and a check that the outcome is as expected. Recalling and applying these seven steps (and a say–ask–check routine for each) seems a lot to ask of learning-disabled children, but there is evidence that it can work with, at least, those of secondary and middle school age. Teachers may create their own strategies to fit particular needs. Simplicity and regular practice will probably increase the likelihood of success.

A particular problem is presented by students with attention deficit and impulsivity disorders. This manifests itself in behavioural hyperactivity, a short attention span and impetuous responses. Purposeful thought often requires sustained attention and self-restraint and, without these, it is less likely to achieve its goals. Fovet (2007) describes the use of computers, email and the internet to accommodate the conditions and, at the same time, enable useful work to be done. In tasks called Webquests, an 'enquiry-oriented activity' is set. Most of the relevant information for the task is to be found by the student on the internet. The teacher can see the student's progress online and can comment on it verbally and via email, providing prompts electronically. The student's attention may wander but they respond well to the teacher's regular prompts, return to the task in hand and are motivated to finish it and report back to the teacher electronically. There was increased self-esteem, more autonomous learning, less disruption of others' learning and more time for the teacher to attend to others. Fovet points out that using electronic tools for tasks that teachers already do well ignores the potential of such tools for new ways of supporting learning. Teachers cannot give all their time to one student but, aided by a computer, they are able to engage such students productively. Some conditions, however, give rise to profound difficulties in particular kinds of productive thought. Schizophrenia spectrum disorders, for instance, can impair the ability to recognize that others may have different views (Lysaker & Buck, 2009), with clear implications for, for example, understanding, wise actions and critical thinking. Children with autistic or Asperger's syndrome conditions also tend to have anxiety and depressive problems, which can affect their purposeful thought (Kim et al., 2012).

Other exceptional students include the able and gifted. There may be a tendency to see these as unlikely to benefit from instruction in self-regulation – they have already demonstrated that they can succeed without it. Able and gifted students do tend to draw on useful strategies to support their purposeful thinking more than other students. For instance, they may routinely analyse a task into discrete subtasks and put these in an order that facilitates its completion (Jackson & Butterfield, 1986). They also tend to work like this spontaneously, from an early age, and apply their strategies widely. But they do not always use the most effective strategies or use what they have to the best advantage. Even gifted students can benefit from consciously reflecting on and acquiring additional strategies to help them maximize their achievement (Risemberg & Zimmerman, 1992; Zimmerman & Martinez-Pons, 1986, 1990). This means that instruction in self-regulation should not be restricted to average and low achievers, although the kind of instruction should reflect the students' capacity for acquiring and managing the strategies.

And challenging

So far, there has been the assumption that there is some willingness to engage in purposeful thought. Inevitably, some students may not be willing and exhibit various degrees of unwelcome behaviour, aggression and disruption, Their beliefs, values and goals are not those of the teacher. Instead, their priorities are, for example, enhancing their self- and public image and seeking immediate pleasure (e.g. Thompson & Perry, 2005). Unfortunately, their behaviour can be very effective in achieving their own goals, while leaving those of the teacher out in the cold. The temptation is to attack only the symptoms, the behaviour, and to do so with aggression and coercion. While it is not possible to ignore some behaviour, a longer-lasting change can only happen if these students are brought to believe that learning goals are worth the effort and are not inherently inimical to their needs, beliefs, goals and values. It may be easier to establish beliefs during childhood, but circumstances do not always cooperate. In the short term, attempting to change such students' beliefs is likely to call for strong self-regulation on the part of the teacher. Students are not the only ones with a concern for their self-worth and public image, and teachers are likely to feel these threatened by some students' behaviour (which is, of course, what is intended). While most teachers probably regulate – or at least conceal – their emotions routinely (e.g. Hutton, 2004), this is likely to call for a conscious effort to stay calm and present a firm, resolute appearance while sidestepping attempts at provocation and avoiding heated arguments. The longer term, however, calls for work on beliefs. Pintrich (1999) has described three sets of students' beliefs that encourage engagement with a task:

1. *Self-efficacy* – a student's judgment of his or her capability to do a task
2. *Task value* – relating to perceptions of the task's personal relevance
3. *Goal orientation* – of two kinds: intrinsic, aiming to master or understand the topic, be creative or wise or evaluate ideas for their own sake; and extrinsic, aiming for good grades to please others, outdo peers or to open doors to other opportunities.

As the problem involves a reluctance to engage with the task, it may be better to begin with task value and make its short-term relevance explicit. Initially, this may mean relying on the practical utility of the topic or the skills being developed, such as 'good working habits' (Boekaerts & Corno, 2005). An initial attraction, however small, may have to be reinforced quickly by addressing pessimistic beliefs about self-efficacy. Careful consideration of traits should inform a plan and the design of materials that ensures some success. Pointing to that success sets the scene for the next lesson where the students should be reminded of it. Over time, slowly and carefully, the aim would be to accumulate these small gains and, eventually, foster interest regardless of utility, because much that has to be taught is not immediately useful. One way could be to highlight and illustrate the need for good working habits in life. While this process may lead to an increased value for educational goals, it is unrealistic to imagine that the problem will fade quickly. Nevertheless, when other goals in school offer some satisfaction, problematic goals may become less pressing and the associated behaviours more amenable to self-regulation. If some willingness to engage develops, self-regulation of the thinking processes can be initiated as with other students. It probably helps, however, if the burden is shared by colleagues who agree on a common approach. This can be where emotional labour is at its hardest, but not all teaching is easy.

In conclusion

Although people have, broadly speaking, much in common, they are also different. Partly genetic, partly learned, these differences can be the cause of this year's failed lesson, a lesson that went well with a different class last year. Teachers do respond to differences in temperament (Pullis & Cadwell, 1982), and self-regulation promises some amelioration of the effects of the differences; students who can make their emotion–cognition partnership productive, in spite of those differences, are more likely to be successful. Strategies that help them do this can be taught. This is an area that is open to a teacher's creativity, crafting ideas to suit particular needs. Keeping such strategies simple and making them memorable probably increases the chance that they will be used spontaneously.

Chapter 11

Emotional labour

Moods, emotions and the teacher

Teaching is an emotionally charged occupation involving considerable emotional labour and, at times, disagreeable labour pains (Golby, 1996; Schutz & Zembylas, 2009). The endeavour calls for a sizeable commitment to the task and a large personal investment in relationships. The emotional wear and tear can cause exhaustion, absenteeism, burnout, dropout and early retirement, effects which have been recognized around the world (e.g. Frenzel et al., 2009; Richardson et al., 2013; Wilson, 2004). But, when things go well, teaching can be rewarding, even exhilarating. Richmond et al. (1987) maintain that there is no escaping emotion in the teacher–student relationship or, as Hargreaves (1998: 835) has put it, 'emotions are at the heart of teaching'. Teachers' moods and emotions and how they handle them are important, both for themselves and their students. They can influence events and thought as much as or more than the students' moods and emotions.

At the heart of teaching is emotional labour

Teachers bring their beliefs, values, goals and aspirations with them to the classroom. Some teachers are intrinsically motivated, valuing the psychological rewards teaching offers, such as the satisfaction of success, the pleasure of sharing an interest and the delight in broadening a student's horizons and raising their aspirations. Students in the USA who were taught by such teachers tended to show more interest and enjoyment in their work (Wild et al., 1997). But other teachers are extrinsically motivated, presumably teaching for financial reward or because the work schedule suits them or some similar reason. In the study, their students tended to show less interest and less enjoyment, even when taught the same material in the same way. Atkinson (2000) found comparable effects in the UK. The teachers' motivation influences the relationships they do (or do not) develop with their students and this affects academic emotions.

At the same time, teachers also bring moods and emotions to the classroom. Davis (2003) and Cubukcu (2013) found that, when the teacher's prevailing mood was clearly positive, students made more effort and were more engaged in their work than when it was negative. It may be that students feel less need for vigilance in a positive emotional climate, so are free to give mental resources to the task in hand. When learners are more engaged, the teacher's mood is likely to be sustained or even enhanced. But when the teacher's mood is negative or no better than apathetic, engagement by both teacher and students can be half-hearted with less learning, effects that could reinforce an already gloomy emotional climate (Sutton & Wheatley, 2003; Wanzer & McCroskey, 1998). Teachers' prevailing moods also affect their judgments of students. A teacher in a good mood is more likely to see a student as 'generally well-behaved' and 'often hard-working'. On a teacher's bad mood day, reprimands tend to be more severe. Given such effects, it is not surprising to find that a teacher's ability to foster a positive emotional climate in a classroom is seen as very important for the learning that takes place there (Garner, 2010; Sutton & Wheatley, 2003). Certainly, preparation for teaching, including the physical arrangement and appearance of the classroom, a concern for understanding, enthusiasm, and a confident, pleasant demeanour, and praise where it is due, can foster learning (Everston, 1989).

Teachers also respond emotionally to classroom events. Often unconsciously, they appraise their teaching as it progresses and feel how well it is going. Their emotional response reflects the outcome of that appraisal. A negative turn in mood serves as a red light, warning that events are not going as hoped; a positive turn is a green light. For example, one teacher tried to use collective formative feedback to give advice to a class on writing assignments. The students responded with open hostility because they felt threatened by the teacher's public disclosure of their inadequacies. The surge of apprehension felt by the teacher was a clear 'Stop' light which prompted an immediate change in approach. She gave feedback individually in a more time-consuming way but without further emotional red lights (Stough & Emmer, 1998).

Interacting with students in a lesson can produce a stream of affect in a teacher (e.g. Hargreaves, 1998, 2000, 2005). Positive emotions (like pride, joy, excitement, pleasure, surprise) tend to be produced by, for instance,

- students' intellectual growth
- successful relationships with students, especially those who are responsive
- students' successes in life
- a job well done
- supportive colleagues
- parents of students who are supportive
- feeling in control and competent.

Negative emotions (like anger, frustration, sadness, helplessness) tend to be produced by, for example,

- student misbehaviour, laziness and inattention
- unsupportive colleagues

- uncaring or irresponsible parents
- administrative distractions and frustrations
- paperwork
- preparation for and inspections of teaching quality
- fatigue, stress and anxiety
- perceived impediments created by school managers.

Student behaviour and compliance is a widespread concern of teachers, so the feelings of anxiety, annoyance and frustration which they generate are not uncommon – for instance, in the UK (Griva & Joekes, 2003), Sweden (Ahlgren & Gådin, 2011), Hong Kong (Tang et al., 2012), China (Liu & Onwuegbuzie, 2012), Malaysia (Samad et al., 2010), Greece (Antoniou et al., 2006), Canada (Klassen, 2010) and the USA (Greenglass & Burke, 2003) – although this is not to say that the precise concern is the same everywhere (Emmer & Stough, 2001; Sutton, 2007). In addition, a teacher is likely to feel irritated by a lazy student but have sympathy with an innate lack of ability (Pullis, 1985). Negative emotions, like annoyance and frustration, distract a teacher's attention from the task in hand and focus it on the cause of the emotion, such as bad behaviour. The danger is that an angry outburst could make a situation worse. Minor disruptions, for instance, may be dealt with by the mere proximity of the teacher.

Teachers' thoughts are also subject to the effects of their own emotions. For instance, emotional classroom incidents will tend to be remembered when others are forgotten. A bad lesson looms large in a teacher's experience and, at the end of the week, will be the one remembered in spite of the good lessons that outnumber it. Emotions also attach themselves to memories about students, and these will be recalled more readily than others. A student who, in spite of personal difficulties, is successful may generate sympathy. Recollections of that student will tend to reflect that feeling. Similarly, a student who behaves badly, even only once, is more likely to be recalled as a miscreant than as someone who is reputable. This selective recall can shape how the teacher interacts with those students in the future. And again, just as with students, moods and emotions affect a teacher's productive thought, such as his creativity: anxiety and its intrusive worries can drain a teacher's mental resources so that lesson plans are less imaginative. Similarly, a teacher becomes less able to cope with the unexpected or to adapt a plan to meet new needs (Hargreaves, 2000).

Even experienced teachers do not always meet perceived threats with stoicism. They have built up a repertoire of behaviours and practices that has generally served them well. Imposed changes, such as new programmes or ways of working, are potential threats to these tried and tested practices. If a change is appraised as supporting the status quo, they are likely to feel positive and support it. If not, they feel negative, resist it and may subvert it. A new approach, for instance, may be adopted superficially but, in reality, teaching goes on as before. Unconscious emotional responses can determine the success or failure of teaching initiatives yet their designers are often blind to them (Hargreaves,

2005). Teachers, like most other people, do not seek to make life difficult, uncomfortable or threatening for themselves, so whatever emotions they anticipate shape the decisions they make (Sutton & Wheatley, 2003). How to respond to events is often determined emotionally and then justified later (Golby, 1996; Tversky & Kahneman, 1974).

Using emotions to good effect

Enthusiasm

Students' emotional expression affects teachers, but the other side of the coin is that teachers' emotional expression affects students. It has long been known that tone of voice, speed of talking, facial expression, posture, gesture and degree of animation can tell others how you feel (e.g. Rosenberg & Langer, 1965). One emotion that reveals itself in this way is enthusiasm. An early study by Rosenshine (1970) found that enthusiastic teachers tend to have students who achieved more but, of course, it would be easy to be enthusiastic with high achieving students – is the teacher's enthusiasm the cause or the result of the achievement? Bettencourt et al. (1983) trained teachers to show enthusiasm and compared them with those who were not trained. The enthusiastic teachers obtained more on-task behaviour when they were interacting directly with their students and also when the students were working on the tasks themselves. Showing enthusiasm, therefore, can increase engagement. It may work because it tells students that today's topic is potentially interesting. It may also produce some emotional contagion, that is, the students 'catch' the enthusiasm and feel curiosity and pleasurable anticipation (Hatfield et al., 1993). Nevertheless, it should be used in moderation; if overdone, it can make the teacher look like a clown and it becomes counterproductive. Frenzel et al. (2009) measured teacher and student enjoyment of a lesson and found that the key factor relating the two was teacher enthusiasm, which resulted in an emotionally positive atmosphere. Frenzel and her colleagues argue that this positive atmosphere is conducive to effective teaching and also to teachers' emotional well-being. While teaching is not simply about making students happy, there are times when this is conducive to productive thought, such as being creative. Research on the effects of enthusiasm does not always distinguish between the teachers' enthusiasm for the subject and enthusiasm for the students' learning. It would be prudent, therefore, to show enthusiasm for both. Striving to display enthusiasm when none is felt, however, takes a lot of emotional labour; it can be wearing and could lose its effect through overuse. Additional strategies are, therefore, potentially useful.

Immediacy behaviour

More general than showing enthusiasm are non-verbal immediacy behaviours, which reduce the physical or psychological distance between teacher and learner (Babab, 2007; Richmond et al., 1987). A teacher who comes out from behind his desk and moves amongst the students is showing immediacy behaviour. While this reduces physical distance, simply smiling or adopting a relaxed posture reduces psychological distance. Such behaviours are associated with student learning (Richmond et al., 1987). Once again, there can be a reciprocal relationship between what the teacher does and what the students do. More learning is likely to make the teacher feel happier, and, interpreting that as a green light, it prolongs immediacy behaviour.

Self-disclosure

While immediacy behaviours are non-verbal forms of communication, there are also verbal forms which motivate students, such as humour, self-disclosure and narrative (Downs et al., 1988; Javidi et al., 1988; Nussbaum, 1992; Nussbaum et al., 1987). It is not uncommon for teachers to use humour in the classroom, often spontaneously; it can defuse annoyance, alleviate boredom, refresh attention and make some relevant point about the topic in hand. Humour does, however, need to be handled with care; there is a distinction between fostering productive thought and entertainment. Self-disclosure is when teachers seem to reveal something of themselves, such as likes, dislikes, interests and snippets of experience. Once again, care is needed, as it may encourage an excessive familiarity, which can be an impediment to class management, although this is probably less of a problem with voluntary, mature students. Teacher narratives are accounts of real or fictitious events and include anecdotes supposedly about personal experiences. While they can be spontaneous stories, those that are chosen and carefully planned can make a teaching point, illustrate an idea or set a scene for the topic of the day. So, for example, when teaching a science class about the stability of objects, a teacher might recount the time he opened his wardrobe doors and the wardrobe toppled on him. Real or imaginary anecdotes of this kind offer safe humour, reduce psychological distance and provide relevance and meaning for the students' studies. Male and female teachers, however, may not see the role of emotions in the classroom in the same way, and women are more likely to use emotion-centred tactics to maintain students' perseverance (Demetriou & Winterbottom, 2009).

Silent signals

Teachers form beliefs about students' abilities and have expectations of them based on those beliefs. If the beliefs are well founded, it helps the teacher provide appropriate learning tasks. The learner, however, may sense those expectations and be content to perform within their limits. Some time ago, Conn et al. (1968) demonstrated that the sensing of those expectations is through the student's perception of emotion in the teacher's vocal expression.

This warns us that we may say one thing while the undertone says something else. 'Can you not explain that?' can be said with hopeful anticipation, disappointment, sympathy or resignation. The first may motivate effort, while the last may terminate it. Of course, whether or not those expectations are sensed depends on the student's ability to perceive emotion. Conn and his colleagues showed that students who are good at it tend to perform much better than those who are not. Atkinson (2000) argues that some teachers habitually see students' progress in a negative light. The students sense it, feel less happy about the subject and show less effort in it. It is, therefore, important to convey an appropriate emotional message alongside the verbal message. It may be necessary to reinforce this verbally for some students. Learners generally prefer teachers who care about their progress and performance (Sutton & Wheatley, 2003). For instance, students feeling anxious about their performance value a compassionate and understanding teacher who balances objectivity with empathy (Crossman, 2007).

Managing emotional labour

Emotional labour can be wearing. Loud expressions of discontent at misbehaviour, bullying or lesson disruption can make a point, but, like scarecrows, they lose their effect if always on display. An overuse of aggressive signals is wearing and stressful for the teacher and, in the long term, bad for health (McPherson et al., 2003). Controlling such emotions is wise and these are the ones teachers try to regulate in themselves (Sutton & Wheatley, 2003). Positive emotions are managed less often, as in the general population (Gross et al., 2006). The extent to which we show positive emotions is a matter of personality and disposition; some people are generally more restrained or gloomy than others and so dampen their classroom's emotional climate (Gross, 2001; Rothbart & Jones, 1998). For them, managing emotional labour may be harder than for others but the rewards can be worth it.

Whatever good a concerned, empathetic, enthusiastic, story-telling teacher does, it does not automatically carry forward to later years or transfer to other teachers. Each teacher has to renew and maintain it him- or herself (Frenzel et al., 2009). Neither does emotional labour make up for bad planning and exposition (Mottet et al., 2008). Strategies for managing moods and emotions and fostering productive thought need to go hand in hand. Being full of enthusiasm is futile when the steps in the argument are too large to follow, rest on understandings not yet present, or when there is a constant badgering of the student to be creative. At the same time, boys and girls may react differently to the teacher's emotional labour (Conn et al., 1968; Keenan & Shaw, 1997), responses may vary with culture and they could change as students become older (Gross, 2001; Gross et al., 2006; John & Gross, 2004). Generally, teacher training has not concerned itself to any great extent with emotional labour (Garner, 2010; Hoy, 2013).

New teachers

The first five years of teaching are crucial for the development of a teacher (Feinman-Nemser & Rémillard, 1996); experience during that time shapes the kind of teacher he or she will be. New teachers, in particular, can experience strong and mixed emotions in their teaching, something which Erb (2002) has likened to an emotional whirlpool. They feel these emotions in anticipation of, during and in reflecting upon teaching. Friedman (2000: 598), working with new teachers in Israel, described the negative aspects of this whirlpool. He listed words used by these teachers to describe their feelings – 'shock, night-mare, catastrophe, collapse, suffering, despair, crisis, and pressure' told the tale of their first few weeks. Feelings of overload, fatigue, exhaustion and blame followed and then there was a period of adjustment in which the situation and its relationships were simplified. For instance, less able students came to be seen as beyond help, a coping strategy that, presumably, makes teaching them less demanding. With such experience, it is not surprising that a number of these teachers were unsure about continuing, and such feelings are not unusual (see, for example, Emmer & Stough, 2001).

Ria et al. (2003), observing new teachers in France, saw that emotions were generated by appraisals of minute-by-minute events in their lessons and that a given lesson produced a stream of emotions, some positive and some negative. These novices were particularly affected by what they saw as 'threats' to their lesson plans, even when the threat was relatively trivial and something an expe-rienced teacher would hardly notice. Plans were perceived as obligatory sequences of events from which there could be no deviation. This is, perhaps, an inevitable consequence of lack of experience, adaptive strategies and self-confidence, but it generated a lot of anxious moments for these novices when students and materials did not behave quite as expected.

Anxiety is particularly common amongst new teachers. Teaching is, for them, a threat to their private and public image and they tend to worry about being unable to perform like their more experienced colleagues (Sutton & Wheatley, 2003). Each lesson they teach has the potential to expose their lack of skill. The stream of emotions guides the experienced teacher, often auto-matically, to deploy strategies that switch off the red lights and switch on the green lights. Rapidly deciding to change direction can make all the difference in a lesson that is going downhill. Novice teachers need knowledge and strate-gies that guide how they intervene and change a lesson's direction.

In Australia, Hastings (2004) identified some of the emotions experienced by teachers whose role was to support such trainee teachers in the classroom. Again, she found the relationship to be an emotion-inducing one. There was guilt and frustration because of the lack of time given to the task, anxiety about the quality of teaching experience and the trainee's perceptions, stress when working with a less competent trainee, relief at the novice's success, sympathy for the one who failed and satisfaction at a job well done. Emotions are not confined to novices and their supervisors. Experienced teachers also feel them, although probably not always with the same intensity if they have acquired coping strategies. Frenzel et al. (2009: 706) exemplify this by reference to a middle school teacher who still finds teaching 'almost scary'. Novices would probably omit the word 'almost'. Coping with emotions like these is important for the well-being of the teacher and the success of the students.

Stress and job satisfaction

Job satisfaction and stress are not opposites, although stress is one factor which produces job dissatisfaction, depression, absenteeism and dropout (Greenglass & Burke, 2003). Job satisfaction tends to be associated with feeling competent (self-efficacy) and believing in the collective will and effectiveness of colleagues to support teaching and learning (collective efficacy) and student achievement. Stress is associated with low self-efficacy, low levels of collegiality, poor teacher–student rapport, student misbehaviour, being taxed beyond mental or physical resources without the prospect of respite or of gaining control, and aiming to be the perfect teacher (Demetriou & Wilson, 2012; Gamefski et al., 2001; Klassen, 2010). While a little stress can be motivating, a lot is bad for health, for teaching and for learning. It occupies teachers' minds, curtails effort at finding solutions and reduces the capacity to engage productively with students (Schutz et al., 2009).

Some have higher stress thresholds than others, but to reduce the risk of stress school leaders should foster their teachers' self- and collective efficacy and collegiality to serve as 'a job resource' (Klassen, 2010: 343). Teachers may draw on this resource for social support and advice and note that they are not the only ones to feel under stress. It is also important to identify what does and does not matter and avoid sweating the small stuff or, at least, choose to ignore it (Schonfeld, 1990). Support of this nature has been found to lower stress, but it probably depends on the colleagues consulted and the teacher's determination to address the cause with planned action (Bakker et al., 2007; Cecil & Forman, 1990).

It is, however, rare for everything to be stressful. Zautra (2003: 203–4), writing about emotions in the workplace more broadly, reminds us that, 'Job involvement can be one of the greatest sustainable resources of joy and fulfilment in our lives … By attending to our own feelings during the process of work and staying aware of the value of our goals, we remain mindful of our interests.' What counts in teacher retention is the balance between positive and negative emotions, which needs to be fairly heavily weighted in favour of positive emotion (Sutton & Wheatley, 2003). Burnout, on the other hand – a work-related syndrome that, amongst other things, is associated with exhaustion from overload – leaves little time to feel or savour whatever positive emotions there are (Friedman, 2000).

Coping

Ways of coping with the wear and tear of emotional labour are needed, both for the experienced and the novice teacher (McCarthy, 2009). Garner (2010) adds a need for resilience, a tendency to respond to adversity with reasonable optimism, persistence and determination – what some simply call 'bouncing back'. In the USA, Tugade and Fredrickson (2004) found that those with resilience used optimism and humour to maintain a positive mood, which helped them reappraise situations constructively. In Australia, Howard and Johnson (2004) found that those who coped tended to reflect on practices and construct strategies for dealing with problems. Some teachers said they had acquired this disposition from their experience in childhood and early adulthood. Those who show a talent for emotional labour could be described as having emotional intelligence but, as Colvin (2008) has described, so-called innate talent is often the result of experience and practice early in life. This suggests that providing knowledge of the emotion–cognition partnership, strategies for emotional self-regulation and practice in using them could supplement whatever talents they have. Turner and Braine (2013) describe the promising effects of 'therapeutic training' aimed at increasing the resilience of new teachers. This training comprised three two-hour sessions on matters of mental health, personal needs, transactional analysis and case studies and coping strategies. A significant element may have been the sharing of experiences within the groups of nine to twelve teachers.

Some implications for practice

A teacher's moods and emotions can usefully contribute to and facilitate learning, provided that they are the right ones at the right time (Aldao et al., 2009; Fried, 2011). As Gross (2002) has pointed out, getting them right is not always easy. Emotion regulation is what people do to manage their emotions and their expression so that they suit the needs of the situation (Gameŝki et al., 2001; Gross, 2002; see also Chapter 10). This can be a conscious act, as when we count to ten when provoked, or an unconscious response, as when we discover the world beyond the window as we sit in another interminable meeting. Gross (1998, 2001, 2002) has described a way of thinking about the self-regulation of emotion as an event presents itself and unfolds, and it can be adapted to reflect teaching events. In teaching, self-regulation may take place before, during and after the event (or, as Cleary and Zimmerman (2004) put it, in forethought, performance control and self-reflection). Before a lesson, a teacher may look forward with confidence, or dread, or feel any of the emotional shades in between. If the first, she may reinforce the feeling by thinking about the lesson and seeking additional materials to support it. If the second, she may distract her attention by checking students' work, talking about something else or by delaying going to the classroom. During a lesson with an excitable class, a teacher may moderate his expression of delight at a child's success in order to maintain a particular emotional climate, and he might count to ten as a child misbehaves so that his response is not immoderate. After a lesson, a teacher may reflect on it with satisfaction, relief or annoyance. She might prolong a pleasurable feeling by relating events to colleagues or reduce negative feelings by sounding off in the staffroom, going for a run or overeating. Lessons with particular groups are rarely one-off occurrences, so the before, during and after emotions and the degree of success in managing them is part of a repeating cycle of events, each informed by the experience of what went before.

Some ways of managing emotions and their expression are effective and some may make matters worse. For example, self-blame and blaming others are not conducive to a teacher's health and well-being. Ruminating about events and continually dwelling on them is also maladaptive; it improves little and can lead to depression. Catastrophizing, inflating the negative side of events, is similar. Resigning yourself to the inevitable and simply accepting it may be realistic and can reduce immediate negative feelings, but some find it difficult. Similarly, thinking happy thoughts may work for some but tends to leave the problem unsolved. Negative emotions are the result of perceived threats to our values and goals, but if we reappraise the situation we may find that these are not really under threat: a verbal insult, for instance, can be seen as telling the world more about the insulter than the insulted. Reappraisal, seeing things in a different light, can reduce negative feelings and replace them with positive ones. Putting things in perspective is similar – many events are of little significance in the long run (Gamefski et al., 2001).

One effective strategy, however, is particularly relevant to the repeating cycle of events. Problem solving offers a powerful way of taking control of teaching (Aldao et al., 2009). Instead of ruminating about failures and failing again, seeing an event as a problem and constructing a course of action with some potential to solve the problem – perhaps with the help and advice of others – can replace anxiety with hope, interest and a feeling of security and competence. A lesson may then be approached more confidently and more positively. Of course, like designing a new product, the solution may need testing, tuning and some persistence to make it effective. Teaching is a risky, public performance and parallels can be drawn with students' oral performance in second language learning and the emotions it generates. Reflecting on it after the event in order to inform planning for the next session, however, can be an effective way of bringing about change (Pennington, 1996).

In conclusion

Tickle (1991) argues for a curriculum for the emotions in teacher education. He considers that skill in managing moods and emotions amounts to enabling a 'personal competence', a term coined by Zimpher and Howey (1987). This personal competence involves being able to recognize moods and emotions in themselves and others, knowing how emotion and cognition interact and managing that interaction in ways which increase the likelihood of productive thought (Garner, 2010). How training could contribute to this personal competence is considered in the final chapter.

Chapter 12

Two minds are better than one

In productive thought, the intellect is not everything; moods and emotions also have their say. This is not to say that logical thought does not exist. It simply recognizes the fact that the emotional system both stimulates thought and leaves its stamp on it. What is stored in memory and recalled from it – engagement with a task, attention given to it, the interpretation of information, the process of making inferences and the manipulation of ideas – are all potentially open to the influence of emotions. There may be a tendency to see emotions only as sand thrown into the cogs and gears of the mind. Sometimes, emotions are like that, but at other times they wind up the spring and provide the oil which makes those cogs run more smoothly and for longer. Immordino-Yang and Damasio (2007: 5) explain: 'emotions are not just messy toddlers in a china shop, running around breaking … delicate cognitive glassware.' In education, this has been ignored or been a matter for impromptu consideration, but it needs to be a part of a teacher's knowledge and integrated with their forethought and teaching skills.

On reflection

We think for a variety of purposes. Those described here illustrate some that are, or arguably should be, familiar in education. Reasoning, causal understanding, creative, wise and critical thinking are complex constructs not so much distinguished by their range of mental resources and processes as by their aim and emphasis. These illustrative examples of productive thought form a teleological collection of practical relevance and meaning for teachers, educationalists and programme compilers in a wide range of contexts. While it may direct attention to particular thinking purposes and guide practice, it is not intended to suggest that there are sharp divisions between these kinds of thought. Understanding and creative thinking have a lot in common, wise thinking integrates thinking for various purposes in order to arrive at an action and critical thinking can be all-embracing in its evaluative role. Purposeful, productive thought has survival value and it can enhance and enrich our lives. It can, at times, also be demanding. When it is, the student's frame of mind can help or hinder it and shape the product. Moods and emotions are major contributors to that frame of mind.

The emotional system concerns itself with our best interests or, more precisely, what we believe, consciously or unconsciously, to be our best interests. According to its appraisal, attention, thought and action are directed by moods and emotions with the aim of promoting those interests. It is true that, at times, moods and emotions are an impediment to sound thinking. Strong emotions can make it difficult to focus on a task and give it the mental resources it needs. Anxiety before and during tests and in public performance can reduce some students' success considerably. When what matters to students is not the same as what matters in the classroom, the conflict of interests can rule out learning. But to see moods and emotions only in this light is too simplistic. Emotion can also motivate thought and increase the likelihood that thought will be productive.

The emotional system can detect matters of personal consequence, filter out what is personally irrelevant, direct attention and prompt thought. It can indicate when a line of thought has become unproductive and prompt a change in direction. A happy mood can put people at ease and favour wide-ranging thought, which generates ideas (Fredrickson et al., 2003). A sad mood can foster detailed, analytical thinking to support evaluation while events of emotional significance receive preferential treatment in memory.

At times, however, the students' frames of mind do not always suit the current needs of productive thought. Students bring moods and emotions with them that may not suit the needs of the task, and their moods may spread to others and adversely affect the emotional climate of the classroom. Those in a good mood may not think critically when it is needed, strong emotions may distract attention and occupy mental resources, and moods may unwittingly bias interpretation and inferencing. While thinking, moods and emotions may change in response to events and may no longer provide support. There is a tendency to plan for and manage students' intellectual engagement with tasks. There are times, however, when students' moods and emotions have more to do with their success than their intellectual powers, and the contribution of moods and emotions, for better and for worse, should not be ignored. Some teachers may have an intuitive feel for managing frames of mind and this is useful, but, as with the intellect, dealing with frames of mind should receive conscious attention in planning, action and afterthought. In this way, the emotional and intellectual systems may be brought together to facilitate productive thought. Two minds are better than one.

Interaction between emotions and thought is not one way. For example, thought can make an inference which, when shared with the emotional system, is judged to be a threat and so generates feelings. We are all familiar with the cold spread of dread when we think something through and finally see the unwanted consequences of a proposal. Later, reason may be applied to reduce the threat. In other words, there can be a beneficial, two-way partnership between thinking and feeling or, more formally, emotion and cognition. When it comes to productive thought, the intellect is not everything but, it should be said, moods and emotions do not complete the set. For instance, feelings are also associated with bodily states, such as temperature, thirst, hunger, tiredness and illness. These, too, can affect our readiness for and effectiveness in purposeful thought, because 'the way the human mind thinks and reasons is not independent of the human body in which it resides' (Spellman & Schnall, 2009: 118). Physical comfort, for instance, may affect productive thought, although not everyone is like the hardy, starving poet, able to create in the cold garret.

The emotional climate needs to be considered when designing learning environments. Learning environments often contain a teacher who, like students, is subject and sensitive to moods and emotions. The teacher's manner and interaction contribute significantly to that climate and to the emotions students feel (Hascher, 2010). But the physical appearance of a learning environment also contributes to the climate, as do teaching resources, the topic and other students, although rarely as much as the teacher. Planning for and preparing the environment with some care can set the tone for a lesson and the teacher's modeling of the expected frame of mind can help through emotional contagion. Given the importance of the thinking–feeling partnership, it is not surprising that some designers of information technology for the classroom attempt to make it sensitive to the emotions of students and able to respond to them (e.g. Daradoumis & Caballe, 2011). This makes it even more important for teachers to be aware of, plan for and manage the partnership themselves, as well as understand what their resources are trying to do.

Some might be reluctant to involve themselves with emotions and see education as being about fostering logical reasoning skills and the intellect. Surely, they argue, tinkering with students' emotions is to interfere with fundamentals of human nature and personality. First, human thinking, unlike the processing of an electronic computer, is intimately involved with the emotions. It is simply inefficient to ignore this and it does the student a disservice to pretend otherwise. Second, if the objection is on the ethical grounds that we are 'messing' with someone's mind, fundamental nature is generally robust and resistant and the teacher's 'messing' amounts to, at most, helping students make the best of their abilities. But that does need to be ethically acceptable.

Teacher education and training

There is evidence that teaching can be more effective for many students and teachers if it is responsive to moods and emotions of the student and of the teacher. The emotion–cognition interaction has, however, been largely ignored in classrooms, other than with unplanned reactions. Acknowledging the importance of emotions and moods in teaching and learning and doing something about it is unlikely to happen spontaneously. The need has to be recognized and the notion included in teacher education and training.

Selecting student teachers

The selection of teachers and trainees is not an exact science. Objectively, evidence of a certain level of education can be obtained from examination results and, more subjectively, a judgment of potential and aptitude might be made by observing and listening to applicants. As with most things in life, it helps if some beliefs and tendencies are present at the outset, then these can be developed and practised in training. Those who select would-be teachers could, therefore, look for evidence of such attributes, albeit embryonic. For instance, is there evidence that the teacher or trainee is aware of academic emotions? Does he recognize that these affect thought and can determine its productivity? Does she see value in anticipating such effects? Does he show some enthusiasm for teaching and learning, and are there hints of, for instance, incipient immediacy behaviours? Is there evidence of resilience and a problem-solving inclination? Given an indication that there is something to build on, teachers and trainees need an opportunity to learn about thinking with feeling and develop expertise in managing it.

Matters to consider in a teacher education and training programme

- An understanding of kinds of productive thought as commonly referred to in practical educational contexts (e.g. deductive reasoning, causal understanding, creativity and problem solving, wisdom and critical thinking) in broad terms and in specific subjects like mathematics, language and literature, the sciences, humanities and arts
    - Common misconceptions about kinds of productive thought and thinkers
    - Strategies for developing productive thinking in these contexts
    - Assessing productive thinking
- Moods and emotions and their functions
    - Recognizing moods and emotions in the classroom
    - Common misconceptions about moods and emotions
    - Innate and learned responses, age and cultural variation
    - The role of beliefs, goals and values in generating emotions
    - Special considerations, such as test anxiety, affective filters, adaptive and maladaptive behaviours
- The 'thinking–feeling' partnership in various kinds of productive thought, helpful and otherwise, evident and less apparent

- o   Strategies and learning environments for managing the partnership through planning, in preparation, while teaching, and on reflection (in conjunction with strategies for fostering cognition)

- o   The development of self-regulation of the partnership

- o   Ethical matters

- Emotional labour and teaching

- o   The self-regulation of emotions in teaching

- o   Coping with emotional labour

As will be expected, the inclusion of such matters on a teacher training course brings with it something of an obligation to teach in a way that reflects them and exemplifies their application. For a teacher, it is important that learning does not remain inert, but should be interpreted and practised in very specific teaching contexts which the teacher will meet in the classroom. This means that the items listed above could have different interpretations in different contexts.

Terms, notions and principles

Certain potentially useful terms, notions and principles may enter into training.

1. Deduction, causal understanding, creative, wise and critical thinking are examples of *valued kinds of purposeful thought* and worthy goals of education. Fostering them may not always be easy, but what they have to offer makes the effort worthwhile.
2. Successful, productive thought depends on more than the intellect. All thought is open to interaction with moods and emotions. A supportive *emotion–cognition partnership* helps ensure that thought will take place and in a form which is productive.
3. Moods and emotions have the potential *to support and to impede* purposeful thought according to the nature of that thought.
4. Everyone has *matters of personal consequence*. These may be held consciously or unconsciously or somewhere in between, and are the interests against which the emotional system makes its judgments.
5. During purposeful thinking, moods and emotions may change in response to events and progress in a *stream of affect*. A frame of mind that supported a particular kind of thought may no longer be appropriate. There is the potential for *emotion–cognition tensions* when, for instance, critical thought is applied too assiduously during idea generation and, in effect, stifles creative thought.

6.   The *emotional climate* is the general, prevailing emotional tone of a learning environment produced by a teacher's example, emotional contagion, convergence or similar processes. If appropriate, it can be an emotional baseline around which a teacher works to support productive thought.

7.   Ultimately, raising an awareness of the effect of frames of mind on thought could help students manage or *regulate* their own emotion–cognition partnership.

8.   Strong anxieties produced by responses to matters of personal consequence, as in *public performance*, can be debilitating. Care is needed to avoid or alleviate these.

9.   Instead of moods and emotions being like the elephant in the classroom, something of enormous consequence yet studiously ignored, it is important to *plan* for both the intellect and emotions, and to make the partnership between them successful.

10. The teacher is not exempt from the effect of emotions; teaching amounts to *emotional labour* and the teachers need to look to their own needs.

To these might be added terms from the glossary.

Figure 12.1 provides an *aide memoire* for some central themes. In particular, students bring their moods and emotions to the environment, responding and contributing to its emotional climate. The task and situation is appraised for matters of personal concern that may generate emotions affecting motivation and thought in a variety of ways, for better or worse. The appraisal is continuous and the consequent stream of effective experience makes the emotion–cognition interaction a dynamic one. Mental products may vary with time and student. Making the emotion–cognition partnership productive can call for forethought, mindful action and reflection on the part of the teacher in a process of emotional labour. This sketch has to be elaborated with the detail provided in earlier chapters.

Planning for an emotion–cognition partnership

Table 12.1 illustrates, in general terms, some of the things that might be considered when planning, preparing, teaching and reflecting. For convenience, matters to do largely with cognition and largely with emotions and moods have been separated, but, in practice, they are integrated and bear upon one another. Planning relates to preparatory thinking about the session ahead, such as what the topic is to be, what level of demand would be appropriate (as, for instance, reflected in the zone of proximal development (Vygotsky, 1978) and how it will be presented, developed and acquired by the students. But it also includes explicit planning for, for instance, motivation and mood management. Note, however, that the two concerns are not entirely separable. Allowing some autonomy in learning, for example, would need to be planned into an activity but could be very motivating for the students.

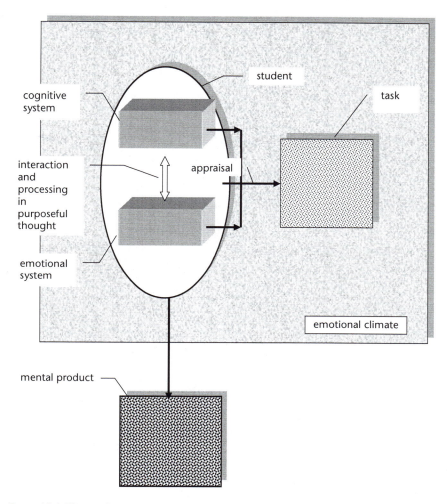

Figure 12.1 The student in action – *an aide memoire.*

Preparation relates to the physical environment and the materials or objects to be used in it. In practice, changes to these are often limited by circumstances and resources. Teaching refers to the educational act in which knowledge is developed and consolidated. While some strategies for fostering productive thought may be useful broadly, others may be more or less subject-specific (e.g. Janssen & de Hullu, 2008; Perkins, 1995). But, when using these, a teacher should also be sensitive to the students' emotional reactions to them and respond appropriately to maintain progress (e.g. Ng, 2012).

Both cognitive and emotional activity may not go as planned, so there is a need for flexibility and a readiness to adapt to developing circumstances. Reflection is what should happen after the event so that any difficulties can be resolved and incorporated in the next plan. Some speedy reflection during the act of teaching is possible when students are engaged with a learning activity. This can indicate a need for a change of plan and what that change should be. There is a tendency for teachers, education policies, programmes of study and standards frameworks to direct their attention to the cognition column of the table (Darder, 2013; Freiberg et al., 2013; Hoy, 2013; Schutz & Lanehart, 2002). If they do anything in the emotion column, it can be unplanned, unstructured and improvised. A table such as this cannot, of course, include the detail of earlier chapters, which may be consulted, as needed.

A self-assessment tool

A checklist to prompt a teacher to consider the emotion–cognition partnership is easy to construct, and one is offered below. Although not intended to be a rigorous, quantifiable assessment, it could serve to make a teacher aware of potential areas for consideration and help to establish new habits and practices. To use it, a teacher should recall a specific teaching event, such as a lesson, a discussion, an activity, the provision of feedback, examination preparation or some other discrete teaching activity in direct contact with students. With this in mind, teachers rate themselves, as follows:

Rate your planning on a scale of 0 to 5.

(0 = most unlike you; 5 = very much like you)

I was clear about the kinds of thought I wanted the students to use	0 1 2 3 4 5
I chose an approach to develop that kind of thinking and learning	0 1 2 3 4 5
I checked/adapted the approach to motivate so that it fostered engagement	0 1 2 3 4 5
I chose strategies to foster moods/emotions which support that kind of thought	0 1 2 3 4 5
I made myself aware of parts which might stimulate adverse moods/emotions	0 1 2 3 4 5
I planned to provide/maintain a supportive classroom environment	0 1 2 3 4 5
Other	0 1 2 3 4 5

Table 12.1 A general framework listing some cognitive and emotional matters to consider when supporting productive thought

Stage	Supporting cognitive engagement	Supporting emotional engagement
1. Planning	Topic identification and clarification; identifying suitable, desired outcomes/central kinds of thinking/prerequisite knowledge/knowhow and teaching strategies/learning activities; provision for high and low achievers; ways of judging the quality of learning	Consideration of motivation: interest, student relevance, relation to values and goals; suitable states of mind for recall, expected kinds of thought and activities; mood/emotion promotion strategies; expectations of student self-regulation; identification of potentially emotive content in the topic and, if necessary, deciding how to treat this; consideration of students with particular emotion/mood tendencies which affect engagement/thought/learning
2. Preparation	Selecting/collecting exemplars and choosing materials to support teaching and learning	Removing distractions and major physical discomforts; arranging materials and objects to foster the desired climate
3. Teaching	Eliciting prior knowledge; developing knowledge for application to the topic; exposition/instructions/questioning/learning activities; providing individual support; reviewing and confirming learning	Sensing the general mood, responding to it; sensing individual moods and responding to them; setting an example; exemplifying self-regulation; fostering engagement through temperate enthusiasm; being explicit about the relevance of the topic for the students; using immediacy behaviours; reinforcing perceptions of self-efficacy; monitoring the flow of affective experience and responding in order to maintain progress; adjusting approaches in response to adverse affective filters and individual traits; encouraging seeing failure as generally remedial, rarely hopeless; taking opportunities to foster student self-regulation; sensing responses to feedback and assessment and adjusting approaches accordingly
4. Reflection	Comparing desired and actual learning outcomes; identifying any significant need for remedial work; identifying intellectual consequences to carry forward	Appraising the engagement of the students with tasks; considering the suitability of the teaching environment and the general ethos in it with a view to improving them, if needed; considering the management of affect in general and for particular students; deciding what affective matters to address subsequently, when to do it (pressing or otherwise) and how to do it; considering your own flow of affect and how you feel about the session and, if you are unhappy with it, making changes/seeking advice

Rate your teaching on a scale of 0 to 5

(0 = most unlike you; 5 = very much like you)

I sensed the general mood of the students at the outset	0 1 2 3 4 5
My behaviour/expectations supported the desired classroom climate	0 1 2 3 4 5
I avoided initiating adverse moods/emotions	0 1 2 3 4 5
If emotions became unsupportive, I fostered/reinforced those needed	0 1 2 3 4 5
I made the students aware of the emotion–cognition partnership, as appropriate	0 1 2 3 4 5
Other	0 1 2 3 4 5

Rate your reflection on the lesson on a scale of 0 to 5

(0 = most unlike you; 5 = very much like you)

I considered the quality of emotion–cognition in the lesson	0 1 2 3 4 5
I devised a plan to deal with significant deficiencies in subsequent lessons	0 1 2 3 4 5
I identified my own feelings produced by the lesson	0 1 2 3 4 5
I devised a plan to deal with stressful/unwelcome personal emotions	0 1 2 3 4 5
Other	0 1 2 3 4 5

This will not suit all occasions or all of the kinds of emotion–cognition interaction that might occur. For instance, when a teacher is struggling with unruly, wilful students, the checklist would need to reflect more of the immediate needs of the situation.

Policy and practice: making it happen

As well as classroom climate, there is also a school climate, broadly formed by the physical environment and the staff's and students' behaviour collectively (Fried, 2011). This overarching climate may influence students' approaches to learning, particularly through the mood they bring to a lesson. Equally, another teacher who does things differently may produce moods and emotions in students that they take to the next lesson. Just as it is good manners to leave a room in a usable state for the next teacher, so a teacher should try to leave a class in a frame of mind that is generally amenable to learning or easily adapted.

Well-worn practices, however, have inertia of their own, and old practices seem able to outlive us all. In the meantime, they are adopted by would-be teachers who were taught themselves by them and see them still in daily use. Simply agreeing to change may not be enough. Evidence that attending to the effects of moods and emotions makes a difference to student productive thinking can, however, tip the balance (Guskey, 1985). This may be one of the keys to developing practices in a profession where so much is absorbed unconsciously through personal experience, past and present. School managers may find that giving attention to the emotion–cognition partnership goes against the inertia of decades of a narrower practice, even their own. If those responsible for education in all its phases want to see teaching adapt to the needs of the twenty-first century, with an emphasis on productive thought, then the continuous cycle of transmitted practice needs to be broken. This is another key role for which universities and similar institutions are well suited: the introduction and integration of innovation into existing practice. Without that, teacher training is little more than a cloning process that replicates what has gone before.

To conclude

Moods and emotions can make or break teaching and learning and even teachers and students. Nevertheless, when the interaction of emotion and cognition is studied, it is often in the context of the workplace and by testing ideas on readily available students, like undergraduates. This is useful, but more studies are needed in schools and in particular disciplines, and in designing, testing and collating strategies, approaches and learning environments which aim to enhance the emotion–cognition partnership in students of different ages. Such studies need to relate readily to or translate meaningfully into the concepts and constructs used by teachers and to be supported by practically meaningful frameworks. Teachers need to be educated and trained to use such strategies, approaches and environments. Resources are needed to support this process and also teaching in schools. The cooperation of schools is needed in such an enterprise but, to introduce new practices, it cannot be confined to schools and must involve a wide range of educational specialists and other professionals in all phases of education.

Glossary

Terms in italic have their own entry.

belief Something accepted as true, although the warrant for it may be lacking.

collaborative dialogue Verbal interaction to support *productive thought*.

disposition A long-term state of mind, rather like a *mood* of very long duration, to which the person returns when shorter-term states have ended.

emotion A fairly short-term, mental state resulting from an evaluation of some situation or event perceived to bear upon the individual.

emotion–cognition partnership A mutually supportive relationship between thinking and *feeling*.

emotional climate The prevailing affective tone in a learning environment produced largely by those in it.

emotional labour Work involving, generating and managing *moods* and *emotions* in self and others.

engagement Working on the task in hand in the manner intended.

feeling A bodily sensation produced by a *mood* or *emotion*.

frame of mind A broad set of mental settings, including *moods* and emotional states, which contribute to responses.

goal Some state of affairs to be achieved.

intellect Capacity for *productive thought* excluding *emotions*, *moods* and similar states.

matters of personal consequence *Beliefs*, *goals*, *values* and related mental possessions that someone holds dear.

mood A more or less extended mental state reflecting perceptions of personal well-being.

moral judgment Deciding whether an action is right or wrong.

performance emotions *Emotions* generated by the need to respond to someone or demonstrate competence; of particular concern are those that adversely affect the performance, such as embarrassment and anxiety.

productive thought The successful, *purposeful* mental processing of information that goes beyond what is given.

purposeful thought Thought directed at a particular end.

regulation The control and management of mental processes.

stream of affect The temporal sequence of emotional states in an event.

temperament A characteristic collection of tendencies of which *traits* can be particulars.

thought Mental activity excluding *emotions*, *moods* and similar states; the product of this activity.

trait A personal tendency to behave or respond in a particular way.

values Those relationships with the world, animate and inanimate, held to be worth preserving.

References

Abrami, P.C., Bernard, R.M., Borokhovski, E., Wade. A., Surkes, M.A. Tamin, R. and Zhang, D. (2008) 'Instructional interventions affecting critical thinking skills and dispositions', *Review of Educational Research*, 78(4): 1102–34.

Adey, P. and Shayer, M. (1994) *Really Raising Standards*, London: Routledge.

Adey, P. and Yates, C. (1989) *Thinking Science: The curriculum materials of the CASE project*, London: Thomas Nelson.

Adhami, M., Johnson, D.C. and Shayer, M. (1998) *Thinking Maths*, Oxford: Heinemann.

Adler, P.S. and Obstfeld, D. (2007) 'The role of affect in creative projects and exploratory search', *Industrial and Corporate Change*, 16(1): 19–50.

Ahlgren, C. and Gådin, K.G. (2011) 'Struggle for time to teach', *Work*, 40(1): 111–18.

Akinola, M. and Mendes, W.B. (2008) 'The dark side of creativity', *Personality and Social Psychology Bulletin*, 34(12): 1677–86.

Alain-Fournier (Alban, H.) (1913/1966) *Le Grand Meaulnes*, trans. F. Davison, London: Penguin.

Albert, D. and Steinberg, L. (2011) 'Judgment and decision making in adolescence', *Journal of Research in Adolescence*, 21(1): 211–24.

Aldao, A., Nolen-Hoeksema, S. and Schweizer, S. (2009) 'Emotion-regulation strategies across psychopathology', *Clinical Psychology Review*, 30: 217–37.

Al-Karasneh, S.M. and Saleh, A.M. (2010) 'Islamic perspectives of creativity', *Procedia Social and Behavioural Sciences*, 2: 412–26.

Alsop, S. and Watts, M. (2000) 'Interviews-about-scenarios', *Research in Education*, 63: 21–33.

Alter, A.L., Oppenheimer, D.M., Epley, N. and Eyre, R.N. (2007) 'Overcoming intuition', *Journal of Experimental Psychology: General*, 136(4): 569–76.

Altshuller, G.S. (2000) *The Innovation Algorithm*, Worcester: Technical Innovation Center.

Ames, D.L., Jenkins, A.C., Banaji, M.R. and Mitchell, J.P. (2008) 'Taking another person's perspective increases self-referential neural processing', *Psychological Science*, 19: 642–4.

Amabile, T.M. (1996) *Creativity and Innovation in Organizations*, Harvard: Harvard Business School.

Amsterlaw, J., Lagattuta, K.H. and Meltzoff, A.N. (2009) 'Young children's reasoning about the effects of emotional and physiological performance', *Child Development*, 80(1): 115–33.

Anderson, A.K. (2005) 'Affective influences on attentional dynamics supporting awareness', *Journal of Experimental Psychology: General*, 134: 258–81.

Anderson, R., Halliday, J., Howe, C. and Soden, R. (1997) *Bridging the Academic/Vocational Divide by Integrating Critical Thinking*, Swindon: ESRC.

Andrade, E.B. and Ariely, D. (2009) 'The enduring impact of transient emotions on decision making', *Organizational Behavior and Human Decision Processes*, 109(1): 1–8.

Andrade, M. and Williams, K. (2009) 'Foreign language learning anxiety in Japanese EFL university classes', *Sophie Junior College Faculty Journal*, 29: 1–4.

Andreasen, N.C. (1995) 'Symptoms, signs, and diagnosis of schizophrenia', *Lancet*, 346: 477–81.

Andrews, P.W. and Thomson, J.A. (2009) 'The bright side of being blue', *Psychological Review*, 116(3): 620–54.

Antoniou, A.S., Polychroni, F. and Vlachakis, A.N. (2006) 'Gender and age differences in occupational stress and professional burnout between primary and high-school teachers in Greece', *Journal of Managerial Psychology*, 21(7): 682–90.

Ardelt, M. (2004) 'Wisdom as an expert knowledge system', *Human Development*, 47: 257–85.

Ardelt, M. and Oh, H., (2010) 'Wisdom', in C.A. Depp and D.V. Jeste (eds) *Successful Cognitive and Emotional Aging*, Arlington: American Psychological Publishing, 87–113.

Arlin, P.K. (1993) 'Wisdom and expertise in teaching', *Learning and Individual Differences*, 5(4): 341–9.

Armony, J.L., Chochol, C., Fecteau, S. and Belin, P. (2007) 'Laugh (or cry) and you will be remembered', *Psychological Science*, 18(2): 1027–9.

Arum, R. and Roksa, J. (2011) *Academically Adrift*, Chicago: University of Chicago.

Astleitner, H. (2000) 'Designing emotionally sound instruction', *Instructional Science*, 28: 169–98.

Asuncion, Z.S. (2010) 'Filipino college freshman students' oral compensatory strategies', *Philippine ESL Journal*, 5: 2–21.

Atkinson, E.S. (2000) 'An investigation into the relationship between teacher motivation and pupil motivation', *Educational Psychology*, 20(1): 45–57.

Augustine, A.A. and Hemenover, S.H. (2009) 'On the relative effectiveness of affect regulation strategies', *Cognition & Emotion*, 23(6): 277–303.

Averil, J.R., Chon, K.K. and Hahn, D.W. (2001) 'Emotions and creativity, East and West', *Asian Journal of Social Psychology*, 4: 165–83.

Avey, J.B., Luthans, S.T., Sweetman, D. and Peterson, C. (2012) 'Impact of employees' character strengths of wisdom on stress and creative performance', *Human Resource Management Journal*, 22(2): 165–81.

Avramova, Y.R., Stapel, D.A. and Lerouge, D. (2010) 'Mood and context-dependence', *Journal of Personality and Social Psychology*, 99(2): 203–14.

Aylesworth, A.B. and MacKenzie, S.B. (1998) 'Context is the key', *Journal of Advertising*, 27(2): 17–31.

Baas, M., De Dreu, C.K.W. and Nijstad, B.A. (2008) 'A meta-analysis of 25 years of mood-creativity research', *Psychological Bulletin*, 134(6): 779–806.

Babab, E. (2007) 'Teachers' nonverbal behavior and its effects on students', in R. Perry and J.C. Smart (eds) *The Scholarship of Teaching and Learning in Higher Education*, New York: Springer, 201–61.

Badcock, P.B.T. and Allen, N.B. (2003) 'Adaptive social reasoning in depressed mood and depressive vulnerability', *Cognition & Emotion*, 17(4): 647–70.

Baddeley, A.D. (1976) *The Psychology of Memory*, New York: Basic Books.

Bailin, S. (1998) 'Critical thinking and drama education', *Research in Drama Education*, 3(2): 145–53.

Bailin, S. (2006) 'An inquiry into inquiry', in D. Vokey (ed.) *Philosophy of Education*, Urbana, Philosophy of Education Society, 1–12.

Bakker, A.B., Hakanen, J.J., Demerouti, E. and Xanthopuolu, D. (2007) 'Job resources boost work engagement, particularly when job demands are high', *Journal of Educational Psychology*, 99: 274–84.

Baltes, P.B. and Smith, J. (2008) 'The fascination of wisdom', *Perspectives on Psychological Science*, 3(1): 56–64.

Baltes, P.B. and Staudinger, U.M. (1993) 'The search for the psychology of wisdom', *Current Directions in Psychological Science*, 2(3): 75–80.

Baltes, P.B. (2000) 'Wisdom', *American Psychologist*, 55(1): 122–36.

Bamford, C. and Lagattuta, K.H. (2012) 'Looking on the bright side', *Child Development*, 83(2): 667–682.

Bandura, A. (1997) *Self-Efficacy: The exercise of control*, New York: Freeman.

Barkley, R.A. (1996) 'Linkages between attention and executive function', in G.R. Lyon and N. Krasnegor (eds), *Attention, Memory and Executive Function*, Baltimore: Paul Brookes, 307–25.

Barkley, R.A. (2006) *Attention Deficit Hyperactivity Disorder*, New York: Guilford.

Barnett, J.E. and Francis, A.L. (2012) 'Using higher order thinking questions to foster critical thinking', *Educational Psychology*, 32(2): 201–11.

Barnier, A.J., Hung, L. and Conway, M.A. (2004) 'Retrieval-induced forgetting of emotional and unemotional autobiographical memories', *Cognition & Emotion*, 18(4): 457–77.

Baron, R.A. (2008) 'The role of affect in the entrepreneurial process', *Academy of Management Review*, 33(2): 328–40.

Barry, E.S., Baus, M.J. and Rehm, L.P. (2004) 'Depression and implicit memory', *Cognitive Therapy and Research*, 28: 387–414.

Bassett, C. (2007) 'Becoming OtherWise™', in P. Cranton and E. Taylor (eds) *Transformative Learning*, Albuquerque: Seventh International Transformative Learning Conference, 358–68.

Bassett, C. (2011) 'Understanding and teaching practical wisdom', *New Directions for Adult and Continuing Education*, 131: 35–44.

Baum, G. (2010) 'The response of a theologian to Charles Taylor's *A Secular Age*', *Modern Theology*, 26: 363–81.

Baumeister, R.F. and Vohs, K.D. (2007) 'Self-regulation, ego depletion, and motivation', *Social and Personality Psychology Compass*, 10: 1–13.

BBC (2013) 'Puppy room bid to beat exam stress for Aberdeen students'. Online. Available at http:www.bbc.co.uk/news/uk-scotland-north-east-orkney-shetland-22508773 (accessed 29 May 2013).

Beasley, C. and Cao, B. (2012) 'Transforming first-year university politics students into critical thinkers', *Ergo*, 2(3): 41–52.

Becker, M.W. and Leinenger, M. (2011) 'Attentional selection is biased toward mood-congruent stimuli', *Emotion*, 11(5): 1248–54.

Beghetto, R.A. (2007) 'Does creativity have a place in classroom discussions?' *Thinking Skills and Creativity*, 2(1): 1–9.

Benor, D.J., Ledger, K., Toussaint, L., Hett, G. and Zaccaro, D. (2009) 'Pilot study of emotional freedom techniques', *Explore*, 5(6): 338–40.

Benson, J. (1983) 'Who is the autonomous man?' *Philosophy*, 58(223): 5–17.

Bereiter, C. and Scardamalia, M. (1989) 'Intentional learning as a goal of instruction', in L.B. Resnick (ed.) *Knowing, Learning, and Instruction*, Alexandria: Association for Supervisors and Curriculum Development, 361–91.

Berger, A., Kofman, O., Livneh, U. and Henik, A. (2007) 'Multidisciplinary perspectives on attention and the development of self-regulation', *Progress in Neurobiology*, 82: 256–86.

Berk, L.E. (2012) *Child Development*, London: Pearson.

Bettencourt, E.M., Gillett, M.H., Gall, M.D. and Hull, R.E. (1983) 'Effects of teacher enthusiasm training on student on-task behavior and achievement', *American Educational Research Journal*, 20: 435–50.

Bissell, A.N. and Lemons, P.P. (2006) 'A new method for assessing thinking in the classroom', *BioScience*, 56(1): 66–72.

Black, B. (ed.) (2012) *An A–Z of Critical Thinking*, London: Continuum.

Black, B. ,Chislett, J., Thomson, A., Thwaites, G. and Thwaites, J. (2008) 'Critical thinking', *Research matters 6*, Cambridge: Cambridge Assessment Publications.

Blair, C. (2010) 'Stress and the development of self-regulation in context', *Child Development Perspective*, 4(3): 181–8.

Blanchette, I. (2006) 'The effect of emotion on interpretation and logic in a conditional reasoning task', *Memory & Cognition*, 34: 1112–25.

Blanchette, I. and Campbell, M. (2012) 'Reasoning about highly emotional topics', *Journal of Cognitive Psychology*, 24(2): 157–64.

Blanchette, I. and Richards, A. (2010) 'The influence of affect on higher level cognition', *Cognition & Emotion*, 24(4): 561–95.

Blanchette, I., Richards, A., Melnyk, L. and Lavda, A. (2007) 'Reasoning about emotional contents following shocking terrorist attacks', *Journal of Experimental Psychology: Applied*, 13: 47–56.

Bless, H. and Igou, E.R. (2005) 'Mood state and the use of general knowledge structures in judgment and decision making', in T. Betsch and S. Haberstroh (eds) *The Routines of Decision Making*, San Diego: Academic Press, 193–210.

Bleyl, M.E. (2007) 'Becoming wiser through proverb and story', in P. Cranton and E. Taylor (eds) *Transformative Learning*, Albuquerque: Seventh International Transformative Learning Conference, 47–52.

Bluck, S. and Glück, J. (2004) 'Making things better and learning a lesson', *Journal of Personality*, 72: 543–72.

Bluck, S. and Glück, J. (2005) 'From the inside out', in R.J. Sternberg and J. Jordan (eds) *A Handbook of Wisdom*, New York: Cambridge University Press, 84–109.

Boden, M.A. (2004) *The Creative Mind: Myths and mechanisms*, London: Routledge.

Bodrova, E. and Leong, D.J. (2006) *Tools of the Mind*, Columbus: Prentice Hall.

Böhmig-Krumhaar, S.A., Staudinger, U.M. and Baltes, P.B. (2002), 'Mehr Toleranz tut Not', *Zeitschrift für Entwicklungspsychologie und Pädagogische Psychologie*, 34: 30–43.

Boekaerts, M. and Corno, L. (2005) 'Self-regulation in the classroom', *Applied Psychology: An International Review*, 54(2): 199–231.

Bonaccio, S. and Reeve, C.L. (2010) 'The nature and relative importance of students' perceptions of the sources of test anxiety', *Learning and Individual Differences*, 20: 617–25.

Bonawitz, E.B. and Lombrozo, T. (2012) 'Occam's rattle: Children's use of simplicity and probability to constrain inference', *Developmental Psychology*, 48(4): 1156–64.

Bourg, T., Risden, K., Thompson, S. and Davis, R.C. (1993) 'The effects of an empathy-building strategy on 6th graders' causal inferencing in narrative text', *Poetics*, 22: 117–33.

Bower, G.H. (1981) 'Mood and memory', *American Psychologist*, 36(2): 129–48.

Bower, G.H. (1992) 'How emotions affect learning', in S.-A. Christianson (ed.) *The Handbook of Emotion and Memory*, Hillsdale: Lawrence Erlbaum, 3–31.

Bowkett, S. (2007) *100+ Ideas for Teaching Creativity*, London: Continuum.

Bradley, R.T. (2009) *Facilitating Emotional Self-Regulation in Pre-School Children*, Boulder Creek: Institute of HeartMath®.

Bradley, R.T., McCraty, R., Atkinson, M., Tomasino, D., Daugherty, A. and Arguelles, L. (2010) 'Emotion self-regulation, psychophysiological coherence, and test anxiety', *Applied Psychophysiology and Biofeedback*, 35(4): 261–83.

Bransford, J.D. and Stein, B (1984) *The IDEAL Problem Solver*, New York: Freeman.

Brehms, S.S. and Brehms, J.W. (1966) *Psychological Reactance: A theory of freedom and control*, New York: Academic Press.

Brem, S.K. (2003) 'Structure and pragmatics in informal argument', *Trends in Cognitive Science*, 7(4): 147–9.

Brookfield, S. (1994) 'Tales from the dark side', *International Journal of Lifelong Education*, 13(3): 203–16.

Brookfield, S. (1997) 'Assessing critical thinking', *New Directions for Adult and Continuing Education*, 75: 17–29.

Brookfield, S. (2013) 'What does it mean to act critically?' *Explorations in Adult Higher Education*, 2: 3–10.

Brown, S.C. (2006) 'The wisdom development scale', *Journal of College Student Development*, 47(1): 1–19.

Brugman, C.M. (2006) 'Wisdom and aging', in J.E. Birren and K.W. Schaie (eds) *Handbook of the Psychology of Aging*, Elsevier: Burlington, 445–76.

Burns, R. (2002) *The Adult Learner at Work*, Sydney: Allen & Unwin.

Buss, D.M. (2001) 'Cognitive biases and emotional wisdom in the evolution of conflict between the sexes', *Current Directions in Psychological Science*, 10: 219–23.

Buzan, T. and Buzan, B. (2006) *The Mind Map Book*, London: BBC.

Bylsma, L.M., Morris, B.H. and Rottenberg, J. (2008) 'A meta-analysis of emotional reactivity in major depressive disorder', *Clinical Psychology Review*, 28: 676–91.

Byrne, R.M.J., Segura, S., Culhane, R., Tasso, A. and Berrocal, P. (2000) 'The temporality effect in counterfactual thinking about what might have been', *Memory & Cognition*, 28(2): 264–81.

Cahill, L., Haier, R.J., Fallon, J., Alkire, M.T., Cheuk, T., Keator, D., Wu, J. and McGaugh, J.L. (1996) 'Amygdala activity at encoding correlated with long-term, free recall of emotional information', *Proceedings of the National Academy of Sciences*, 93: 8016–21.

Cambria, E., Hussain, AA., Havasi, C. and Eckl, C. (2009) 'Affective space', in *Proceedings of the 1st Workshop on Opinion Mining and Sentiment Analysis*, *CAEPIA-TTIA Conference*, Seville, 32–41.

Cambridge International Examinations (2013) 'A & AS level: Thinking skills'. Online. Available at http://www.cie.org.uk (accessed 30 May 2013).

Capie, W. and Tobin, K. G. (1981) 'Pupil engagement in learning tasks', *Journal of Research in Science Teaching*, 18(5): 409–17.

Carr, D. (2010) 'Revisiting the liberal and vocational dimensions of university education', *British Journal of Educational Studies*, 57(1): 1–17.

Carruthers, P. (2002) 'Human creativity', *British Journal of the Philosophy of Science*, 53: 225–49.

Carthy, T., Horesh, N., Apter, A. and Gross, J.J. (2010) 'Patterns of emotional reactivity and regulation in children with anxiety disorders', *Journal of Psychopathology & Behavioral Assessment*, 32: 23–36.

Carver, C.S. and Connor-Smith, J. (2010) 'Personality and coping', *Annual Review of Psychology*, 61: 679–704.

Cassady, J.C. and Johnson, R.E. (2002) 'Cognitive test anxiety and academic performance', *Contemporary Educational Psychology*, 27: 270–95.

Cecil, M.A. and Forman, S.G. (1990) 'Effects of stress inoculation training and coworker support groups on teachers' stress', *Journal of School Psychology*, 28(2): 105–18.

Channon, S. and Baker, J. (1994) 'Reasoning strategies in depression', *Personality and Individual Differences*, 17(5): 707–11.

Chapell, M.S., Blanding, Z.B., Silverstein, M.E., Takahashi, M., Newman, B., Gubi, A. and McCann, N. (2005) 'Test anxiety and academic performance in undergraduate and graduate students', *Journal of Educational Psychology*, 97(2): 268–74.

Charland, L.C. (1998) 'Is Mr Spock mentally competent?' *Philosophy, Psychiatry and Psychology*, 5: 67–81.

Charles, S.T., Mather, M. and Carstensen, L.L. (2003) 'Aging and emotional memory', *Journal of Experimental Psychology: General*, 132(2): 310–24.

Chekhov, A. (1888/1991) *The Steppe and Other Stories*, trans. C. Garnett, London: Everyman's Library.

Chi, M.T.H., De Leeuw, N., Chio, M.-H. and Lavacher, C. (1994) 'Eliciting self-explanations improves understanding', *Cognitive Science*, 18: 439–77.

Chon, K.K., Kim, K.H. and Ryoo, J.B. (2000) 'Experience and expression of anger in Korea and America', *Korean Journal of Rehabilitation Psychology*, 7: 61–75.

Christopher, J.C. and Hickinbottom, S. (2008) 'Positive psychology, ethnocentrism, and the disguised ideology of individualism', *Theory and Psychology*, 18(5): 563–89.

Cismas, S.C. (2009) 'Test anxiety and motivational incentives in web-based learning', in I. Rudas, M. Demivalp and N. Mastorakis (eds) *Proceedings of the 9th WSEAS Conference on Distance Learning and Web Engineering*, Stevens Point: WSEAS, 77–82.

Cleary, T.J. and Zimmerman, B.J. (2004) 'Self-regulation empowerment program', *Psychology in Schools*, 41(5): 537–50.

Clements, J. (2008) *Confucius: A biography*, Stroud: Sutton.

Clore, G., Gasper, K. and Garvin, E. (2001) 'Affect as information', in J.P. Forgas (ed.) *Handbook of Affect and Social Cognition*, Mahwah: Lawrence Erlbaum, 121–41.

Clore, G. and Huntsinger, J.R. (2007) 'How emotions form judgment and regulate thought', *Trends in Cognitive Science*, 11(9): 393–9.

Clore, G. and Huntsinger, J.R. (2007) 'How the object of affect gives its impact', *Emotion Review*, 1(1): 39–54.

Clore, G.L. and Palmer, J. (2009) 'Affective guidance of intelligent agents: How emotion controls cognition', *Cognitive Systems Research*, 10: 21–30.

Cohen, Y. and Norst, M.M.J. (1989) 'Fear, dependence and loss of self-esteem', *RELC Journal*: 20(2): 61–77.

Cole, M. and Cole, S.R. (2001) *The Development of Children*, New York: Worth.

Colman, A.M. (2003) *Oxford Dictionary of Psychology*, Oxford: Oxford University Press.

Colvin, G. (2008) *Talent is Overrated*, London: Nicholas Brealey.

Conn, L.K., Edwards, C.N., Rosenthal, R. and Crowne, D. (1968) 'Perception of emotion and response to teachers' expectancy by elementary school children', *Psychological Reports*, 22: 27–34.

Connell, J. (1990) 'Context, self, and action', in D. Cicchetti and M. Beeghly (eds) *The Self in Transition: From infancy to childhood*, Chicago: University of Chicago Press, 61–7.

Connors, L., Putwain, D., Woods, K. and Nicholson, L. (2009) 'Causes and consequences of test anxiety in Key Stage 2 pupils', paper presented at the BERA Conference, September, Manchester.

Conrad, J. (1904/1994) *Nostromo*, London: Penguin.

Converse, B.A., Shuhong, L., Keysar, B. and Epley, N. (2008) 'In the mood to get over yourself', *Emotion*, 8(5): 725–30.

Cowan, N., Elliott, E.M., Saults, J.S., Morey, C.C., Mattox, S. and Hismjatullina, A. (2005) 'On the capacity of attention', *Cognitive Psychology*, 51: 42–100.

Cowcher, H. (1988) *Rain Forest*, London: Corgi/André Deutsch.

Crano, W.D. (1995) 'Attitude strength and vested interest', in R.E. Petty and J.A. Krosnick (eds) *Attitude Strength: Antecedents and consequences*, Mahwah: Erlbaum, 131–58.

Craft, A. (1999) 'Creative development in the early years', *Curriculum Journal*, 10: 135–50.

Craft, A. (2002) *Creativity and Early Years Education*, London: Continuum.

Craft, A. (2008) 'Nurturing creativity, wisdom, and trusteeship in education', in A. Craft, H. Gardner and G. Claxton (eds) *Creativity, Wisdom and Trusteeship*, Thousand Oaks: Corwin, 1–15.

Croker, S. and Buchanan, H. (2011) 'Scientific reasoning in the real-world context', *British Journal of Developmental Psychology*, 29: 409–24.

Cropley, A.J. (2001) *Creativity in Education and Learning*, London: RoutledgeFalmer.

Cropley, D.H., Cropley, A.J., Kaufman, J.C. and Runco, M.A. (2010) *The Dark Side of Creativity*, Cambridge: Cambridge University Press.

Crossman, J. (2007) 'The role of relationships and emotions in student perceptions of learning and assessment', *Higher Education and Research Development*, 26(3): 313–27.

Crozier, W.R. and Hostettler, K. (2003) 'The influence of shyness on children's test performance', *British Journal of Educational Psychology*, 73: 317–28.

Csikszentmihalyi, M. (1996) *Creativity: Flow and the psychology of discovery and invention*, New York: HarperCollins.

Cubukcu, F. (2013) 'The significance of teachers' academic emotions', *Procedia: Social and Behavioral Sciences*, 70: 649–53.

Cupchik, G. and Krista, P. (2005) 'The scent of literature', *Cognition & Emotion*, 19(1): 101–19.

Curnow, T. (1999) *Wisdom, Intuition and Ethics*, Aldershot: Ashgate.

Curnow, T. (2007) *Wisdom in the Ancient World*, London: Duckworth.

Dalgleish, T., Yiend, J., Schweizer, S. & Dunn, B.D. (2009) 'Ironic effects of emotion suppression when recounting distressing memories', *Emotion*, 9(5): 744–9.

Damasio, A. (1994) *Descartes' Error*, New York: Avon Books.

Damasio, A. (2000) 'A second chance for emotion', in R.D. Lane and L. Nadel (eds) *Cognitive Neuroscience of Emotion*, Oxford: Oxford University Press, 12–23.

Daniels, L.M. and Stupnisky, R.H. (2012) 'Not that different in theory', *Internet & Higher Education*, 15: 222–6.

Danovitch, J.H. and Keil, F.C. (2008) 'Young Humeans: The role of emotions in children's evaluation of moral reasoning abilities', *Developmental Science*, 11(1): 33–9.

Daradoumis, T. and Caballe, S. (2011) 'Endowing e-learning systems with emotion awareness', *Intelligent Networking and Collaborative Systems (INCoS), Third International Conference on Intelligent Networking and Collaborative Systems*, New York: IEEE, 68–75.

Darby, L. (2005) 'Science students' perceptions of engaging pedagogy', *Research in Science Education*, 35: 425–45.

Darder, P. (2013) 'Education, emotion, complexity', in A. Massip-Bonet and A. Bastardas-Boarda (eds) *Complexity Perspectives on Language, Communication and Society*, Berlin: Springer, 95–102.

Davis, E.L., Levine, L.J., Lench, H.C. and Quas, J.A. (2010) 'Metacognitive emotion regulation', *Emotion*, 10(4): 498–510.

Davis, H. (2003) 'Conceptualizing the role and influence of student–teacher relationships on children's social and cognitive development', *Educational Psychologist*, 38: 207–34.

Davis, M.A. (2009) 'Understanding the relationship between mood and creativity', *Organizational Behavior and Human Decision Processes*, 108: 25–38.

de Bono, E. (1985) *Six Thinking Hats*, New York: Key Porter Books.

de Bono, E. (1987) *Letters to Thinkers*, New York: Key Porter Books.

de Bono, E. (1995) Serious creativity, *Journal of Quality and Participation*, 18(5): 12–18.

de Carvalho, M. (1997) *A God Strolling in the Cool of the Evening*, trans. G. Rabassa, London: Orion.

De Dreu, C.K.W., Baas, M. and Nijstad, B.A (2008) 'Hedonic tone and activation level in the mood-creativity link', *Journal of Personality and Social Psychology*, 94(5): 739–56.

De Dreu, C.K.W., Nijstad, B.A. and Baas, M. (2011) 'Behavioral activation links to creativity because of increased cognitive flexibility', *Social Psychological & Personality Science*, 2: 72–80.

Demetriou, H. and Wilson, E. (2012) 'It's bad to be too good', *Procedia – Social and Behavioral Sciences*, 46: 1801–5.

Demetriou, H. and Winterbottom, M. (2009) 'The role of emotion in teaching', *Educational Studies*, 35(4): 449–73.

Deutscher, M. (2011) 'Sting of reason', *Parrhesia*, 13: 79–95.

DeWall, C.N., Baumeister, R.F. and Masicampo, E.J. (2008) 'Evidence that logical reasoning depends on conscious processing', *Consciousness and Cognition*, 17: 628–45.

Dewey, J. (1916) *Democracy and Education*, New York: Macmillan.

Dewey, J. (1938/1998) *Experience and Education*, West Lafayette: Kappa, Delta, Pi Honorary Society in Education.

DfES (Department for Education and Skills) (2003) *Excellence and Enjoyment*, London: DfES.

Dick, O.L. (1972) *Brief Lives*, Harmondsworth: Penguin.

Diener, E. and Lucas, R.E. (2000) 'Subjective emotional well-being', in M. Lewis and J.M. Haviland (eds) *Handbook of Emotions*, New York: Guilford, 325–37.

Dirkx, J.M. (2001) 'The power of feelings', *New Directions for Adult and Continuing Education*, 89: 63–72.

Djamasbi, S., Strong, D.M. and Dishaw, M. (2010) 'Affect and acceptance', *Decision Support Systems*, 48(2): 383–94.

D'Mello, S., Taylor, R., Davidson, K. and Graesser, A. (2008) 'Self versus teacher judgments of learner emotions during a tutoring session with AutoTutor', *Intelligent Tutoring Systems, Lecture Notes in Computer Science*, 5091: 9–18.

Dogan, H. (2012) 'Emotion, confidence, perception and expectation: case of mathematics', *International Journal of Science and Mathematics Education*, 10: 49–69.

Dolan, R.J. (2002) 'Emotion, cognition, and behavior', *Science*, 298(5596): 1191–4.

Donnelly, P. and Hogan, J. (2013) 'Encouraging students in the classroom', *European Journal of Political Science*, Online. Available at doi: 10.1075/eps.2013.12 (accessed 30 May 2013).

Dosher, B.A. (2003) 'Working memory', in L. Nadel (ed.) *Encyclopedia of Cognitive Science*, London: Nature Publishing Group, 569–77.

Dowens, M.G. and Calvo, M.G. (2003) 'Genuine memory bias versus response bias in anxiety', *Cognition & Emotion*, 17(6): 843–57.

Downs, V.C., Javidi, M. and Nussbaum, J.F. (1988) 'An analysis of teachers' verbal communication within the college classroom', *Communication Education*, 37: 127–41.

Dreisbach, G. and Goschke, T. (2004) 'How positive affect modulates cognitive control', *Journal of Experimental Psychology: Learning, Memory and Cognition*, 30: 343–53.

Du, X. (2009) 'The affective filter in second language learning', *Asian Social Science*, 5(8): 162–5.

Duncan, S. and Barrett, L.F. (2007) 'Affect is a form of cognition', *Cognition & Emotion*, 21, 1184–211.

Dunn, J. (2003) 'Emotional development in early childhood', in R.J. Davidson, K.R. Scherer and H.H. Goldsmith (eds) *Handbook of Affective Sciences*, Oxford: Oxford University Press, 332–46.

Durkin, K. (1995) *Developmental Social Psychology*, Oxford: Blackwell.

Duvall, S.J. and Hays. D.J. (2005) *Grasping God's Word*, Grand Rapids: Zondervan.

Eastwood, J.D., Smilek, D. and Merikle, P.M. (2001) 'Differential attentional guidance by unattended faces expressing positive and negative emotion', *Perception & Psychophysics*, 63: 1004–13.

Efklides, A. and Petkaki, C. (2005) 'Effects of mood on students' metacognitive experiences', *Learning and Instruction*, 15: 415–31.

Eisenberg, N., Spinrad, T.L. and Eggum, N.D. (2010) 'Emotion-related self-regulation and its relation to children's maladjustment', *Annual Review of Clinical Psychology*, 6: 495–525.

Ekman, P. and Friesen, W.V. (2003) *Unmasking the Face: A guide to recognizing emotions from facial clues*, Cambridge: Malor.

Elder, L. (1996) 'Critical thinking and emotional intelligence', *Inquiry: Critical Thinking across the Disciplines*, 16(2): 35–49.

Elfenbein, H.A. and Ambady, N. (2003) 'Universals and cultural differences in recognizing emotions', *Current Directions in Psychological Science*, 12(5): 159–64.

Elfenbein, H.A., Marsh, A.A. and Ambady, N. (2002) 'Emotional intelligence and the recognition of emotion from facial expressions', in L.F. Barrett and P. Salovey (eds) *The Wisdom of Feelings: Processes underlying emotional intelligence*, New York: Guilford, 37–59.

Elias, M.J., Hunter, L. and Kress, J.S. (2001) 'Emotional intelligence in education', in J. Ciarrocchi, J.P. Forgas and J.D. Mayer (eds) *Emotional Intelligence in Everyday Life*, Philadelphia: Psychology Press, 133–49.

Embse, N., Barterian, J. and Segool, N. (2013) 'Test anxiety interventions for children and adolescents', *Psychology in the Schools*, 50(1): 57–71.

Emmer, E.T. and Stough, L.M. (2001) 'Classroom management', *Educational Psychologist*, 36(2): 103–12.

Ennis, R. (2001) 'Goals for a critical thinking curriculum and its assessment', in A. Costa (ed.) *Developing Minds: A resource book for teaching thinking*, London: Association for Supervision and Curriculum Development, 44–6.

Ennis, R. (2011) 'Critical thinking and reflection', *Inquiry*, 26(1): 15.

Entwistle, A. and Entwistle, N. (2002) 'Experience of understanding in revising for degree examinations', *Learning and Instruction*, 2(1): 1–22.

Entwistle, N. (2009) *Teaching for Understanding at University*, London: Palgrave.

Epley, N., Keysar, B., Van Boven, L. and Gilovich, T. (2004) 'Perspective taking as egocentric anchoring and adjustment', *Journal of Personality and Social Psychology*, 87: 327–39.

Erb, C.S. (2002) 'The emotional whirlpool of beginning teachers' work', paper presented at the annual meeting of the Canadian Society of Studies in Education, Toronto, May.

Erickson, H.L. (2007) *Concept-Based Curriculum and Instruction for the Thinking Classroom*, Thousand Oaks: Corwin.

Escobedo, J.R. and Adolphs, R. (2010) 'Becoming a better person', *Emotion*, 10(4): 511–18.

Evans, D. (2004) 'The search hypothesis of emotion', in D. Evans and P. Cruse (eds) *Emotions, Evolution and Rationality*, Oxford: Oxford University Press, 179–92.

Evans, D. and Cruse, P. (2004) *Emotions, Evolution and Rationality*, Oxford: Oxford University Press, xii.

Evans, D. and Rothbart, M.K. (2007) 'Developing a model for adult temperament', *Journal of Research in Personality*, 41: 868–88.

Evans, J. St B.T. (2008) 'Dual-processing accounts of reasoning, judgment and social cognition', *Annual Review of Psychology*, 59: 255–78.

Evans, S., Ferrando, S., Findler, M., Stowell, C., Smart, C. and Haglin, D. (2008) 'Mindfulness-based cognitive therapy for generalized anxiety disorder', *Journal of Anxiety Disorders*, 22: 716–21.

Everston, C. (1989) 'Improving elementary classroom management', *Journal of Educational Research*, 82(2): 82–90.

Eysenck, H.J. and Eysenck, M.W. (1985) *Personality and Individual Differences*, New York: Plenum Press.

Eysenck, M.W. (1997) *Anxiety and Cognition: A unified theory*, Hove: Psychology Press.

Eysenck, M.W. and Calvo, M.G. (1992) 'Anxiety and performance', *Cognition & Emotion*, 6: 409–34.

Eysenck, M.W. and Payne, S. (2005) 'Trait anxiety, visuospatial processing, and working memory', *Cognition & Emotion*, 19(8): 1214–28.

Eysenck, M.W., Payne, S. and Derakshan, N. (2005) 'Trait anxiety, visuospatial processing, and working memory', *Cognition & Emotion*, 19(8): 1214–28.

Facione, P.A. (2011) *Critical Thinking: What it is and why it counts*, Millbrae: Insight Assessment.

Fartoukh, M., Chanquoy, L. and Piolet, A. (2013) 'Emotion and complex tasks', *Neural Nets & Sourroundings*, 19: 357–65.

Fehr, B. and Russell, J.A. (1984) 'Concept of emotion viewed from a prototype perspective', *Journal of Experimental Psychology: General*, 113: 464–86.

Feinman-Nemser, S. and Rémillard, J. (1996) 'Perspectives on learning to teach', in F.B. Murray (ed.) *The Teacher Educator's Handbook*, San Francisco: Jossey-Bass, 63–91.

Ferrari, M. (2009) 'Teaching for wisdom in public schools to promote personal giftedness', *International Handbook of Giftedness*, Part 11, 1099–112.

Ferré, P. (2003) 'Effects of level of processing on memory for affectively valenced words', *Cognition & Emotion*, 17(6): 859–80.

Fetchenhauer, D., Groothuis, T. and Pradel, J. (2010) 'Not only states but traits – humans can identify permanent altruistic dispositions in 20s', *Evolution and Human Behavior*, 31: 80–6.

Fiedler, K. (1988) 'Emotion and mood, cognitive style and behavior regulation', in K. Fielder and J.P. Forgas (eds) *Affect, Cognition and Social* Behavior, Toronto: Hogrefe, 100–19.

Finn, J. D. (1993) *School Engagement and Students at Risk*, Washington: National Center for Education Statistics.

Fischer, H.R. (2001) 'Abductive reasoning as a way of understanding', *Foundations of Science*, 6(4): 361–83.

Fischer, K.W., Daniel, D.B., Immordino-Yang, M.H., Stern, E., Battro, A. and Koizumi, H. (2007) 'Why mind, brain, and education? Why now?' *Mind, Brain and Education*, 1(1): 1–2.

Fisher, A. (2001) *An Introduction to Critical Thinking*, Cambridge: Cambridge University Press.

Fisher, M. and Baird, D.E. (2005) 'Online learning design that fosters student support, self-regulation, and retention', *Campus-Wide Information Systems*, 22(2): 88–107.

Fivush, R., Sales, J.M. and Bohanek, J.G. (2008) 'Meaning making in mothers' and children's narratives of emotional events', *Memory*, 16: 579–94.

Florez, I.R. (2011) 'Developing young children's self-regulation through everyday experiences', *Young Children*, July: 46–51.

Fogel, A., Nwokah, E, Dedo, J.Y., Messinger, D., Dickson, K.L., Matusov, E. and Holt, S.A. (1992) 'Social process theory of emotion', *Social Development*, 2: 122–42.

Forgeard, M.J.C. (2011) 'Happy people thrive on adversity', *Personality and Individual Differences*, 51: 904–9.

Forgas, J.P. (1995) 'Mood and judgment: the affect infusion model (AIM)', *Psychological Bulletin*, 117(1): 39–66.

Forgas, J.P. (2007) 'When sad is better than happy', *Journal of Experimental Social Psychology*, 43: 513–28.

Forgas, J.P. and Locke, J. (2005) 'Brief report', *Cognition & Emotion*, 19(7): 1071–81.

Forgas, J.P. and Vargas, P.T. (2000) 'The effects of mood on social judgment and reasoning', in M. Lewis and J.M. Haviland-Jones (eds) *Handbook of Emotions*, New York: Guilford, 350–67.

Fovet, F. (2007) 'Using distance learning electronic tools within the class to engage ADHD students', paper presented at the 3rd ASEE/IEEE Frontiers in Education Conference, Milwaukee, October.

Frank, R.H. (1988) *Passions within Reason*, New York: Norton.

Frederickson, N.L. and Furnham, A.F. (2004) 'Peer-assessed behavioural characteristics and sociometric rejection', *British Journal of Educational Psychology*, 74: 391–410.

Fredricks, J., Blumenfeld, P. and Paris, A. (2004) 'School engagement', *Review of Educational Research*, 74(1): 59–109.

Fredrickson, B.L. (2001) 'The role of positive emotions in positive psychology', *American Psychologist*, 56(3): 218–26.

Fredrickson, B.L. (2003) 'The value of positive emotions', *American Scientist*, 91(4): 330–5.

Fredrickson, B.L. (2004) 'The broaden-and-build theory of positive emotions', *Philosophical Transactions of the Royal Society: Biological Sciences*, 359: 1367–77.

Fredrickson, B.L. and Branigan, C. (2005) 'Positive emotions broaden the scope of attention and thought-action repertoires', *Cognition & Emotion*, 19(3): 313–32.

Fredrickson, B.L., Tugade, M.M., Waugh, C.E. and Larkin, G.R. (2003) 'What good are positive emotions in a crisis?' *Journal of Personality and Social Psychology*, 84(2): 365–76.

Freeman, S. (2000) *Ethics: An introduction to philosophy and practice*, Sydney: Wadsworth.

Freiberg, H.J., Stacey, M.T. and Helton, S. (2013) 'Classroom management', *Advances in Research on Teaching*, 18: 203–25.

Frenzel, A.C., Goetz, T., Lüdtke, O., Pekrun, R. and Sutton, R.E. (2009) 'Emotional transmission in the classroom', *Journal of Educational Psychology*, 101(3): 705–16.

Fried, L. (2011) 'Teaching teachers about emotion regulation in the classroom', *Australian Journal of Teacher Education*, 36(3): 117–27.

Friedman, I.A. (2000) 'Burnout in teachers', *Journal of Clinical Psychology*, 56(5): 595–606.

Frijda, N.H. (1986) *The Emotions*, Cambridge: Cambridge University Press.

Frijda, N.H. (1988) 'The laws of emotion', *American Psychologist*, 43(5): 349–58.

Frijda, N.H. (2004) 'Emotions and action', in A.S.R. Manstead, N. Frijda and A. Fischer (eds) *Feelings and Emotions*, Cambridge: Cambridge University Press, 158–73.

Frith, U., Morton, J. and Leslie, A.M. (1991) 'The cognitive basis of a biological disorder: Autism', *Trends in Neuroscience*, 14: 433–8.

Fry, S. (1998) *Moab in my Washpot*, London: Arrow.

Gable, P. and Harmon-Jones, H. (2010) 'The motivational dimensional model of affect', *Cognition & Emotion*, 24(2): 322–37.

Galvez, J.F., Thommi, S. and Ghaemi, S.N. (2009) 'Positive aspects of mental illness: a review of bipolar disorder', *Journal of Affective Disorders*, 128: 185–90.

Gamefski, N., Kraaij, V. and Spinhoven, P. (2001) 'Negative life events, cognitive emotion regulation and emotional problems', *Personality and Individual Differences*, 30(8): 1311–27.

Garcia-Retamero, R. and Rieskamp, J. (2008) 'Adaptive mechanisms for treating missing information', *Psychological Record*, 58: 547–68.

Gardner, M.P. (1985) 'Mood states and consumer behaviour', *Journal of Consumer Research*, 12(3): 281–300.

Garety, P.A., Freeman, D., Jolley, S., Dunn, G., Bebbington, P.E., Fowler, D.G., Kuipers, E. and Dudley, R. (2005) 'Reasoning, emotions, and delusional conviction in psychosis', *Journal of Abnormal Psychology*, 114(3): 373–84.

Garner, P.W. (2010) 'Emotional competence and its influence on teaching and learning', *Educational Psychology Review*, 22: 297–321.

Garner, R. (2007) 'Schools "must do more for creativity"', *Independent*, 31 October, 12.

Garnham, A. and Oakhill, J. (1994) *Thinking and Reasoning*, Oxford: Blackwell.

Garrett, M.T. and Wilbur, M.P. (1999) 'Does the worm live in the ground? Reflections on Native American Spirituality', *Journal of Multicultural Counseling & Development*, 27: 193–206.

Gasper, K. (2004a) 'Do you see what I see?' *Cognition & Emotion*, 18: 405–21.

Gasper, K. 2004b) 'Permission to seek freely? The effect of happy and sad moods on generating old and new ideas', *Creativity Research Journal*, 16(2/3): 215–29.

Gasper, K. and Clore, G.L. (2002) 'Attending to the big picture', *Psychological Science*, 13(1): 34–40.

Gasper, K. and Zawadzki, M.J. (2012) 'Want information?' *Motivation and Emotion*, 37(2): 308-22.

George, J.M. (2007) 'Dual tuning in a supportive context', *Academy of Management Journal*, 50(3): 605–22.

George, J.M. (2009) 'The illusion of will in organizational behaviour research', *Journal of Management*, 35(6): 1318–39.

George, J.M. and Zhou, J. (2002) 'Understanding when bad moods foster creativity and good ones don't', *Journal of Applied Psychology*, 87(4): 687–97.

Giddy. P. (2012) 'Philosophy for children in Africa', *South African Journal of Education*, 32: 15–25.

Giedd, J.N. (2008) 'The teen brain: Insights from neuroimaging' *Journal of Adolescent Health*, 42(4): 335–43.

Gilbert, M.A. (1995) 'Arguments and arguers', *Teaching Philosophy*, 18(2): 125–38.

Gilhooly, K.J. (1996) *Thinking: Directed, undirected and creative*, London: Academic Press.

Gilkey, R., Caceda, R. and Kilts, C. (2010) 'When emotional reasoning trumps IQ', *Harvard Business Review*, 88(9): 27.

Gino, F., Agote, L., Miron-Spektor, E. and Todorova, G. (2009) 'First get your feet wet: The effects of learning from direct and indirect experience on team creativity', *Organizational Behavior and Human Decision Processes*, 11: 102–15.

Gläser-Zikuda, M., Fuß, S., Laukenmann, K. M. and Randler, C. (2005) 'Promoting students' emotions and achievement – instructional design and evaluation of the ECOLE-approach', *Learning and Instruction*, 15(5): 481–95.

Glassman, M. and Kang, M.J. (2011) 'The logic of wikis', *Computer-Supported Collaborative Learning*, 6: 93–112.

Glatthorne, A.A. and Barron, J. (1991) 'The good thinker', in A.L. Costa (ed.) *Developing Minds*, Vol. 1, Alexandria: ASCD Publications, 49–53.

Glück, J. and Bluck, S. (2011) 'Laypeople's conceptions of wisdom and its development', *Psychological Science and Social Sciences*, 66(3): 321–5.

Glück, J., Bischof, B. and Siebenhüner, L. (2012) '"Knows what is good and bad", "Can teach you things", "Does lots of crosswords": Children's knowledge about wisdom', *European Journal of Developmental Psychology*, 9(5): 582–98.

Glück, J., Ernst, R. and Unger, F. (2002) 'How creatives define creativity', *Creativity Research Journal*, 14(1): 55–67.

Goel, V. and Vartanian, O. (2011) 'Negative emotions can attenuate the influence of beliefs on logical reasoning', *Cognition & Emotion*, 25(1): 121–31.

Goetz, T., Frenzel, A.C., Pekrun, R., Hall, N.C. and Lüdke, O. (2007) 'Between and within-domain relations of students' academic emotions', *Journal of Educational Psychology*, 4: 715–33.

Golby, M. (1996) 'Teachers' emotions', *Cambridge Journal of Education*, 26(3): 423–5.

Golding, C. (2011) 'Educating for critical thinking', *Higher Education Research & Development*, 30(3): 357–70.

Goleman, D. (1995) *Emotional Intelligence*, New York: Bantam Books.

Good, R. (1993) 'The many forms of constructivism', *Journal of Research in Science Teaching*, 30(9): 1015.

Goodall, A. (2012) 'Creative vs accounting', *Times Higher Educational Supplement*, 2042: 43–4.

Graesser, A., McDaniel, B., Chipman, P., Witherspoon, A., D'Mello, S. and Gholson, B. (2006) 'Detection of emotions during learning with AutoTutor', in R. Son (ed.) *Proceedings of the 28th Annual Meeting of the Cognitive Science Society*, Mahwah: Lawrence Erlbaum, 285–90.

Grawitch, M.J. and Munz, D.C. (2005) 'Individual and group affect in problem-solving workgroups', in C.E.J. Hartel, W.J. Zerbe and N.M. Ashkenasy (eds) *Emotions in Organizational Behavior*, Mahwah: Lawrence Erlbaum, 119–88.

Grayling, A.C. (2003) *What is Good?* London: Weidenfeld & Nicolson.

Grazziano, P.A., Reavis, R.D., Keane, S.P. and Calkins, S.D. (2007) 'The role of emotion regulation in children's early academic success', *Journal of School Psychology*, 45: 3–19.

Greenberg, L.S. and Pascual-Leone, J. (1998) 'Emotion in the creation of personal meaning', in M. Power and C.R. Brewin (eds) *The Transformation of Meaning in Psychological Therapies*, Chichester: John Wiley, 160–73.

Greene, J. and Haidt, J. (2002) 'How (and where) does moral judgment work?' *Trends in Cognitive Sciences*, 6(12): 517–23.

Greenglass, E.R. and Burke, R.J. (2003) 'Teacher stress', in M.F. Dollard, A.H. Winefield and H.R. Winefield (eds) *Occupational Stress in the Service Professions*, New York: Taylor & Francis, 213–36.

Gregersen, T.S. and Horwitz, E.K. (2002) 'Language learning and perfectionism', *Modern Language Journal*, 86(4): 562–70.

Gregorian, V. (2007) 'A sense of elsewhere', *American Libraries*, 38(10): 46–8.

Gregory, M. (2009) 'Ethics education and the practice of wisdom', *Teaching Ethics*, Spring: 105–30.

Gregory, R.L. (1998) *The Oxford Companion to the Mind*, Oxford: Oxford University Press.

Griva, K. and Joekes, K. (2003) 'UK teachers under stress', *Psychology and Health*, 18(4): 457–71.

Gross, J.J. (1998) 'The emerging field of emotion regulation', *Review of General Psychology*, 2(3): 271–99.

Gross, J.J. (2001) 'Emotion regulation in adulthood', *Current Directions in Psychological Science*, 10(6): 214–19.

Gross, J.J. (2002) 'Emotion regulation', *Psychophysiology*, 39: 281–91.

Gross, J.J. and Thompson, R.A. (2007) 'Emotion regulation', in J.J. Gross (ed.) *Handbook of Emotion Regulation*, New York: Guilford, 3–26.

Gross, J.J., Richards, J.M. and John, O.P. (2006) 'Emotion regulation in everyday life', in D.K. Snyder, J.A. Simpson and J.N. Hughes (eds) *Emotion Regulation in Couples and Families*, Washington: American Psychological Association, 13–35.

Gumora, G. and Arsenio, W.F. (2002) 'Emotionality, emotion regulation and school performance in middle school', *Journal of School Psychology*, 40(5): 395–413.

Guskey, T.R. (1985) 'Staff development and teacher change', *Educational Leadership*, 42(7): 57–60.

Guthrie, J.T. and Wigfield, A. (2000) 'Engagement and motivation in reading', in M. Kamil and P. Mosenthal (eds) *Handbook of Reading Research*, Vol. 3, Mahwah: Lawrence Erlbaum, 403–22.

Haddon, M. (2004) *The Curious Incident of the Dog in the Night-Time*, London: Vintage.

Hadwin, J., Brogan, J. and Stevenson, J. (2005) 'State anxiety and working memory in children', *Educational Psychology*, 25(4): 379–93.

Hadwin, J. and Perner, J. (1991) 'Pleased and surprised: Children's cognitive theory of emotion', *British Journal of Developmental Psychology*, 9: 215–34.

Hahn, D.-W., Lee, K. and Ashton, M.C. (1999) 'A factor analysis of the most frequently used Korean personality trait adjectives', *European Journal of Personality*, 13(4): 261–82.

Haidt, J. (2001) 'The emotional dog and its rational tail', *Psychological Review*, 108(4): 814–34.

Haidt, J. (2002) 'Dialogue between my head and my heart: Affective influences on moral judgement', *Psychological Inquiry*, 13(1): 54–6.

Halford, G.S. (1993) *Children's Understanding*, Hillsdale: Lawrence Erlbaum.

Halpern, D.F. (1997) *Critical Thinking Across the Curriculum*, Mahwah: Lawrence Erlbaum.

Halpern, D.F. (2001) 'Why wisdom', *Educational Psychologist*, 36(4): 253–6.

Hammerly, H. (1975) 'The deduction/induction controversy', *Modern Language Journal*, 59(1/2): 15–18.

Hänze, M. (2003) 'Productive functions of emotions in classroom learning', in P. Mayring and C. von Rhoeneck (eds) *Learning Emotions*, Frankfurt am Main: Peter Lang, 185–92.

Harðarson, A. (2012) 'Why the aims of education cannot be settled', *Journal of Philosophy of Education*, 42(2): 223–35.

Hardy, J., Gammage, K. and Hall, K.A. (2001) 'A descriptive study of athletes' self-talking', *Sport Psychologist*, 15: 306–18.

Hargreaves, A. (1998) 'The emotional practice of teaching', *Teacher and Teacher Education*, 14(8): 835–54.

Hargreaves, A. (2000) 'Mixed emotions: Teachers' perceptions of their interactions with students', *Teaching and Teacher Education*, 16(8): 811–26.

Hargreaves, A. (2005) 'The emotions of teaching and educational change', in A. Hargreaves (ed.) *Extending Educational Change*, Dordrecht: Springer, 278–95.

Harman, G. (2011) 'Notes on practical reasoning', *Cogency*, 3(1): 127–45.

Hascher, T. (2010) 'Learning and emotion: perspectives for theory and research', *European Educational Research Journal*, 9(1): 13–28.

Harris, S. (2011) *The Moral Landscape: How science can determine human values*, Detroit: Free Press.

Haselton, M.G. and Ketelaar, T. (2006) 'Irrational emotions or emotional wisdom? The evolutionary psychology of emotions and behavior', in J. Forgas (ed.) *Hearts and Minds*, New York: Psychology Press, 21–40.

Hastings, W. (2004) 'Emotions and the practicum', *Teachers and Teaching: Theory and Practice*, 10(2): 135–48.

Hatfield, E., Cacioppo, J.T. and Rapson, R.L. (1993) 'Emotional contagion', *Current Directions in Psychological Science*, 2(3): 96–9.

Hattaway, M. (1968) 'Paradoxes of Solomon', *Journal of the History of Ideas*, 29(4): 499–530.

Hauser, M.D. (2006) *Moral Minds*, New York: HarperCollins.

Havlick, D. and Hourdequin, M. (2005) 'Practical wisdom in environmental education', *Ethics, Place and Environment*, 8(3): 385–92.

He, D. (2013) 'What makes learners anxious while speaking English', *Educational Studies*, Online. Available at http://dx.doi.org/10.1080/03055698.2013.764819 (accessed 28 May 2013).

Heath, W.P. and Erickson, J.R. (1998) 'Memory for central and peripheral actions and props after varied post-event presentation', *Legal and Criminological Psychology*, 3: 321–46.

Hembree, R. (1988) 'Correlates, causes, effects, and treatment of test anxiety', *Review of Educational Research*, 58: 47–77.

Higgins, S.E. (2012) *The Teaching and Learning Toolkit: Technical appendices*, Durham: Sutton Trust/Durham University.

Higgins, S.E., Hall, E., Baumfield, V. and Moseley, D. (2005) *A Meta-Analysis of the Implementation of Thinking Skills Approaches on Pupils*, London: Social Science Research Unit.

Hirt, E.R., Devers, E.E. and McCrea, S.M. (2008) 'I want to be creative: Exploring the role of hedonic contingency theory in the positive mood–cognitive flexibility link', *Journal of Personality and Social Psychology*, 94(2): 214–30.

Holland, A.C. and Kensinger, E.A. (2010) 'Emotion and autobiographical memory', *Physics of Life Reviews*, 7: 88–131.

Holliday, S. and Chandler, M. (1986) 'Wisdom: Explorations in adult competence', in J. Meacham (ed.) *Contributions to Human Development*, Basel: Karger, 17: 1–96.

Hollon, E.W. (1971) 'Thoughts toward a Socratic philosophy of education', *Peabody Journal of Education*, 49(1): 53–9.

Holmes, E. (1977) *Amy's Goose*, New York: Vintage/Harper Row.

Holmes, E.A., Lang. T. and Shah, D.M. (2009) 'Developing interpretation bias modification as a "cognitive vaccine" for depressed mood', *Journal of Abnormal Psychology*, 118(1): 76–88.

Hom, H.L. and Arbuckle, B. (1988) 'Mood induction effects upon goal setting and performance in young children', *Motivation and Emotion*, 12: 113–22.

Hood, P. (2008) 'What do we teachers need to know to enhance our creativity?' *Education 3–13*, 36(2): 139–51.

Horwitz, E.K. (2010) 'Foreign and second language anxiety', *Language Teaching*, 43(2): 154–67.

Hovanitz, C.A., Hursh, A.N. and Hudepohl, A.D. (2011) 'Dimensions of affect modulation by perceived mood regulation ability', *Applied Psychophysiological Biofeedback*, 36: 113–19.

Howard, S. and Johnson, B. (2004) 'Resilient teachers: Resisting stress and burnout', *School Psychology of Education*, 7: 399–420.

Howe, M.L. and Malone, C. (2011) 'Mood-congruent true and false memory', *Memory*, 19(2): 192–201.

Hoy, A.W. (2013) 'A reflection on the place of emotion in teaching and teacher education', *Advances in Research on Teaching*, 18: 255–70.

Hu, W., Shi, Q.Z., Han, Q., Wang, X. and Adey, P. (2010) 'Creative scientific finding and its developmental trend', *Creativity Research Journal*, 22(1): 1–7.

Hua, Z. (2012) 'Turning to the pedagogy of "listening"', *Complicity*, 9(1): 57–74.

Huang, P. and Hwang, Y. (2013) 'An exploration of EFL learners' anxiety and e-learning environments', *Journal of Language Teaching and Research*, 4(1): 27–35.

Hullett, C.R. (2005) 'The impact of mood on persuasion', *Communication Research*, 32(4): 423–42.

Hume, D. (1739/1978) *Treatise of Human Nature*, Oxford: Oxford University Press.

Hurson, T. (2008) 'Hurson's productive thinking model'. Available at http://www.mindtools.com/pages/article/productive-thinking-model.htm (accessed 9 October 2013).

Hutton, R.E. (2004) 'Emotional regulation goals and strategies for teachers', *Social Psychology of Education*, 7: 379–98.

Immordino-Yang, M.H. and Damasio, A. (2007) 'We feel, therefore we learn', *Mind, Brain and Education*, 1(1): 3–10.

Isbell, L.M., Lair, E.C. and Rovenpor, D.R. (2013) 'Affect as information about process-ing styles', *Social and Personality Psychology Compass*, 7: 93–114.

Isen, A. (1990) 'The influence of positive and negative affect on cognitive organization', in N. Stein, B. Leventhal and T. Trabasso (eds) *Psychological and Biological Processes in the Development of Emotion*, Hillsdale: Lawrence Erlbaum, 75–94.

Isen, A. (2008) 'Some ways in which positive affect influences decision making and problem solving', in M. Lewis, J.M. Haviland-Jones and L.F. Barrett (eds) *Handbook of Emotions*, New York: Guilford, 548–73.

Isen, A., Daubman, K.A. and Nowicki, G.P. (1987) 'Positive affect facilitates creative problem solving', *Journal of Personality and Social Psychology*, 52(6): 1122–31.

Isen, A., Horn, N. and Rosenham, D.L. (1973) 'Effects of success and failure on childen's generosity', *Journal of Personality and Social Psychology*, 21(3): 384–88.

Isen, A., Johnson, M.M.S., Mertz, E. and Robinson, G.F. (1985) 'The influence of posi-tive affect on the unusualness of word associations', *Journal of Personality and Social Psychology*, 48(6): 1413–26.

Izard, C.E. (1991) *The Psychology of Emotions*, New York: Plenum.

Izard, C.E. (2007) 'Basic emotions, natural kinds, emotion schemas, and a new para-digm', *Perspectives on Psychological Science*, 2: 260–80.

Izard, C.E. (2010) 'The many meanings/aspects of emotion', *Emotion Review*, 2: 363–70.

Jackson, N.E. and Butterfield, E.C. (1986) 'A conception of giftedness designed to pro-mote research', in R.J. Sternberg and J.E. Davidson (eds) *Conceptions of Giftedness*, Cambridge: Cambridge University Press, 151–81.

Janssen, F. and de Hullu, E. (2008) 'A toolkit for stimulating productive thinking', *Journal of Biological Education*, 43(1): 21–6.

Javidi, M., Downs, V.C. and Nussbaum, J.F. (1988) 'A comparative analysis of teachers' use of dramatic style behaviors at higher and secondary educational levels', *Communication Education*, 37: 278–88.

Jeste, D.V., Ardelt, M., Blazer, D., Kraemer, H.C., Vaillant, G. and Meeks, T.W. (2010) 'Expert consensus on characteristics of wisdom, a Delphi method study', *Gerontologist*, 50(5): 668–80.

Jeste, D.V. and Harris, J.C. (2010) 'Wisdom – a neuroscience perspective', *Journal of the American Medical Association*, 304(14): 1602–3.

Jewell, P. (1996) 'A reasoning taxonomy for gifted children', paper presented at the Australian Association for the Education of the Gifted and Talented, Adelaide. Online. Available at http://www.eric.ed.gov/ERICWebPortal/detail?accno=ED442248_(accessed 30 May 2013).

John, O.P. and Gross, J.J. (2004) 'Healthy and unhealthy emotion regulation', *Journal of Personality*, 72(6): 1301–33.

Johnson, D.W. and Johnson, R.T. (1993) 'Creative and critical thinking through aca-demic controversy', *American Behavioral* Scientist, 37(1): 40–53.

Johnson-Laird, P.N. (1983) *Mental Models*, Cambridge: Cambridge University Press.

Johnson-Laird, P.N. (2010) 'Mental models and human reasoning', *Proceedings of the National Academy of Science*, 107(43): 18243–50.

Jones, A. (2007) 'Multiplicities or manna from heaven?' *Australian Journal of Education*, 51(1): 84–103.

Jones, A. (2009) 'Redisciplining generic attributes', *Studies in Higher Education*, 34(1): 85–100.

Jones, M.G. and Wheatley, J. (2006) 'Gender differences in teacher–student interactions in science classrooms', *Journal of Research in Science Teaching*, 27(9): 861–74.

Jump, P. (2012) 'Renaissance man's word to the wise', *Times Higher Education*, 2034: 22–3.

Just, M.A. and Carpenter, P.A. (1996) 'A capacity theory of comprehension', *Psychological Review*, 103: 773–80.

Kahneman, D. (2012) *Thinking, Fast and Slow*, London: Penguin.

Kahneman, D. and Tversky, A. (1979) 'Prospect Theory', *Econometrica*, 47(2), 263–93.

Kant, E. (1785/2002) *Critique of Practical Reason*, Cambridge: Hackett.

Kapoor, A., Mota, S. and Picard, R.W. (2001) 'Towards a learning companion that recognizes affect', *AAAI Technical Report FS-01-02*.

Katz, M.S. (2009) 'R.S. Peters' normative conception of education and educational aims', *Journal of Philosophy of Education*, 43: 97–108.

Kaufman, R. (2009) 'Becoming your own leader', *Performance Improvement*, 8(4): 29–34.

Kaufmann, G. (2003) 'Expanding the mood–creativity equation', *Creativity Research Journal*, 15(2/3): 131–5.

Kaufmann, G. and Vosburg, S.K. (1997) 'Paradoxical mood effects on creative problem solving', *Cognition & Emotion*, 11(2): 151–70.

Kaufmann, G. and Vosburg, S.K. (2002) 'The effects of mood on early and late idea production', *Creativity Research Journal*, 14(3/4): 317–30.

Kaviani, H., Javaheri, F. and Hatami, N. (2011) 'Mindfulness-based cognitive therapy reduces depression and anxiety induced by real stressful setting in non-clinical population', *International Journal of Psychology and Psychological Therapy*, 11(2): 285–96.

Keenan, K. and Shaw, D. (1997) 'Developmental and social influences on young girls' early problem behaviour', *Psychological Bulletin*, 121: 95–113.

Kell, D.B. and Oliver, S.G. (2003) 'Here is the evidence, now what is the hypothesis?' *BioEssays*, 26: 99–105.

Keltner, D., Ekman, P., Gonzago, G.C. and Beer, J. (2003) 'Facial expression of emotion', in R.J. Davidson, Scherer, K.R. and H.H. Goldsmith (eds) *Handbook of Affective Sciences*, Oxford University Press: Oxford, 415–32.

Kensinger, E.A. (2009) 'Remembering the detail: Effects of emotion', *Emotion Review*, 1(2): 99–113.

Kim, J.A., Szatmari, P., Bryson, S.E., Streiner, D.L. and Wilson, F.J. (2012) 'The prevalence of anxiety and mood problems among children with autism and Asperger syndrome', *Autism*, 4(2): 117–32.

King, M.I., Ollendick, T.H. and Gullone, E. (1991) 'Test anxiety in children and adolescents', *Australian Psychologist*, 26: 25–32.

Klassen, R.M. (2010) 'Teacher stress: The mediating role of collective efficacy beliefs', *Journal of Educational Research*, 103: 342–50.

Kliegel, M., Jäger, T., Phillips, L.H., Federspiel, E., Imfeld, A., Keller, M. and Zimprich, D. (2005) 'Effects of sad mood on time-based prospective memory', *Cognition & Emotion*, 19(8): 1199–213.

Knauff, M. and Wolf, A.G. (2010) 'Complex cognition: The science of human reasoning, problem-solving, and decision-making', *Cognitive Processes*, 11: 99–102.

Kohlberg, L., Levine, C. and Hewer, A. (1983) *Moral Stages*, Karger: New York.

Kołakowski, L. (1972) 'Intellectuals and change', *Daedalus*, 101(3): 1–15.

Koo, M., Clore, G.L., Kim, J. and Incheol, C. (2012) 'Affective facilitation and inhibition of cultural influences on reasoning', *Cognition & Emotion*, 26(4): 680–9.

Koole, S. L. (2009) 'The psychology of emotion regulation', *Cognition & Emotion*, 23(1): 4–41.

Kort, B., Reilly, R. and Picard, R.W. (2001) 'An affective model of the interplay between emotions and learning', *Proceedings of the IEEE International Conference on Advanced Learning Technologies*, Madison, August.

Kramer, D.A. (1990) 'Conceptualizing wisdom', in R. Sternberg (ed.) *Wisdom: Its nature, origins and development*, Cambridge: Cambridge University Press, 279–309.

Kramer, J. (2009) 'The study of proverbs in Anglo-Saxon literature', *Literature Compass*, 6(1): 71–96.

Krashen, S.D. (1988) *Second Language Acquisition and Second Language Learning*, New York: Prentice-Hall.

Kristjánsson, K. (2007) *Aristotle, Emotions and Education*, Aldershot: Ashgate.

Kröper, M., Fay, D., Lindberg, T. and Meinel, C. (2011) 'Interrelations between motivation, creativity and emotions in design thinking processes', in T. Taura and Y. Nagai (eds) *Design Creativity 2010*, London: Springer-Verlag, 97–104.

Kuhn, D. and Udell, W. (2001) 'The path to wisdom', *Educational Psychologist*, 36(4): 261–64.

Kunau, K.A. (2011) 'Borrowing the wings of Daedalus', Master's thesis, University of Iowa.

Kwok, D.W.Y. (1989) *The Chinese Tradition: An essay, Occasional Papers, No. 3*, Honolulu: Center for Chinese Studies.

Kyaga, S., Lichtenstein, P., Boman, M., Hultman, C. and Långström, N. (2011) 'Creativity and mental disorder', *British Journal of Psychiatry*, 199: 373–9.

LaBanca, F. and Ritchie, K.C. (2011) 'The art of scientific ideas', *Science Teacher*, 78(8): 48–51.

LaBar, K.S. and Phelps, E.A. (1998) 'Arousal-mediated memory consolidation', *Psychological Science*, 9(6): 490–93.

Labouvie-Vief, G. (1990) 'Wisdom as integrated thought', in R. Sternberg (ed.) *Wisdom*, New York: Cambridge University Press, 52–83.

Lagattuta, K.H. (2007) 'Thinking about the future because of the past', *Child Development*, 78(5): 1492–509.

Lahikainen, A.R., Kirmanen, T., Kraav, I. and Taimalu, M. (2003) 'Studying fears in young children', *Childhood*, 10: 83–104.

Laidlaw, E. (2012) 'Plato's neurobiology', *Philosophy Now*, 90: 18–19.

Lane, R.D. and Nadel, L. (2000) *Cognitive Neuroscience of Emotion*, New York: Oxford University Press.

Laney, C., Heuer, F. and Reisberg, D. (2003) 'Thematically induced arousal in naturally occurring emotional memories', *Applied Cognitive Psychology*, 17: 995–1004.

Lang, P.J. (1988) 'What are the data of emotions?' in V. Hamilton, G.H. Bower and N. Frijda (eds) *Cognitive Perspectives on Emotion and Motivation*, Vol. 41, Dordrecht: Kluwer, 173–91.

Lau, J. (2009) *A Mini Guide to Critical Thinking*, Hong Kong: University of Hong Kong.

Lazarus, R.S. (1991) *Emotion and Adaptation*, New York: Oxford University Press.

LeDoux, J. (1998) *The Emotional Brain*, London: Wiedenfeld & Nicolson.

LeDoux, J. (1989) 'Cognitive–emotional interactions in the brain', *Cognition & Emotion*, 3(4): 267–89.

LeDoux, J. (2000) 'Emotion circuits in the brain', *Annual Review of Neuroscience*, 23: 155–84.

Lee, G., Kwon, J., Park, S.-S., Kim, J.-W., Kwon, H-G. and Park, H.-K. (2003) 'Development of an instrument for measuring cognitive conflict in secondary-level science classes', *Journal of Research in Science Teaching*, 40(6): 585–603.

Lehrer, J. (2009) *The Decisive Moment*, Edinburgh: Canongate.

Lehtinen, E. (2010) 'The potential of teaching and learning supported by ICT for the acquisition of deep conceptual knowledge and the development of wisdom', in E. De Corte and J.E. Fenstad, *From Information to Knowledge; From knowledge to wisdom*, London: Portland Press, 79–88.

Lench, H.C., Flores, S.A. and Bench, S.W. (2011) 'Discrete emotions predict changes in cognition, judgment, experience, behavior, and physiology', *Psychological Bulletin*, 137(5): 834–55.

Levenson, R.W. (1999) 'The intrapersonal function of emotions', *Cognition & Emotion*, 13(5): 481–504.

Levine, L.J. and Edelstein, R.S. (2009) 'Emotion and memory narrowing', *Cognition & Emotion*, 23(5): 833–75.

Levinson, M. (1999) *The Demands of a Liberal Education*, Oxford: Oxford University Press.

Ley, K. and Young, D.B. (2001) 'Instructional principles for self-regulation', *Educational Technology Research and Development*, 49(2): 93–103.

Liggett, S. (1991) 'Creativity and non-literary writing: The importance of problem finding', *Journal of Teaching Writing*, 10(2): 165–79.

Lindström, B.R. and Bohlin, G. (2011) 'Emotion processing facilitates working memory performance', *Cognition & Emotion*, 25(7): 1196–204.

Lindzey, G. and Byrne, D. (1968) 'Measurement of social choice and interpersonal alternatives', in G. Lindzey and E. Aronson (eds) *Handbook of Social Psychology*, Reading: Addison-Wesley, 452–525.

Linnenbrink, E.A. (2007) 'The role of affect in student learning', in P.A. Schultz and R. Pekrun (eds) *Emotion in Education*, San Diego: Elsevier, 107–24.

Linnenbrink-Garcia, L., Pugh, K., Koskey, K.L.K. and Stewart, V.C. (2012) 'Developing conceptual understanding of natural selection', *Journal of Experimental Education*, 80(1): 45–68.

Lipman, M. (1973) *Philosophy for Children*, Upper Montclair: Institute for the Advancement of Philosophy for Children.

Lipman, M. (2003) *Thinking in Education*, Cambridge: Cambridge University Press.

Lipman, M., Sharp, A.M. and Olscanyon, F.S. (1980) *Philosophy in the Classroom*, Philadelphia: Temple University Press.

Liu, S. and Onwuegbuzie, A.J. (2012) 'Chinese teachers' work stress and their turnover intention', *International Journal of Educational Research*, 53: 160–70.

Lombardi, D. & Sinatra, G.M. (2013) 'Emotions about teaching about human-induced climate change', *International Journal of Science Education*, 35(1): 167–91.

Lombrozo, T. (2007) 'Simplicity and probability in causal explanation', *Cognitive Psychology*, 55: 232–57.

Lönnqvist, J.-E., Paunonen, S., Nissinen, V. and Verkasalo, M. (2006) 'Conformism moderates the relations between values, anticipated regret, and behavior', *Personality and Social Psychology Bulletin*, 32: 1469–81.

Lovelock, J. (2006) *The Revenge of Gaia*, London: Penguin.

Lowe, P.A. and Ang, R.P. (2012) 'Cross-cultural examination of test anxiety among US and Singapore students on the Test Anxiety Scale for elementary students', *Educational Psychology*, 32(1): 107–26.

Lubart, T. and Getz, I. (1998) 'The influence of heuristics on psychological science', *Journal for the Theory of Social Behavior*, 28(4): 435–57.

Lupien, S.J., McEwen, B.S., Gunnar, M.R. and Heim, C. (2009) 'Effects of stress throughout the lifespan on the brain, behaviour and cognition', *Nature Reviews: Neuroscience*, 10: 434–45.

Lysaker, P.H. and Buck, K.D. (2009) 'Metacognition in schizophrenia spectrum disorders', *Giornale Italiano di Psicopatologia*, 15(2): 2–12.

McCarthy, C.J. (2009) 'The relationship between elementary teachers' experience, stress, and coping resources to burnout symptoms', *Elementary School Journal*, 109(3): 282–300.

McClowry, S.G., Snow, D.L. and Tamis-LeMonda, C.S. (2005) 'An evaluation of the effects of INSIGHTS on the behaviour of inner city primary school children', *Journal of Personality*, 69(6): 819–46.

McDonald, A.S. (2001) 'The prevalence and effects of test anxiety in school children', *Educational Psychology*, 21(1): 89–101.

McGhee, P. (1997) 'Problem Solving within the age group 5–14', *School Science Review*, 79: 103–10.

McGregor, D. (2007) *Developing Thinking; Developing Learning*, Maidenhead: Open University Press.

McGregor, D. and Gunter, B. (2006) 'Invigorating pedagogic change', *European Journal of Teacher Education*, 29(1): 23–48.

Mackintosh, B. and Mathews, A. (2003) 'Don't look now', *Cognition and Emotion*, 17: 623–46.

MacLeod, C., Tata, P. and Mathews, A. (1987) 'Perception of emotionally valenced information in depression', *British Journal of Clinical Psychology*, 26: 67–8.

McPherson, M.B., Kearney, P. and Plax, T.G. (2003) 'The dark side of instruction: Teacher anger at classroom norm violations', *Journal of Applied Communication Research*, 31: 76–90.

Madjar, N. and Oldham, G.R. (2002) 'Preliminary tasks and creative performance on a subsequent task', *Creativity Research Journal*, 14(2): 239–51.

Maiden, N., Gizikis, A. and Robertson, S. (2004) 'Provoking creativity', *IEEE Software*, Sept/Oct: 68–75.

Mameli, M. (2004) 'The role of emotions in ecological and practical rationality', in D. Evans and P. Cruse (eds) *Emotions, Evolution, and Rationality*, Oxford: Oxford University Press, 159–78.

Manz, C.C. and Neck, C.P. (1991) 'Inner leadership: Creating productive thought patterns', *Academy of Management Executive*, 5(3): 87–95.

Marchand, H. (2003) 'An overview of the psychology of wisdom', *Journal of the Philosophy of Education*, 46(2): 223–35.

Martin, A. and Marsh, H. (2005) 'Student motivation and engagement in mathematics, science and English', paper presented at the Australian Association for Research in Education, Sydney, November/December.

Martin, E.A. and Kerns, J.G. (2011) 'The influence of positive mood on different aspects of cognitive control', *Cognition & Emotion*, 25(2): 265–79.

Martin, L. and Stoner, P. (1996) 'Mood as input', In L. Martin and A. Tesser (eds) *Striving and Feeling*, Hillsdale: LEA, 279–301.

Martin, L.L., Ward, D.W., Achee, J.W. and Wyer, R.S. (1993) 'Mood as input: People interpret the motivational implications of their moods', *Journal of Personality and Social Psychology*, 64: 317–26.

Marzano, R., Pickering, D. and Pollock, J. (2001) *Classroom Instruction that Works*, Alexandria: Association for Supervision and Curriculum Development.

Mason, M. (2000) 'Integrated critical thinking', in T. McLaughlin (ed.) *Proceedings of the Thirty-Fourth Annual Conference of the Philosophy of Education Society of Great Britain*, Oxford: Philosophy of Education Society.

Mason, M. (ed.) (2008) *Critical Thinking and Learning*, Malden: Blackwell.

Matusov, E. and Soslau, E. (2010) 'A structuralist approach to argumentation in education', *Culture & Psychology*, 16(4): 549–57.

Maxfield, L. and Melnyk, W.T. (2000) 'Single session treatment of test anxiety with eye movement desensitization and reprocessing', *International Journal of Stress Management*, 7(2): 87–101.

Maxwell, N. (1984) *From Knowledge to Wisdom*, Oxford: Blackwell.

Mayer, J.D. and Cobb, C.D. (2000) 'Educational policy on emotional intelligence', *Educational Psychology Review*, 12(2): 163–83.

Mayer, J.D., Roberts, R.D. and Barsade, S.G. (2008a) 'Human abilities: Emotional intelligence', *Annual Review of Psychology*, 59: 507–36.

Mayer, J.D., Salovey, P. and Caruso, D.R. (2008b) 'Emotional intelligence', *American Psychologist*, 63(6): 503–17.

Mayring, P. (2003) 'Introduction: Importance of affective factors', in P. Mayring and C. von Rhoeneck (eds) *Learning Emotions*, Frankfurt am Main: Peter Lang, 7–8.

Meinhardt, J. and Pekrun, R. (2003) 'Attentional resource allocation to emotional events', *Cognition & Emotion*, 17(3): 477–500.

Menezes, I. and Campos, B.P. (1998) 'Students' perceptions of classroom climate', in P. Lang, Y. Katz and I. Menezes (eds) *Affective Education*, London: Cassell, 237–50.

Mercer, N., Wegerif, R. and Dawes, L. (1999) 'Children's talk and the development of reasoning in the classroom', *British Educational Research Journal*, 25(1): 95–111.

Meri, J.W. and Bacharach, J.L. (2006) *Medieval Islamic Civilization*, London: Routledge.

Merleau-Ponty, M. (1964) *Signs*, Evanston: Northwestern University Press.

Mestre, J. P. (2005) 'Facts and myths about pedagogies of engagement in science', *Peer Review*, 7: 24–7.

Meyer, D.K. and Turner, J.C. (2002) 'Discovering emotion in classroom motivation research', *Educational Psychologist*, 37(2): 107–14.

Meyer, D.K. and Turner, J.C. (2006) 'Re-conceptualizing emotion and motivation to learn in classroom contexts', *Educational Psychology Review*, 18: 377–90.

Miceli, M. and Castelfranchi, C. (2005) 'Anxiety as an "epistemic" emotion', *Anxiety, Stress and Coping*, 18: 291–319.

Milbank, J. (1996) 'The sublime in Kierkegaard', *Heythrop Journal*, 37: 298–321.

Milne, I. (2007) Children's science, *Primary Science Review*, 100: 33–4.

Miron-Shatz, T. Stone, A. and Kahneman, D. (2009) 'Memories of yesterday's emotions', *Emotion*, 9(6): 885–91.

Mok, C.K., Whitehill, T.L. and Dodd, B.J. (2008) 'Problem-based learning, critical thinking and concept mapping in speech-language pathology education', *International Journal of Speech-Language Pathology*, 10(6): 438–48.

Moldin, S.O., Reich, T. and Rice, J.P. (1991) 'Current perspectives on the genetics of unipolar depression', *Behavioral Genetics*, 21: 211–42.

Montague, M. (2008) 'Self-regulation strategies to improve mathematical problem solving for students with learning disabilities', *Learning Disability Quarterly*, 31(1): 37–44.

Morgan, J. (2010) 'Autobiographical memory biases in social anxiety', *Clinical Psychology Review*, 30: 288–97.

Moseley, D., Baumfield, V., Elliott, J., Gregson, M., Miller, J. and Newton, D.P. (2005) *Frameworks for Thinking*, Cambridge: Cambridge University Press.

Moss, M., Cook, J., Wesnes, K. and Duckett, P. (2003) 'Aromas of rosemary and lavender: Essential oils differentially affect cognition and mood in healthy adults', *International Journal of Neuroscience*, 113: 15–38.

Mottet, T.P., Garza, R., Beebe, S.A., Houser, M.L., Jurrells, S. and Furler, L. (2008) 'Instructional communication predictors of ninth-grade students' affective learning in math and science', *Communication Education*, 57(3): 333–55.

Mulligan, K. and Scherer, K.R. (2012) 'Towards a working definition of emotion', *Emotion Review*, 4(4): 345–57.

Mumford, M.D. (2003) 'Where have we been, where are we going: Taking stock in creativity research', *Creativity Research Journal*, 15: 107–20.

Ndirangu, G.W., Muola, J.M., Kithuka, M.R. and Nassiuma, D.K. (2009) 'An investigation of the relationship between test anxiety and academic performance in secondary schools in Nyeri District, Kenya', *Global Journal of Educational Research*, 8(1/2): 1–7.

Neumann, A. (2012) 'Research as thought and emotion in researchers' learning', *Research Intelligence*, 118: 8–9.

Newton, D.P. (1988) *Making Science Education Relevant*, London: Kogan Page.

Newton, D.P. (2010a) 'Assessing the creativity of scientific explanations in elementary science', *Research in Science and technological Education*, 28(3): 187–201.

Newton, D.P. (2010b) 'Quality and peer review of research: an adjudicating role for editors', *Accountability in Research*, 17: 130–45.

Newton, D.P. (2012a) *Teaching for Understanding*, London: Routledge.

Newton, D.P. (2012b) 'Recognizing creativity', in L. Newton (ed.) *Creativity for a New Curriculum*, London, Routledge, 108–19.

Newton, D.P. (2013) 'Moods, emotions and creative thinking', *Thinking Skills and Creativity*, 8: 34–44.

Newton, D.P. and Donkin, H. (2011) 'Some notions of artistic creativity amongst history of art students acquired through incidental learning', *International Journal of Education through Art*, 7(3): 283–98.

Newton, D.P. and Newton, L.D. (1995) 'Using analogy to help young children understand', Newton, D.P. and Newton, L.D. (2000) 'Do teachers support causal understanding through their discourse when teaching primary science?' *British Educational Research Journal*, 26: 599–613.

Newton, D.P. and Newton, L.D. (2001) 'Choosing and judging teachers', *Research in Education*, 66: 54–64.

Newton, D.P. and Newton, L.D. (2006) 'Could elementary textbooks serve as models of practice to help new teachers and non-specialists attend to reasoning in music', *Music Education Research*, 8(1): 3–16.

Newton, D.P. and Newton, L.D. (2009) 'Some student teachers' conceptions of creativity in school science', *Research in Science & Technological Education*, 27(1): 45–60.

Newton, D.P. and Newton, L.D. (2010a) 'Engaging science: Pre-service primary teachers' notions of engaging science lessons', *International Journal of Science and Mathematics Education*, 32(15): 1989–2005.

Newton, D.P. and Newton, L.D. (2010b) 'What teachers see as creative incidents in elementary science lessons', *International Journal of Science Education*, 32(15): 1989–2005.

Newton, L.D. (2012) *Creativity for a new curriculum: 5–11*, London: Routledge.

Newton, L.D. (2013a) 'Teachers questions: can they support understanding and higher-level thinking?' *Research Journal*, 1: 6–17.

Newton, L.D. (2013b) *From Teaching for Creative Thinking to Teaching for Productive Thought*, Ulm: International Centre for Innovation in Education.

Ng, K.S. (2012) 'Emotional intelligence of teachers', *Indian Journal of Education and Information Management*, 1(2): 68–72.

Ng, K., Lay, Y.F., Areepattamannil, S., Treagust, D.F. and Chandrasegaran, A.L. (2012) 'Relationship between affect and achievement in science and mathematics in Malaysia and Singapore', *Research in Science & Technological Education*, 30(3): 225–37.

Nickerson, R.S. (1985) 'Understanding understanding', *American Journal of Education*, 93: 201–39.

Niiniluoto, I. (1999) 'Defending abduction', *Philosophy of Science*, 66, Supplement, S436–51.

Niu, L. (2013) 'Do instructional interventions influence college students' critical thinking skills? A meta-analysis', *Educational Research Review*, 9, 114–128

Niu, W. (2009). 'Development of creativity research in Chinese societies', in J.C. Kaufman and R.J. Sternberg (eds) *The International Handbook of Creativity*, New York: Cambridge University Press, 374–94.

Norman, D.A. (2002) 'Emotions and design: Attractive things work better', *Interactions*, 9(4): 36–42.

Novak, J.D. (2010) *Learning, Creating and Using Knowledge: Concept Maps as Facilitative Tools in Schools and Corporations*, London: Routledge.

Nussbaum, J.F. (1992) 'Effective teacher behaviors', *Communication Education*, 41: 167–80.

Nussbaum, M.C. (2001) *Upheavals of Thought*, New York: Cambridge University Press.

Nussbaum, J.F., Comadena, M.E. and Holladay, S.J. (1987) 'Classroom verbal behavior of highly effective teachers', *Journal of Thought*, 2: 73–80.

O'Quin, K. and Besemer, S. P. (1989) 'The development, reliability and validity of the Revised Creative Product Semantic Scale' *Creativity Research Journal*, 2: 268–79.

O'Regan, K. (2003) 'Emotion and e-learning', *Journal of Asynchronous Learning Networks*, 7(3): 78–92.

Oaksford, M., Morris, F., Grainger, B. and Williams, J.M.G. (1996) 'Mood, reasoning and central executive processes', *Journal of Experimental Psychology: Learning, Memory and Cognition*, 22(2): 476–92.

Oatley, K. (2002) 'Emotions and the story worlds of fiction', in M.C. Green, J.J. Strange and T.C. Brock (eds) *Narrative Impact*, Mahwah: Lawrence Erlbaum, 39–70.

Oatley, K. (2009) 'Communications to self and others', *Emotion Review*, 1(3): 206–13.

Oatley, K. and Jenkins, J.M. (1996) *Understanding Emotions*, Oxford: Blackwell.

Olitsky, S. (2007) 'Promoting student engagement in science', *Journal of Research in Science Teaching*, 44(1): 33–56.

Onyeizugbo, E.U. (2010) 'Self-efficacy, gender and trait anxiety as moderators of text anxiety', *Electronic Journal of Research in Educational Psychology*, 8(1): 299–312.

Ortner, T.M. and Caspers, J. (2011) 'Consequences of test anxiety on adaptive testing versus fixed item testing', *European Journal of Psychological Assessment*, 27(3): 157–63.

Osborne, T. (2003) 'Against "creativity": A philistine rant', *Economy and Society*, 32(4): 507–25.

Otto, J.H. (2001) 'Mood as input', *Zeitschrift für Sozialpsychologie*, 32(1): 1–11.

Ozoliņš, J.T. (2013) 'R.S. Peters and J.H. Newman on the aims of education', *Educational Philosophy and Theory*, 45(2): 153–70.

Padgett, R. (1994) 'Creative reading', in C. Edgar and R. Padgett (eds) *Educating the Imagination*, New York: Teachers & Writers Collaborative, 244–59.

Palfai, T.P. and Salovery, P. (1993/94) 'The influence of depressed and elated mood on deductive and inductive reasoning', *Imagination, Cognition and Personality*, 13(1): 57–71.

Paris, S.G. (2001) 'Wisdom, snake oil, and the educational marketplace', *Educational Psychologist*, 36(4): 257–60.

Park, S., Soo-Young, L., Oliver, S. and Cramond, B. (2006) 'Changes in Korean science teachers' perceptions of creativity and science teaching after participating in an overseas professional development program', *Journal of Science Teacher Education*, 17(1): 37–64.

Parkinson, B. (1995) *Ideas and Realities of Emotion*, London: Routledge.

Parkinson, B. and Totterdell, P. (1999) 'Classifying affect-regulation strategies', *Cognition & Emotion*, 13(3): 277–303.

Pascual-Leone, J. (1990) 'An essay on wisdom', in R.J. Sternberg (ed.) *Wisdom: Its nature, origins and development*, Cambridge: Cambridge University Press, 160–77.

Paul, R. (1993) *Critical Thinking*, Santa Rosa: Foundation for Critical Thinking.

Payne, M.A. (2010) 'Use-it-or-lose-it? Interrogating an educational message from the teen brain research', *Australian Journal of Teacher Education*, 35(5): 79–91.

Pearson, H. (1977) *The Smith of Smiths*, London: The Folio Society.

Peirce, C.S. (1923/1998) *Chance, Love and Logic*, Lincoln: University of Nebraska.

Pêcher, C., Lemercier, C. and Cellier, J-M. (2009) 'Emotions drive attention', *Safety Science*, 47(9): 1254–59.

Pekrun, R. (1992) The impact of emotions on learning and achievement, *Applied Psychology: An International Review*, 41(4): 359–76.

Pekrun, R. (2006) 'The control-value theory of achievement emotions', *Educational Psychology Review*, 18: 315–41.

Pekrun, R. (2011) 'Emotions as drivers of learning and cognitive development', *New Perspectives on Affect and Learning Technologies*, 3(1): 23–39.

Pekrun, R., Elliot, A.J. and Maier, M.A. (2009) 'Achievement goals and achievement emotions', *Journal of Educational Psychology*, 101(1): 115–35.

Pekrun, R., Goetz, T., Titz, W. and Perry, R.P. (2006) 'Academic emotions in students' self-regulated learning and achievement', *Educational Psychologist*, 37(2): 91–106.

Pekrun, R. and Linnenbrink-Garcia, L. (2012) 'Academic emotions and student engagement', in S.L. Christenson, A.L. Reschly and C. Wylie (eds) *Handbook of Research on Student Engagement*, New York, Springer, 259–82.

Pennington, M.C. (1996) 'The "cognitive-affective filter" in teacher development', *System*, 24(3): 337–50.

Perels, F., Gürtler, T., Schmitz, B. (2005) 'Training of self-regulatory and problem-solving competence', *Learning and Instruction*, 15: 123–39.

Perkins, D. (1993) 'Teaching for understanding', *American Educator*, 17, 28–35.

Perkins, D. (1995) *Outsmarting IQ: The emerging science of learnable intelligence*, New York: Free Press.

Perkins, D., Jay, E. and Tishman, S. (1993) 'Beyond abilities: A dispositional theory of thinking', *Merrill-Palmer Quarterly*, 39(1): 1–21.

Perlovsky. L.I. and Levine, S.D. (2010) 'Drive for creativity', paper presented at the International Joint Conference on Neural Networks, Barcelona, July.

Perlstein, W.M., Elbert, T. and Stenger, V.A. (2002) 'Dissociation in human prefrontal cortex of affective influences on working memory-related activity', *Proceedings of the National Academy of Science, USA*, 99: 1736–41.

Perry, N.E., VandeKamp, K.O., Mercer, L.K. and Nordby, C.J. (2002) 'Investigating teacher–student interactions that foster self-regulated learning', *Educational Psychologist*, 37(1): 5–15.

Pessoa, L. (2008) 'On the relationship between emotion and cognition', *Perspectives*, 9, 148–58.

Peters, E., Västfjäll, D., Gärling, T. and Slovic, P. (2006) 'Affect and decision making', *Journal of Behavioral Decision Making*, 19: 79–85.

Peterson, C. and Whalen, N. (2001) 'Five years later: Children's memory for medical emergencies', *Applied Cognitive Psychology*, 15: 17–24.

Peterson, D.S. and Taylor, B.M. (2012) 'Using higher order questioning to accelerate students' growth in reading', *Reading Teacher*, 65(5): 295–304.

Petty, G. (1997) *How to be Better at Creativity*, London: Kogan Page.

Pham, M.T. (2007) 'Emotions and rationality', *Review of General Psychology*, 11(2): 155–78.

Phelps, E.A. (2006) 'Emotion and cognition', *Annual Review of Psychology*, 57: 27–53.

Phillips, H. (2003) 'The pleasure seekers', *New Scientist*, 11 October: 36–43.

Piaget, J. (1952) *The Origins of Intelligence in Children*, New York: International Universities Press.

Piaget, J. (1972) 'Intellectual evolution from adolescence to adulthood', *Human Development*, 15: 1–12.

Piaget, J. (1978) *Success and understanding*, London: Routledge & Kegan Paul.

Pimental, C.F. (2011) 'Should I teach or should I learn? – group learning based on the influence of mood', *Affective Computing and Intelligent Interaction*, 6975: 72–80.

Pink, D.H. (2005) *A Whole New Mind*, New York: Penguin.

Pintrich, P.R. (1999) 'The role of motivation in promoting and sustaining self-regulated learning', *International Journal of Educational Research*, 31(6): 459–70.

Pintrich, P.R. and De Groot, E.V. (1990) 'Motivational and self-regulated learning components of classroom academic performance', *Journal of Educational Psychology*, 82: 33–40.

Pithers, R.T. and Soden, R. (2000) 'Critical thinking in education: A review', *Educational Research*, 42(3): 237–49.

Pleij, H. (2002) 'Restyling 'wisdom', remodelling the nobility, and caricaturing the peasant', *Journal of Interdisciplinary History*, 32(4): 689–704.

Plutchik, R. (1980) 'A general psychoevolutionary theory of emotion', in R. Plutchik, and H. Kellerman (eds) *Emotion: Theory & Research*, Vol. 1, *Theories of Emotion*, New York: Academic Press, 3–33.

Poggiani, F. (2012) 'What makes reasoning sound?' *Transactions of the C.S. Peirce Society*, 48(1): 32–50.

Pooley, J.A. and Cohen, L. (2010) 'Resilience: A definition in context', *Australian Community Psychologist*, 22(1): 30–6.

Popp, P.A., Grant, L.W. and Stronge, J.H. (2011) 'Effective teachers for at-risk or highly mobile students', *Journal of Education for Students Placed at Risk*, 16: 275–91.

Poskiparta, E., Niemi, P., Lepola, J., Ahtola, A. and Laine, P. (2003) 'Motivational-emotional vulnerability and difficulties in learning to read and spell', *British Journal of Educational Psychology*, 73(2): 187–206.

Prinz, J. (2004) 'Which emotions are basic?' in D. Evans and P. Cruse (eds) *Emotions, Evolution and Rationality*, Oxford: Oxford University Press, 69–87.

Pring, R. (2010) 'The need for a wider vision of learning', *International Studies in Sociology of Education*, 20(1): 83–91.

Pullis, M. (1985) 'Students' temperament characteristics and their impact on decisions by resource and mainstream teachers', *Learning Disability Quarterly*, 8: 109–22.

Pullis, M. and Cadwell, J. (1982) 'The influence of children's temperament on teachers' decision strategies, *American Educational Research Journal*, 19(2): 165–81.

Purdie, N. and Hattie, J. (1996) 'Cultural differences in the use of strategies for self-regulated learning', *American Educational Research Journal*, 33(4): 845–71.

Putwain, D.W. (2009) 'Assessment and examination stress in Key Stage 4', *British Educational Research Journal*, 35(3): 391–411.

Putwain, D.W., Connors, L. and Symes, W. (2010) 'Do cognitive distortions mediate the test anxiety–examination performance relationship?' *Educational Psychology*, 30(1): 11–26.

Putwain, D.W., Langdale, H.C., Woods, K.A. and Nicholson, L.J. (2011) 'Developing and piloting a dot-probe measure of attentional bias for test anxiety', *Learning & Individual Differences*, 21: 478–82.

QCA/Qualifications and Curriculum Authority (2005) *Creativity: Find it, promote it!* London: QCA.

Radenhausen, R.A. and Anker, J.M. (1988) 'Effects of depressed mood induction on reasoning performance', *Perceptual and Motor Skills*, 66: 855–60.

Rader, N. and Hughes, E. (2005) 'The influence of affective state on the performance of a block design task in 6- and 7-year-old children', *Cognition & Emotion*, 19(1): 143–50.

Ragozinno, K., Resnik, H., Utne-O'Brien, M. and Weissberg, R.P. (2003) *Educational Horizons*, Summer: 169–71.

Ragozinno, M.E., Km, J., Hassert, D., Minniti, N. and Kiang, C. (2003) 'The contribution of the rat prelimbic-infralimbic areas to different forms of task switching', *Behavioral Neuroscience*, 117: 1054–65.

Rank, J. and Frese, M. (2008) 'The impact of emotion, moods and other affect-related variables on creativity, innovation and initiative in organizations', in N.M. Ashkanasy and C.L. Cooper (eds) *Research Companion to Emotions in Organizations*, Cheltenham: Edward Elgar, 103–19.

Reddy, W.M. (2001) *The Navigation of Feeling*, Cambridge: Cambridge University Press.

Reisenzein, R. (2009) 'Emotions as metarepresentational states of mind', *Cognitive Systems Research*, 10(1): 6–20.

Repetto, R. and Holmes, T. (1983) 'The role of population in resource depletion in developing countries', *Population and Development Review*, 9(4): 609–32.

Reznitskaya, M., Kuo, L.-J., Clark, A.-M., Miller, B., Jadallah, M., Anderson, R.C. and Nguyen-Jahiel, K. (2009) 'Collaborative reasoning', *Cambridge Journal of Education*, 38(1): 29–48.

Ria, L., Sève, C., Saury, J., Theureau, J. and Durand, M. (2003) 'Beginning teachers' situated emotions', *Journal of Education for Teaching*, 29(3): 219–33.

Richards, A., French, C.C., Nash, G., Hadwin, J.A. and Donnelly, N. (2007) 'A comparison of selective attention and facial processing biases in typically developing children who are high and low in self-reported trait anxiety', *Development and Psychopathology*, 19: 481–95.

Richards, H.J. and Hadwin, J.A. (2011) 'An exploration of the relationship between trait anxiety and school attendance in young people', *School Mental Health*, 3(4): 236–44.

Richards, J.C. and Rodgers, T.S. (1986) *Approaches and Methods in Language Teaching*, Cambridge: Cambridge University Press.

Richardson, P.W., Watt, H.M.G. and Devos, C. (2013) 'Types of professional and emotional coping among beginning teachers', Online. Available at doi: 10.1108/S1479-3687(2013)0000018016 (accessed 25 June 2013).

Richmond, V.A., Gorham, J.S. & McCrosky, J.C. (1987) 'The relationship between selected immediacy behaviors and cognitive learning', in M. McLaughlin (ed.) *Communication Yearbook 10*, Beverly Hills: Sage.

Risemberg, R. and Zimmerman, B.J. (1992) 'Self-regulated learning in gifted students', *Roeper Review*, 15(2): 98–101.

Ritchie, K.C., Shore, B.M., LaBanca, F. and Newman, A.J. (2011) 'The impact of emotions on divergent thinking processes', *Mind, Brain and Education*, 5(1): 211–25.

Robinson, M.D. (2000) 'The reactive and prospective function of moods', *Cognition & Emotion*, 14(2): 145–76.

Roca, E. (2008) 'Introducing practical wisdom in business schools', *Journal of Business Ethics*, 82: 607–20.

Rodeiro, C.L.V., Bell, J.F. and Emery, J.L. (2009) *Can Emotional and Social Abilities Predict Differences in Attainment at Secondary School?* Cambridge: Cambridge Local Examinations Syndicate.

Rook, L. and van Knippenberg, D. (2011) 'Creativity and imitation: Effects of regulatory focus and creative exemplar quality', *Creativity Research Journal*, 23(4): 346–56.

Rosenberg, B.G. and Langer, J. (1965) 'A study of postural-gestural communication', *Journal of Personality and Social Psychology*, 2(4): 593–7.

Rosenshine, B. (1970) 'Enthusiastic teaching: A research review', *School Review*, 78: 499–514.

Rosenstein, J.G., Caldwell, J.H., and Crown, W.D. (1996) *New Jersey Mathematics Curriculum Framework*, New Jersey: New Jersey Mathematics Coalition.

Ross, W.D., Ackrill, J.L. and Urmston, J.O. (1980) *Aristotle's Nicomachean Ethics*, New York: Oxford University Press.

Rothbart, M.K. (2012) *Becoming Who We Are*, New York: Guilford Press.

Rothbart, M.K. and Jones, L.B. (1998) 'Temperament, self-regulation and education', *School Psychology Review*, 27(4): 479–91.

Roy, S. (2007) 'Creativity, complexity and physics education', paper presented at the Complexity Science and Educational Research Conference, Vancouver, February.

Rude, S., Gortner, E.-M. and Pennebaker, J. (2004) 'Language use of depressed and depression-vulnerable college students', *Cognition & Emotion*, 18(8): 1121–33.

Rudinow, J. and Barry, V.E. (1999) *Invitation to Critical Thinking*, Fort Worth: Harcourt Brace.

Rueda, M.R., Posner, M.I. and Rothbart, M.K. (2005) 'The development of executive attention', *Developmental Neuropsychology*, 28(2): 573–94.

Russ, S. (1996) 'Development of creative processes in children', *New Directions for Child Development*, 72: 31–42.

Russ, S. and Grossman-McKee, A. (1990) 'Affective expression in children's fantasy play', *Journal of Personality Assessment*, 54: 756–71.

Ryan, S. (1999) 'What is wisdom', *Philosophical Studies*, 93: 119–39.

Saarikallio, S. and Erkkilä, J. (2007) 'The role of music in adolescents' mood regulation', *Psychology in Education*, 35(1): 88–109.

Sadovnichiy, V. (2006) 'Knowledge and wisdom in the globalizing world', *Philosophy Now*, 54: 12–13.

Sakiz, G., Pape, S.J. and Woolfolk, H. (2012) 'Does perceived teacher affective support matter for middle school students in mathematics classes?' *Journal of School Psychology*, 50(2): 235–55.

Samad, N.I.A., Hashim, Z., Moin, S. and Abdullah, H. (2010) 'Assessment of stress and its risk factors among primary school teachers in the Klang Valley, Malaysia', *Global Journal of Health Science*, 2(2): 163–71.

Samson, A.C. and Gross, J.J. (2012) 'Humour as emotion regulation', *Cognition & Emotion*, 26(2): 375–84.

Sánchez-Escobedo, P. (2013) 'A cross comparative international study on the concept of wisdom', *Gifted Education* International, Online. Available at doi: 10.1177/ 0261429413486575 (accessed 25 June 2013).

Sand, G. (1876) *Auteur de la table*, Paris: Lévy Frères.

Sayfan, L. and Lagattuta, K.H. (2008) 'Grown-ups are not afraid of scary stuff but kids are', *Child Development*, 79(4): 821–35.

Scherer, K.R., Johnstone, T. and Klasmeyer, G. (2003) 'Vocal expression of emotion', in R.J. Davidson, K.R. Scherer and H.H. Goldsmith (eds) *Handbook of Affective Sciences*, Oxford: Oxford University Press, 433–56.

Schnall, S. (2011) 'Clean, proper and tidy are more than the absence of dirty, disgusting and wrong', *Emotion Review*, 3(3): 264–66.

Schnall, S., Benton, J. and Harvey, S. (2008a) 'With a clean conscience', *Psychological Science*, 19(12): 1219–22.

Schnall, S., Haidt, J., Clore, G.L. and Jordan, A.H. (2008b) 'Disgust as embodied moral judgment', *Personal Social Psychology Bulletin*, 34(8): 1096–109.

Schnall, S., Jaswal, V.K. and Rowe, C. (2008c) 'A hidden cost of happiness in children', *Developmental Science*, 11(5): F25–F30.

Schnall, S. and Laird, J.D. (2003) 'Keep smiling', *Cognition & Emotion*, 17(5): 787–97.

Schollmeier, P. (1989) 'Aristotle on practical wisdom', *Zeitschrift für philosophische Forschung*, 43(5): 124–32.

Schonfeld, I.S. (1990) 'Coping with job-related stress', *Journal of Occupational Psychology*, 63(2): 141–9.

Schraw, G., Crippen, K.J. and Hartley, K. (2006) 'Promoting self-regulation in science education', *Research in Science Education*, 36: 111–39.

Schunk, D.H. (2012) *Learning Theories*, Boston: Pearson.

Schupp, H., Cuthbert, B., Bradley, M., Hillman, C., Hamm, A. and Lang, P. (2004) 'Brain processes in emotional perception: Motivated attention', *Cognition & Emotion*, 18(5): 593–611.

Schutz, P.A., Aultman, L.P. and Williams-Johnson, M.R. (2009) 'Educational psychology perspectives on teachers' emotions', *Advances in Teacher Emotion Research*, 3: 195–212.

Schutz, P.A. and Lanehart, S.L. (2002) 'Introduction: Emotions in education', *Educational Psychologist*, 37(2): 67–8.

Schutz, P.A. and Zembylas, M. (2009) 'Introduction to advances in teacher emotion research: The impact on teachers' lives', *Advances in Teacher Emotion Research*, 1: 3–11.

Schuwirth, L. (2013) '"Emotions in learning" is more than merely "learning of emotions"', *Medical Education*, 47(1): 14–15.

Schwartz, N. (2002) 'Situation cognition and the wisdom of feelings', in L. F. Barrett and P. Salovey (eds) *The Wisdom in Feeling*, New York: Guilford, 144–66.

Schwartz, N. and Clore, C.L. (1983) 'Mood, misattribution and judgments of well-being', *Journal of Personality and Social Psychology*, 45(3): 513–23.

Schwartz, S.H. (1994) 'Are there universal aspects in the structure and contents of human values?' *Journal of Social Issues*, 50(4): 19–45.

Schwartz, S. (2012) '10,000 books, 10,000 miles: the journey towards wisdom', Macquarie University Research Online. Available at researchonline.mq.edu.au (accessed 8 October 2013).

Scott, R.B.Y. (1961) 'Priesthood, prophecy, wisdom, and the knowledge of God', *Journal of Biblical Literature*, 80(1): 1–15.

Segool, N.K., Carlson, J.S., Gosforth, A.N., Embse, N. and Barterian, J.A. (2013) 'Heightened test anxiety among young children', *Psychology in the Schools*, 50(5): 489–99.

Sercombe, H. (2010) 'The gift and the trap: working the "teen brain" into our concept of youth', *Journal of Adolescent Research*, 25(1): 31–47.

Sergerie, K., Lepage, M. and Armony, J.L. (2007) 'Influence of emotional expression on memory recognition bias', *Biological Psychiatry*, 62: 1126–33.

Shaheen, R. (2010) 'Creativity and education', *Creative Education*, 1(3): 166–9.

Sharp, C. and Le Métais, J. (2000) *The Arts, Creativity and Cultural Education: An International Perspective*, London: QCA.

Siegel, H. (with S. Johnson, ed. C. Winch) (2010) *Teaching Thinking Skills*, London: Continuum.

Siegesmund, R. (1998) 'Why do we teach art today?' *Studies in Art Education*, 39(3): 197–214.

Signer, M.A. (2008) 'Rabbi and Magister: Overlapping models of the twelfth-century renaissance', *Jewish History*, 22: 114–37.

Silva, Z.B. (2012) 'Saudade: A key Portuguese emotion', *Emotion Review*, 4(2): 203–11.

Simeonova, D.I., Chang, K.D., Strong, C. and Ketter, T.A. (2005) 'Creativity in familial bipolar disorder', *Journal of Psychiatric Research*, 39: 623–31.

Skinner, E.A. and Belmont, M.J. (1993) 'Motivation in the classroom', *Journal of Educational Psychology*, 85(4): 571–81.

Slife, B.D. and Weaver, C.A. (1992) 'Depression, cognitive skill, and metacognitive skill in problem solving', *Cognition & Emotion*, 6(1): 1–22.

Small, D.A., Lerner, J.S. and Fischhoff, B. (2006) 'Emotion priming and attribution for terrorism', *Political Psychology*, 27(2): 289–98.

Smallwood, J., Fitzgerald, A., Lynden, K. and Phillips, L.H. (2009) 'Shifting moods, wandering minds', *Emotion*, 9(2): 271–76.

Smith, J., Staudinger, U.M. and Baltes, P.B. (1994) 'Occupational settings facilitating wisdom-related knowledge', *Journal of Consulting and Clinical Psychology*, 62(5): 989–99.

Sofowara, O.A. (2007) 'The use of educational cartoons and comics in enhancing creativity in primary school pupils in Ile-ife, Osun State, Nigeria', *Journal of Applied Sciences Research*, 3: 913–20.

Sokolon, M.K. (2006) *Political Emotions: Aristotle and the symphony of reason and emotion*, DeKalb: Northern Illinois University.

Southam-Gerow, M.A. and Kendall, P.C. (2002) 'Emotion regulation and understanding', *Clinical Psychology Review*, 22: 189–222.

Spada, M.M., Nikčević, A.V., Moneta, G.B. and Wells, A. (2008) 'Metacognition, perceived stress and negative emotion', *Personality and Individual Differences*, 44: 1172–81.

Spellman, B. and Schnall, B. (2009) 'Embodied rationality', *Queen's Law Journal*, 35(1): 117–64.

Spering, M., Wagener, D. and Funke, J. (2005) 'The role of emotions in complex problem-solving', *Cognition & Emotion*, 19(8): 1252–61.

Spicer, F. (2004) 'Emotional behaviour and the scope of belief-desire explanation', in D. Evans and P. Cruse (eds) *Emotions, Evolution and Rationality*, Oxford: Oxford University Press, 51–68.

Spielberger, C.D. and Vagg, P.R. (1995) *Test Anxiety: Theory, assessment and treatment*, Washington: Taylor & Francis.

Sripada, C.S. and Stich, S. (2004) 'Evolution, culture, and the irrationality of emotions', in D. Evans and P. Cruse, *Emotions, Evolution and Rationality*, Oxford: Oxford University Press, 133–58.

Stanger-Hall, K.F. (2012) 'Multiple-choice exams: An obstacle for higher-level thinking in introductory science classes', *Life Sciences Education*, 11(3): 294–306.

Stanko-Kaczmarek, M. (2012) 'The effect of intrinsic motivation on the affect and evaluation of the creative process among fine art students', *Creativity Research Journal*, 24(4): 304–10.

Stanovich, K.E. (2010) 'The rationality of teaching for wisdom', *Educational Psychologist*, 36(4): 247–51.

Staudinger, U.M. and Glück, J. (2011) 'Psychological wisdom research', *Annual Review of Psychology*, 62: 215–41.

Stedman, N.L.P. and Adams, B.L. (2012) 'Identifying faculty's knowledge of critical thinking concepts and perceptions of critical thinking in instruction in Higher Education', *NACTA Journal*, June: 9–14.

Stein, N.L. and Albro, E.R. (2001) 'The origins and nature of arguments', *Discourse Processes*, 32(2/3): 113–33.

Stein, N.L. and Levine, L.J. (1999) 'The causal organization of emotional knowledge', *Cognition and Emotion*, 3: 343–78.

Steinberg, L. (2007) 'Risk taking in adolescence', *Current Directions in Psychological Science*, 16(2): 55-9.

Sternberg, R.J. (1985) 'Implicit theories of intelligence, creativity and wisdom', *Journal of Personality and Social Psychology*, 49: 607–27.

Sternberg, R.J. (2001) 'Why schools should teach for wisdom', *Educational Psychologist*, 36(4): 227–45.

Sternberg, R.J. (2003) *Wisdom, Intelligence and Creativity Synthesized*, New York: Cambridge University Press.

Sternberg, R.J. (2005) 'Older but not wiser? The relationship between age and wisdom', *Ageing International*, 30(1): 5–26.

Sternberg, R.J. (2006) 'The nature of creativity', *Creativity Research Journal*, 18(1): 87–98.

Sternberg, R.J. (2013) 'What is cognitive education?' *Journal of Cognitive Education and Psychology*, 12(1): 45–58.

Stipeck, D. (2002) *Motivation to Learn*, Boston: Allyn and Bacon.

Stollstorff, M., Bean, S.E., Anderson, L.M., Devaney, J.M. and Vaidya, C.J. (2013) 'Rationality and emotionality', *Social, Cognitive and Affective Neuroscience*, 8(4): 404–9.

Stough, L. and Emmer, E. (1998) 'Teacher emotions and test feedback', *International Journal of Qualitative Studies in Education*, 11: 341–62.

Stowell, J.R. and Bennett, D. (2010) 'Effects of online testing on student exam performance and test anxiety', *Journal of Educational Computing Research*, 42(2): 161–71.

Strain, A.C., Azevedo, R. and D'Mello, S.K. (2012) 'Using a false biofeedback methodology to explore relationships between learners' affect, metacognition, and performance', *Contemporary Educational Psychology*, 38: 22–39.

Sutton, R.E. (2007) 'Teachers' anger, frustration and self-regulation', in P.A. Schutz and R. Pekrun (eds) *Emotion in Education*, Burlington: Academic Press, 259–74.

Sutton, R.E. and Wheatley, K.F. (2003) 'Teachers' emotions and teaching', *Educational Psychology Review*, 15(4): 327–58.

Svantesson, I. (1989) *Mind Mapping and Memory*, London: Kogan Page.

Swain, M. (2013) 'The inseparability of cognition and emotion in second language learning', *Language Teaching*, 46(2): 195–207.

Sylvester, R. (1994) 'How emotions affect learning', *Educational Leadership*, October: 60–5.

Takahashi, M. (2000) 'Towards a culturally inclusive understanding of wisdom', *International Journal of Aging and Human Development*, 47(1): 1–19.

Talarico, J.M., Berntsen, D. and Rubin, D.C. (2009) 'Positive moods enhance recall of peripheral details', *Cognition & Emotion*, 23(2): 380–98.

Tamir, M. (2011) 'The maturing field of emotion regulation', *Emotion Review*, 3(1): 3–7.

Tan, A.-G. (2000) 'A review of the study of creativity in Singapore', *Journal of Creative Behavior*, 34(4): 259–84.

Tang, J.J., Leka, S. and MacLennan, S. (2012) 'The psychosocial work environment and mental health of teachers', *International Archives of Occupational and Environmental Health*, 1–10.

Taylor, C. (2007) *A Secular Age*, Cambridge: Belknap.

Tello, N (2010) 'Fostering confidence in speaking through participating in a Radio Show', Master's thesis, Universidad de la Sabana, Colombia.

Thagard, P. and Shelley, C. (1997) 'Abductive reasoning: Logic, visual thinking and coherence', in M.L. Dalla Chiara (ed.) *Logic and Scientific Methods*, Dordrecht: Kluwer, 413–27.

Thayer, R.E., Newman, J.R. and McClain, T.M. (1994) 'Self-regulation of mood', *Journal of Personality and Social Psychology*, 67(5): 910–25.

Thayer-Bacon, B. (1998) 'Transforming and re-describing critical thinking: Constructive thinking', *Studies in Philosophy & Education*, 17(2/3): 123–48.

Thompson, T. and Perry, Z. (2005) 'Is the poor performance of self-worth protective students linked with social comparison goals?' *Educational Psychology*, 25(5): 471–90.

Tickle, L. (1991) 'New teachers and the emotions of learning teaching', *Cambridge Journal of Education*, 21(3): 319–29.

Tiedens, L.Z. and Linton, S. (2001) 'Judgment under emotional certainty and uncertainty', *Journal of Personality and Social Psychology*, 81: 973–88.

Tooby, J. and Cosmides, L. (1990) 'The past explains the present', *Ethology and Sociobiology*, 11: 375–424.

Trickey, S. and Topping, K.J. (2004) 'Philosophy for Children', *Research Papers in Education*, 19(3): 365–80.

Trigwell, K., Ellis, R.A. and Han, F. (2012) 'Relations between students' approaches to learning, experienced emotions and outcomes of learning', *Studies in Higher Education*, 37(7): 811–24.

Truong, G., Turk, D.J. and Handy, T.C. (2013) 'An unforgettable apple', Online. Available at doi: 10.3758/s13415-013-0174-6 (accessed 25 June 2013).

Tucker, D.M., Hartry-Speiser, A. McDougal, L., Luu, P. and de Grandpre, D. (1999) 'Mood and spatial memory', *Biological Psychology*, 50: 103–25.

Tugade, M.M. and Fredrickson, B.L. (2004) 'Resilient individuals use positive emotions to bounce back from negative emotional experiences', *Journal of Personality and Social Psychology*, 86(2): 320–33.

Tugade, M.M. and Fredrickson, B.L. (2007) 'Regulation of positive emotions', *Journal of Happiness Studies*, 8: 311–33.

Turner, S. & Braine, M. (2013) 'Embedding therapeutic training in teacher education', *Teacher Education Network Journal*, 5(1): 4–18.

Turner, J.C., Midgley, C., Meyer, D.K., Gheen, M., Anderman, E.M., Kang and Patrick, H. (2002) 'The classroom environment and students' reports of avoidance strategies in mathematics', *Journal of Educational Psychology*, 94(1): 88–106.

Tversky, A. and Kahneman, D. (1974) 'Judgment under uncertainty: Heuristics and biases', *Science*, 185: 1124–31.

Tversky, A. and Kahneman, D. (1981) 'The framing of decisions and the psychology of choice', *Science*, 211(4481): 453–8.

Um, E., Plass, J.L., Hayward, E.O. and Homer, B.D. (2012) 'Emotional design in multimedia learning', *Journal of Educational Psychology*, 104(2): 485–98.

Valdesolo, P. and DeSteno, D. (2006) 'Manipulations of emotional context shape moral judgment', *Psychological Science*, 17: 476–7.

Valdez, J. (1993) '*Wisdom: A Hispanic perspective*', Doctoral dissertation, Colorado State University.

van der Zee, Thijs, M., and Schakel, L. (2002) 'The relationship of emotional intelligence with academic intelligence and the Big Five', *European Journal of Personality*, 16: 103–25.

van Gelder, T. (2005) 'Teaching critical thinking', *College Teaching*, 53(1): 41–6.

van Goethem, A. and Sloboda, J. (2011) 'The functions of music for affect', *Musicae Scienticiae*, 15(2): 208–28.

van Merriënboer, J.J.G. and Sweller, J. (2005) 'Cognitive load theory and complex learning', *Educational Psychology Review*, 17(2): 147–77.

Vandekerckhove, M. and Panskepp, J. (2009) 'The flow of anoetic to noetic and autonoetic consciousness', *Consciousness and Cognition*, 18(4): 1018–28.

Varga, A. and Stulrajterova, M. (2008) 'Presentations in ESL classes', *Didactica*, 1(1): 25–8.

Venville, G.J. and Dawson, V.M. (2010) 'The impact of a classroom intervention on Grade 10 students' argumentation skills, informal reasoning, and conceptual understanding of science', *Journal of Research in Science Teaching*, 47(8): 952–77.

Vince, R. (2006) 'Being taken over', *Journal of Management Studies*, 43(2): 343–65.

Vitters, J., Overwien, P. and Martinsen, E. (2009) 'Pleasure and interest are differentially affected by replaying versus analyzing a happy life moment', *Journal of Positive Psychology*, 4(1): 14–20.

Vogel, N. (2001) *Making the Most of Plan–Do–Review: The teacher's idea book 5*, Ypsilanti: High/Scope Press.

Vosburg, S.K. (1998) 'Mood and the quantity and quality of ideas', *Creativity Research Journal*, 11(4): 315–24.

Vosgerau, J. (2010) 'How prevalent is wishful thinking? Misattribution of arousal causes optimism and pessimism in subjective probabilities', *Journal of Experimental Psychology: General*, 139(1): 32–48.

Vygotsky, L. (1978) *Mind in Society*, Cambridge, MA: Harvard University Press.

Wachelka, D. and Katz, R.C. (1999) 'Reducing test anxiety and improving academic self-esteem in high school and college students with learning disabilities', *Journal of Behavior Therapy*, 30: 191–8.

Wade, C. (1995) 'Using writing to develop and assess critical thinking', *Teaching of Psychology*, 22(1): 24–8.

Wagner, P.A. and Penner, J. (1984) 'The new approach to teach forms of reasoning to the gifted', *Roeper Review*, 6(4): 188–91.

Walker, W.R., Skowronski, J.J. and Thompson, C.P. (2003) 'Life is pleasant – and memory helps to keep it that way', *Review of General Psychology*, 7(2): 203–10.

Wallas, G. (1926) *The Art of Thought*, New York: Harcourt Brace & World.

Wanzer, M.B. and McCroskey, J.C. (1998) 'Teacher socio-communicative style as a correlate of student affect toward teacher and course material', *Communication Education*, 47: 43–52.

Watkins, C. (2001) 'Learning about learning enhances performance', *National School Improvement Network Bulletin*, 13: 1–7.

Watson, D. (2000) *Mood and Temperament*, New York: Guilford.

Waxman, H.C. and Walberg, H. J. (1986) 'Teaching and productivity', *Education and Urban Society*, 18(2): 211–20.

Webster, J.D. (2010) 'Wisdom and positive psychosocial values in young adulthood', *Journal of Adult Development*, 17: 70–80.

Webster-Stratton (1995) 'Helping children learn to regulate their emotions', Online. Available at http://w.incredibleyears.com/ParentResources/helping-children-regulate-emotions.pdf (accessed 30 May 2013.)

Weems, C.F., Scott, B.G., Taylor, L. K., Cannon, M.F., Romano, D.M., Perry, A.M. and Triplett, V. (2010) 'Test anxiety prevention and intervention programs in schools', *School Mental Health*, 2(2): 62–71.

Weinstein, A. M. (1995) 'Visual ERPs evidence for enhanced processing of threatening information in anxious university students', *Biological Psychiatry*, 37: 847–58.

Weissman, M.M., Canino, G.J., Greenwald, S., Joyce, P.R., Karam, E.G., Lee, C.K., Rubio-Stipec, M., Wells, J.E., Wickramaratne, P.J. and Wittchen, H.U. (1995) 'Current rates and symptom profiles of panic disorder in six cross-national studies', *Clinical Neuropharmacology*, 18: S1–S6.

Wellman, H.M. and Bartsch, K. (1988) 'Young children's reasoning about beliefs', *Cognition*, 30: 239–77.

Wells, J. (2011) 'International education, values and attitudes: A critical analysis of the International Baccalaureate Learner Profile', *Journal of Research in International Education*, 10(2): 174–88.

Wessel, I. and Wright, D.B. (2004) 'Emotional memory failures', *Cognition & Emotion*, 18(4): 449–55.

Whipp, J. and Chiavelli, S. (2004) 'Self-regulation in a web-based course', *Educational Technology Research & Development*, 52(4): 5–22.

White, C. E. (2010) 'Mathematics and anti-mathematics', *School Science and Mathematics*, 19(1): 29–37.

White, D.A. and Robinson, R. (2001) 'Critical thinking and artistic creation', *Journal of Aesthetic Education*, 35(2): 77–85.

White, J. (2007) *What Schools are for and Why*, London: Philosophy Society of Great Britain.

Wild, T.C., Enzle, M.E., Nix, G. and Deci, E.L. (1997) 'Perceiving others as intrinsically or extrinsically motivated', *Personality and Social Psychology Bulletin*, 23: 837–48.

Willis, J. (2007) 'The neuroscience of joyful education', *Educational Leadership*, 64: 1–5.

Wilson, D.F. (2004) *Supporting Teachers Supporting Pupils*, London: RoutledgeFalmer.

Wilson, E., MacLeod, C, Mathews, A. & Rutherford, E.M. (2006) 'The causal role of the interpretive bias in anxiety reactivity', *Journal of Abnormal Psychology*, 115, 103-11.

Wineburg, S.S. and Wilson, S.M. (1991) 'Models of wisdom in the teaching of history', *History Teacher*, 24(4): 395–412.

Winne, P.H., Nesbit, J.C., Kumar, V., Hadwin, A.F., Lajoie, S.P., Azevedo, R. and Perry, N.E. (2006) 'Supporting self-regulated learning with gStudy software', *Technology, Instruction, Cognition and Learning*, 3: 105–13.

Wolters, C.A. (1998) 'Self-regulated learning and college students' regulation of motivation', *Journal of Educational Psychology*, 90(2): 224–35.

Woodhead, C. (2012) 'Talking point', *Independent Schools Magazine*, February, 8.

Worthington, M. and Carruthers, E. (2003) *Children's Mathematics: Making marks, making meaning*, London: Paul Chapman.

Wulf, C. (2011) 'Emotions in the teaching of history', *International Journal of Cultural Research*, 1(2): 89–93.

Wundt (1907) *Outlines of Psychology*, Leipzig: Wilhelm Engelmann.

Wyman, P.A., Cross, W., Hendricks Brown, C., Yu, Q., Tu, X. and Eberly, S. (2010) 'Intervention to strengthen emotional self-regulation in children with emerging mental health problems', *Journal of Abnormal Child Psychology*, 38(5): 707–20.

Yang, S.-Y. (2001) 'Conceptions of wisdom among Taiwanese Chinese', *Journal of Cross-Cultural Psychology*, 32(6): 662–80.

Yang, S.-Y. (2011) 'East meets West: Cross cultural perspectives on wisdom in adult education', *New Directions for Adult and Continuing Education*, 2011(13): 145–54.

Yekovich, F.R., Thompson, M.A. and Walker, C.H. (1991) 'Generation and verification of inferences by experts and trained non-experts', *American Educational Research Journal*, 28: 189–209.

Young, D.J. (1990) 'An investigation of students' perspectives on anxiety and speaking', *Foreign Language Annals*, 26(3): 539–53.

Young, D.J. (1991) 'Creating a low-anxiety classroom environment', *Modern Language Journal*, 75(4): 426–39.

Zajonc, R.B. (1980) 'Feeling and thinking', *American Psychologist*, 35(2): 151–75.

Zarinpoush, F., Cooper, M. and Moylan, S. (2000) 'The effects of happiness and sadness on moral reasoning', *Journal of Moral Education*, 29(4): 397–412.

Zautra, A.J. (2003) *Emotions, Stress and Health*, Oxford: Oxford University Press.

Zeelenberg, M., Nelissen, R.M.A., Breugelmans, S.M. and Pieters, R. (2008) 'On emotion specificity in decision making', *Judgment and Decision Making*, 3(1): 18–27.

Zeidner, M. (2012) 'Adaptive coping with test situations', *Educational Psychologist*, 30(3): 123–33.

Zeidner, M., Matthews, G. and Roberts, R.D. (2012) *What We Know About Emotional Intelligence*, Cambridge: MIT Press.

Zimmerman, B.J. (2008) 'Investigating self-regulation and motivation', *American Educational Research Journal*, 45(1): 166–83.

Zimmerman, B.J. and Martinez-Pons, M. (1986) 'Development of a structured interview for assessing student use of self-regulated learning strategies', *American Educational Research Journal*, 23(4): 614–28.

Zimmerman, B.J. and Martinez-Pons, M. (1990) 'Student differences in self-regulated learning', *Journal of Educational Psychology*, 82(1): 51–9.

Zimpher, N. and Howey, K. (1987) 'Adapting supervisory practices to different orientations of teaching competence', *Journal of Curriculum and Supervision*, 2: 101–27.

Zuck, R.B. (1991) *A Biblical Theology of the Old Testament*, Chicago: Moody.

Subject and author index